Family Support

of related interest

Social Work with Children and Families
Getting into Practice
Ian Butler and Gwenda Roberts
ISBN 1 85302 365 5 pb

Homeless Children
Problems and Needs
Edited by Panos Vostanis and Stuart Cumella
ISBN 1 85302 595 X pb

Child Development for Child Care and Protection Workers
Brigid Daniel, Sally Wassel and Robbie Gilligan
ISBN 1 85302 633 6 pb

Effective Ways of Working with Children and their Families
Edited by Malcolm Hill
ISBN 1 85302 619 0 pb

Residential Child Care
International Perspectives on Links with Families and Peers
Edited by Mono Chakrabarti and Malcolm Hill
ISBN 1 85302 687 5 pb

Child Welfare Services Developments in Law,
Policy, Practice and Research
Edited by Malcolm Hill and Jane Aldgate
ISBN 1 85302 316 7 pb

State Child Care Practice
Looking After Children?
Carol Hayden, Jim Goddard, Sarah Gorin and Niki Van Der Spek
ISBN 1 85302 670 0 pb

Issues in Foster Care
The Personal, the Professional and the Organizational
Edited by Greg Kelly and Robbie Gilligan
ISBN 1 85302 465 1 pb

Making an Impact – Children and Domestic Violence
A Reader
Marianne Hester, Chris Pearson and Nicola Harwin
ISBN 1 85302 844 4 pb

Troubles of Children and Adolescents
Edited by Ved Varma
ISBN 1 85302 323 X pb

Understanding and Supporting Children with Emotional
and Behavioural Difficulties
Edited by Paul Cooper
ISBN 1 85302 666 2 pb

Family Support

Direction from Diversity

*Edited by John Canavan, Pat Dolan
and John Pinkerton*

Jessica Kingsley Publishers
London and Philadelphia

First published in the United Kingdom in 2000 by
Jessica Kingsley Publishers Ltd,
116 Pentonville Road, London
N1 9JB, England
and
325 Chestnut Street,
Philadelphia, PA 19106, USA.

www.jkp.com

© Copyright 2000 Jessica Kingsley Publishers

Library of Congress Cataloging in Publication Data
A CIP catalog record for this book is available from the Library of Congress

British Library Cataloguing in Publication Data
Family support : direction from diversity
1. Child welfare   2. Family
I. Canavan, John 1967–   II. Dolan, Pat 1958–   III. Pinkerton, John, 1953–
362.7
ISBN 1 85302 850 9

ISBN 1 85302 850 9

Printed and Bound in Great Britain by
Athenaeum Press, Gateshead, Tyne and Wear

Contents

List of Tables

List of Figures

Acknowledgements

The authors would like to acknowledge the interest and support of the many people who assisted in bringing this project to fruition. In particular, we would like to thank the Child Care Unit, Community Services, Western Health Board and the Department of Political Science and Sociology, NUI Galway. Their financial and administrative support was crucial to the production of this book and to the International Conference on Family Support which was an important part of that process. We are also most grateful to the chapter contributors for their diligent efforts in meeting our editorial demands, to Christine Moylan for her administrative back-up and to Maria Kelly and Rosaleen Gormley for their work on the preparation of the manuscript.

Introduction

John Canavan, Pat Dolan and John Pinkerton

Why a book on family support?

This book aims to consolidate current knowledge about family support, to clarify its current status, and to elaborate central theoretical and practice themes in its developmental trajectory. It draws on a range of sources from both theory and practice in a variety of national contexts. The book's starting point was the editors' growing awareness of the importance of the family support debate within both the UK and the Republic of Ireland. Their involvement in the debate within the two jurisdictions, along with some knowledge of the relevant US literature, suggested that the term not only could but probably should be interpreted in a variety of ways. An edited book drawing out the range of perspectives on family support in theory and practice seemed an ideal means to explore and share that thesis. As a key stage in the production of such a book, an international conference on family support was held at National University of Ireland, Galway, with the support of the regional health authority for the west of Ireland (Western Health Board) in June 1998. The conference, which was multidisciplinary both in terms of speakers and audience, focused on clarifying and bridging theoretical and practice perspectives on family support and proved to be an important contribution in its own right to the debate.

The conference affirmed the messages emerging from research and practice that family support does not represent a neatly bounded set of concepts and activities. Rather, it is more akin to a repertoire of explanatory and prescriptive ideas drawn from various contexts of intervention and associated academic fields of enquiry. This book accepts, explores and celebrates that diversity. Concepts and experience from different international settings (UK, USA, Germany, Denmark, Republic of Ireland), different levels of analysis (society, community, family) and different sites of intervention (education, social services, local government) are all considered.

In addition to exposing the reader to this rich variety of elements, the book also offers a general framework for thinking about and delivering family support and suggests that it is possible to discern a shared direction within the diversity. At its full potential, the integrative nature of family support theory and practice represents an opportunity for the optimal use of a very broad and diverse range of knowledge in promoting the welfare of children and their families. The editors hope that the book will contribute to the development of a coherent perspective on responses to the many problems facing families in today's world.

Given the wide-ranging nature of family support and the inclusive perspective being taken by the editors, the book should prove useful to an equally broad readership. First, it will be a tool in the education and training of those professions involved in providing services aimed at promoting the welfare of children and families. It should be of particular value in training social workers, psychologists, public health nurses, early years professionals, youth and community workers and teachers. Second, for practising professionals from all of these disciplines, it will be a means of updating and better understanding the theory and practice of family support. Third, the book should act as an important source of ideas for those charged with service development in local government, health, justice and education sectors. Finally, the editors hope that it will be of value to academics, researchers and evaluators in setting out the terms of the debate and the likely future direction for family support.

What is in this book?

In order to contextualize the many valuable messages to be found in this book, at the outset the terrain of family support is charted by Robbie Gilligan. In Chapter 1 he acquaints the reader with the core ingredients of family support, in terms of its conceptual base, how it operates in practice and what the international research evidence says about its value. This strongly argued case provides the setting in which the diversity of family support emerges in subsequent chapters.

The next two chapters make it clear that the family support debate cannot be reduced to a set of purely technical or administrative difficulties. Adopting a sociological perspective, in Chapter 2 Graham Crow and Graham Allan make explicit the complexities behind the concepts of community, family and support which inform a large part of the material in later chapters. Their critical outlook is useful in getting past the rhetoric which is often attached to state pronouncements on family support. Critical appraisal of state sponsorship of family support is an important theme of Chapter 3, in which Joachim

Wieler, writing from a social work practice viewpoint, traces the early history and recent re-emergence of family work in Germany. In addition to providing a picture of family support in Germany, this chapter usefully reminds us that there is much to be gained from tracing its theoretical and practice roots.

Chapters 4 and 5 focus on methods of practice applicable to family support. While it is obvious that service providers should aspire to make parents central to family support, in Chapter 4 Martin Herbert concentrates on the psychosocial technology required to translate such aspirations into practice. Specifically, he sets out in detail approaches to working with out-of-control adolescents through programmes which strengthen parenting. More broadly, in Chapter 5 Carolyn Cutrona explains the process of social support within families. Drawing on both clinical and research evidence from the USA, she distinguishes different sources and types of support and the skills needed to develop and sustain them.

The inclusive nature of family support, both in terms of the problems it tackles and the services that constitute it, is illustrated in the next four chapters. In Chapter 6 John Canavan and Pat Dolan outline the evolution of one Irish community-based family support project which targets at-risk adolescents. They highlight a series of factors essential in the development of a dynamic service, including research and experimentation, listening to and learning from service users, and a reflective practice style. In Chapter 7 Saoirse Nic Gabhainn and Fiona Walsh illustrate the cumulative and multidimensional character of explanations of the problem of drug misuse and responses to it. They identify family as a key locus of intervention and explore the implications which this has for practice. The role of mainstream education systems in supporting families is advocated by Sandra Ryan in Chapter 8. With evidence from Irish and international sources, she demonstrates the ways in which school can be a beneficial site in supporting families. Casting the net wider still, in Chapter 9 Peter Steen Jensen uses the example of the Danish city Odense to highlight the role of local government in supporting families. In addition to the provision of adequate resources, he stresses normalization, organizational dynamism and innovation as important factors in the strategic planning and operation of integrated family support systems.

The final chapter, by John Pinkerton, revisits key themes emerging through the book and plots a possible future direction for family support. It suggests a set of emerging agendas for policymakers, operational managers, practitioners and researchers and argues that if set within an integrated social

policy perspective, these can provide a coherent direction for future developments in the field of family support.

Seeking direction

As an integrated field of theory and practice, family support is relatively new,
with the development of consensus of what constitutes its foundations and
main pillars still being established. This book is a contribution to developing
some coherence within this necessary debate. It does not pretend to have
covered all the areas which need to be drawn together. For example, there are
obvious omissions in relation to target groups, such as individuals with
disabilities, and types of family support provision, such as family centres.
However, it does provide and illustrate suggestions for a framework in which
the full range of the field can be considered. In participating in this project,
the editors and contributors have been motivated by a desire to better
understand the complexities of family support. Accordingly, the book should
stimulate thinking and debate around the key ideas of family support for
policy and practice. But what is most important is that such theoretical debate
makes a contribution to improving the day-to-day lives of children and
families in need.

CHAPTER 1

Family Support

Issues and Prospects

Robbie Gilligan

Introduction

Despite all the justifiable concern about poverty, child abuse, domestic violence and homelessness, and their adverse effects on children, it is still possible for at least some children to do well in difficult circumstances. This can happen if support can interact with the child's natural drive for normal development. Speaking from a North American perspective, Masten and Coatsworth (1998) observe that children can transcend adversity:

> Successful children remind us that children grow up in multiple contexts – in families, schools, peer groups, baseball teams, religious organis- ations, and many other groups – and each context is a potential source of protective as well as risk factors. These children demonstrate that child- ren are protected not only by the self-righting nature of development, but also by the actions of adults, by their own actions, by the nurturing of their assets, by opportunities to succeed and by the experience of success. (Masten and Coatsworth 1998, p.216)

Family support is about mobilizing support for children's normal develop- ment; for normal development in adverse circumstances. It is about mob- ilizing that support in all the contexts in which children live their lives – family, school, peer group, sports team, church, and so on. It is about counteracting the corrosive potential of poverty and other harm that can befall children in disadvantaged communities. Family support is certainly about more than child protection in a narrow sense. It is about more than trying to prevent child abuse, important though that is. Child-focused family support is about supporting children's social, psychological and educational development. It is about supporting their belonging to family, school and neighbourhood. Family support is to child welfare 'what vaccines, clean water, sanitation and food hygiene have been to health care' (Gilligan 1995b).

Family support may take many forms. The following are some Irish examples which each have a different focus. In relation to early childhood, in addition to pre-school programmes (O'Flaherty 1995), there is the Community Mothers scheme in which locally recruited peer health educators are used with vulnerable parents (Johnson and Molloy 1995; Johnson, Howell and Molloy 1993). Homestart is a voluntary visiting and support scheme for isolated parents. There are also family support workers, who work intensively on practical concerns affecting a child and family's quality of life (Opgenhafen 1996). The Neighbourhood Youth Projects provide a range of supports to young people at risk at an individual, group and family level within a neighbourhood context (Clarke, Lahert and McCabe 1994; Dolan 1993).

Given that family support takes on so many different forms, the aim of this chapter is to set them within a shared context. To do this, five basic questions are addressed:

1. What is family support and what does it seek to do?

2. Why is family support important in discussing practice in disadvantaged communities?

3. What core ideas and concepts are important in understanding family support?

4. Does family support work?

5. What are the key issues and challenges facing family support?

What is family support?

Child-focused family support in disadvantaged communities should embrace strategies and approaches which promote the development and safety of children in their own family and promote the conditions in the family, school and neighbourhood which are conducive to such safety and development. It should also help to keep children in their own family by preventing the breakdown of relationships within the family to the point where the children wish to leave for their own safety and welfare or where other responsible adults feel this is the best course. Family support seeks to promote the child's safety and development and prevent the child leaving the family by reducing stressors in the child and family's life, promoting competence in the child, connecting the child and family members to relevant supports and resources and promoting morale and competence in parents.

Family support may, of course, occur naturally through informal support systems of kin, neighbours and friends. It may also be planned, arranged or delivered by professionals or para-professionals in, for instance, the health, social service or education systems. It is helpful to think of three categories of family support when provided formally (Gilligan 1995a). The first of these is *developmental family support*. It seeks to strengthen the social supports and coping capacities of children and adults in the context of their families and neighbourhood. Personal development groups, recreational projects, youth programmes, parent education or other adult education relevant to family living and relationships would be examples of developmental family support. This type of family support is not problem focused and is in principle open to all who are encountering the ordinary challenges of parenting and family living.

The second category is *compensatory family support*. It seeks to compensate family members for the disabling effects of disadvantage or adversity in their present or earlier life. Examples of compensatory family support would include high-quality day nursery programmes for preschoolers from very disadvantaged home circumstances, special youth programmes for those at risk in communities with high rates of truancy and early school leaving. Compensatory family support can serve as one important strand in the range of strategies necessary to counteract the toxic effects on personal, family and neighbourhood life of social exclusion.

Protective family support is the third category. It seeks to strengthen the coping and resilience of children and adults in relation to identified risks or threats experienced within individual families. Examples of protective family support include: day fostering for the children of drug-abusing parents; refuges and support groups for women who are victims of domestic violence; support programmes in child behaviour management for parents encountering serious problems in this area; a discreetly presented 'club' aimed at raising the self-esteem and social skills of young victims of abuse or bullying; the work of a homemaker who seeks to enhance the home management and social networks of an isolated and poorly coping family newly arrived in an area. Protective family support will recognize the value of relationships, routines (such as bedtime) and rituals (like birthdays and Christmas) in giving greater structure and stability to home life for a child in stressful family circumstances.

Family support and practice in disadvantaged communities

What happens to children within their families, both in the home and in the web of wider relationships, is of major influence, if not decisive, in shaping a child's experience and destiny. Stressors within the family and acting on the family have huge implications for a child's welfare and development. As these stressors accumulate, together they begin to bite even deeper in terms of the harm they do. Research findings indicate that mounting stressors greatly increase the risk, for example, of developing conduct disorder (Rutter *et al.* 1995) and reducing IQ over time (Sameroff *et al.* 1993). Happily there is evidence that cumulative protective factors work in the opposite direction – they may have disproportionately positive effects (Runyan *et al.* 1998). Family support is important because it may be able to help reduce stressors and add to protective factors in a child's life.

Family support is also important because family and family relationships mean so much to children, even children who have experienced great harm and hurt in the family. Abused children may still feel great loyalty to the abusive parent. 'You can take the child out of the family, but you cannot take the family out of the child' (Gilligan 1995b). At the end of the day it is very difficult to replace the family satisfactorily for large numbers of children (Toynbee 1998). The legion of sorry tales about state care internationally should induce great humility in those tempted to remove even more children to care and should energize those convinced of the protective and preventive potential of family support.

Core ideas and concepts in understanding family support

In this section a number of broad-brush ideas important to an understanding of family support will be presented, followed by a number of ideas influential for actual practice.

Strengths perspective

In seeking to understand the needs and potential of children and families, a family support perspective is less concerned with deficits, pathology and risk and more concerned to find and value strengths. There are whole sets of questions which never get considered if attention is only on the negatives in a child or family profile. Through actively looking for positive resources, healing and developmental potential become apparent that otherwise go unrecognized. A mother experiencing difficulty with her children may be a gifted musician, or the repository of a rich body of family or cultural lore, or a popular community activist. Validating these strengths may transform the working relationship and open up new vistas of possible solutions. Assessing the child or parent's circumstances without factoring in that kind of detail is to hopelessly miss the rich reality of all that is in the child's life context.

Risk and protective factors as social capital

Clustering of protective factors may serve as 'social capital' which can help a child and family to withstand the stress of living in conditions of economic and social stress. Runyan *et al.* (1998) looked at a sample of 667 two- to five-year-old children (mean age, 4.4 years) and their maternal caregivers who were living in high-risk social conditions in the USA. The researchers wished to identify those young children who were 'doing well' and those 'not doing well' in order to determine whether social capital had a bearing on this. Only 13 per cent of the children were classified as doing well. The individual indicators that best discriminated between levels of child funct-ioning were the most direct measures of social capital as defined – church affiliation, perception of personal social support and support within the neighbourhood. The presence of any social capital indicator increased the odds of doing well by 29 per cent; adding any two increased the odds of doing well by 66 per cent. The researchers suggest that social capital may be most crucial for families who have fewer financial and educational resources. They argue that their findings show the need to search for new and creative ways of supporting interpersonal relationships and strengthening the com-munities in which families carry out their daily activities. The challenge for family support is to achieve a favourable balance between risk and protective factors or, to put it another way, to build up the stock of social capital which a family and child has.

Secure base and arenas of comfort

Attachment theory underlines the importance of stable attachments for the child growing up. Stable attachments teach the growing child that people and the world are trustworthy and reliable and that the child is lovable. For a toddler that sense of a secure base in the world is cultivated and sustained by reliable care of one or more key caregivers. As the child grows older the sense of secure base may also be sustained, for example, by relationships with valued teachers or mentors. It is essential that family support seeks to foster this sense of secure base for a young person. Another useful concept in supporting young people under stress is the idea of providing or finding 'arenas of comfort' separate from stressful domains (Simmons and Blyth 1987, cited in Thiede Call 1996). Where home is stressful the best family support strategy may be to help the young person find an 'arena of comfort' outside the home which may make home bearable. School, a workplace, or sites for sport and hobbies may constitute such arenas of comfort.

Developmental pathways, transitions and turning points

As they grow up from birth, children follow developmental pathways through the various milestones of development. Progress is rather like that of a yacht on a deep-sea journey. The yacht may be blown off course by unfavourable winds, it may be becalmed, it may be seriously damaged by severe conditions. It may be blown back on course by a fortunate coincidence of wind conditions. Similarly, a child growing up may be blown off course by adverse circumstances. Some who veer off may never recover. Others may be fortunate to reach a positive turning point in the form of a positive event, incident or relationship which brings them back on course (Clausen 1995). Turning points may occur serendipitously and change does not always result from in-depth or enduring experiences or relationships. Some turning points are normative and can be anticipated; for example, having a baby, going to school, moving from primary to secondary school. Durlak and Wells (1997) suggest that such normative transitions may be a very fruitful focus for family support intervention.

Rutter *et al.* (1995, p.88) remind us that it is possible to break the links between childhood difficulties and adult adversity if the right actions are taken at the right time along the pathway. Some of those actions may involve key choices made by the growing person, but many will depend on support and help from others. Sometimes turning points may start with something very small:

> Caregivers, teachers and social workers should remember that the detail of what they do counts. The rituals, the smiles, the interest in little things, the daily routines, the talents they nurture, the interests they stimulate, the hobbies they encourage, the friendships they support, the sibling ties they preserve make a difference. All of these little things may foster in a child the vital senses of *belonging*, of *mattering*, of *counting*. All of these little things we do, these details, may prove decisive turning points in a young person's developmental pathway. (Gilligan 1998b)

Based on their longitudinal study in Hawaii, Werner and Smith (1992) remind us of the power of positive relationships in enhancing the resilience of vulnerable youngsters:

> The life stories of the resilient youngsters now grown in to adulthood teach us that competence, confidence and caring can flourish, even under adverse circumstances, if children encounter persons who provide

them with the *secure basis* [emphasis added] for the development of trust, autonomy and initiative. (Werner and Smith 1992, p.209)

Limitations of support

Broadly speaking, support can help prevent stress and dysfunction and reduce the toll stress might otherwise take on health, well-being and functioning (Thompson 1995). But it is important to recognize that social support may be most effective when combined with other services (Thompson 1995). Social support cannot make up for inadequate income, inadequate housing, inadequate educational opportunities for children or adults, or shortcomings in the economy or labour market or in the physical fabric of the local neighbourhood.

Sources of family support

Parental support where it is forthcoming may be very important to the developing young person. American research suggests that parental support not only serves as a buffer against stress for the young person, but also may enhance the effects of protective factors such as academic competence and coping behaviour (Wills and Cleary 1996). Support from within the family may also come from siblings. For children living in circumstances of family stress or breakdown, sibling relationships and support may become very important (Caya and Liem 1998; McTeigue 1998). Grandparents and extended kin may provide very important arenas of comfort when home circumstances are difficult. When home becomes too difficult, placement with relatives may be a desirable alternative. But adults outside the family may also be very important; for instance, teachers, neighbours and mentors (Smith and Carlson 1997). Werner and Smith's famous longitudinal study of young people growing up who proved resilient in the face of adversity found that among the factors associated with resilience in vulnerable youngsters were 'the availability of caring adults outside the home, and supportive teachers in school who acted as role models and assisted the youths with realistic educational and vocational plans' (Werner and Smith 1992, p.186).

Kin may also be an important source of support to parents. While recent British research suggests that kinship contact may be in decline there, it is still notable that researchers have found that relatives, and in particular parents, remain a crucial source of aid and assistance for families with young children. This seems especially so in the case of lone parents (McGlone, Park and Smith 1998). Thompson (1995) also reminds us that non- neighbourhood resources may be very important in informal social support. These may include: extended kin; friends who live outside local neighbourhoods; and social contacts through schools, churches, trade unions and broader community groups. A key role for the family support professional may be to help identify members of a person's social network and the nature of their relationship to that person. The social network map developed by Tracy in the USA is one such tool which seems user-friendly for both client and worker. It has been used in Ireland in a study by Dolan (1997).

Importance of multiplicity of role identities

It is reassuring sometimes when science and research confirm the instincts of common sense. One such instance is the idea that it is protective for mental health to have multiple role identities (Harris 1993; Thoits 1983). Take for example a young lone mother living on a low income. Assume she is isolated from family and community and may only have the role of mother to play in her everyday life. The destructiveness and isolation of her role as mother may have a negative effect on her level of morale and social support and thereby on her parental effectiveness and commitment. If, on the other hand, she has access to good child care, participates in local adult education classes, has a part-time job and is involved in supporting the local girls' football team, then she has social roles as student, employee and football supporter to add to her repertoire of social identities and opportunities. The likelihood is that her mental health and thereby her parenting will be enhanced. She will feel better about herself and will gain encouragement from the interest and support of others whom she encounters in her different roles.

This suggests that a key principle of family support must be to enhance the number of identities available to parents with constrained opportunities. It is clear that adult education, community development, job placement/ training and good quality child care all have a part to play in strengthening the parent–child relationship. The key family support intervention in this instance may be to encourage and support the young woman to tap into these resources which are available in the community. This may take time, sensitivity, skill and much encouragement (Inglis 1994). Personal development courses for women and men are extremely important, not only for the gains they bring to the person, but also to that person as parent and thereby to the child. This argument is supported by the work of Borge (1996), a Norwegian researcher who suggests that in the case of young children, maternal involvement in education may play a secondary prevention role in relation to childhood problems.

Therapeutic alliances

It may take some time for families who have become alienated, disillusioned and disaffected from mainstream services to engage with the service of a family support professional or volunteer. Giving time and attention to the building of relationship as an initial objective becomes crucial (Morrison Dore and Alexander 1996). Unless a therapeutic alliance is formed, it is unlikely that anything very productive will emerge from the helping relationship. To recall Harris's (1993) metaphor, help may be more valuable coming in the form of a milk van – low key, regular and reliable – rather than a fire brigade – sudden, once off and crisis driven.

Importance of school

The tremendous supportive potential of schools for children and families goes largely unrecognized. School affords many developmental opportunities to children through academic, sporting and social experience (Gilligan 1998, 2000; Sylva 1989). Teachers can serve as confidants and mentors and guarantors of a child's welfare. A sense of 'membership' of a school may have great psychological and social value for a vulnerable child. It should not be assumed that school only benefits those with the necessary academic ability and who have no serious social problems. A large New Zealand study, for instance, indicates how positive school experiences were a key factor in helping to distinguish women who had recovered from episodes of sexual abuse in childhood and women who had not (Romans *et al.* 1995). In a British study, Rutter and colleagues (1995) have found that positive school experience may influence the later approach of girls reared in residential care to planning for work and career. They note this positive school experience embraces sports, arts and crafts, music, social relationships and positions of responsibility within the school and more rarely in this ex-care group academic achievement. This evidence reminds us of the wide scope for accomplishment of different kinds which schools can offer, even to children who are not academic high-flyers. The key is for adults – teachers, parents and other professionals – to be alert to the value of school experience in this regard.

Schools may also give parents in difficulty a safe place to air child-care problems and get support (Briggs 1997; Greif 1994; O'Callaghan 1993). It may help pull parents into adult neighbourhood networks and adult educational programmes (Briggs 1997; Thompson 1995, p.175). It may serve as a vital local resource in run-down neighbourhoods drained of other facilities (Thompson 1995) and may help to promote and sustain a sense of community in hard-pressed inner cities. Schools have the potential to serve as a hub for the delivery of a full range of social services to children and families. This is an idea which is being promoted by commentators in the USA (Dryfoos 1994; Hooper-Briar and Lawson 1994).

Importance of neighbourhoods and community development

Wilson (1996) refers to the importance of neighbourhood social organiz-ation in the quality of life of local residents. This clearly has importance for children and child-rearing households in a neighbourhood. He talks of three major dimensions to neighbourhood social organization. The first of these is the prevalence, strength and interdependence of social networks; the second is the extent of collective supervision that the residents exercise and the degree of personal responsibility they assume in addressing neighbourhood problems; the third is the rate of resident participation in voluntary and formal organizations (Wilson 1996).

Wilson (1995) also refers to an adaptation of Bandura's concept of self-efficacy in the individual. Self-efficacy refers to the individual's self-belief in terms of pursuing actions effectively which serve desired goals. At com-munity level, weak self-efficacy among many individuals because of econ-omic and social marginalization may lead to what Wilson terms 'weak collective efficacy', which has an effect, inter alia, on the morale, norms and expectations of parents and children in the community affected. Thompson (1995) argues that strengthening 'needy neighbourhoods' may promise greater success than could piecemeal efforts over a broader geographical net to strengthen non-local social support on a family-by-family basis. Thus community development has to be a central part of any comprehensive family support strategy in disadvantaged communities.

Deliberate family process

Bennet, Wolin and Reiss (1988) highlight the possible protective value for children of structure and routine in families subject to stress. In their study of parental alcoholism they found children were more protected from paternal alcoholism when the family was still intact enough to be able to plan and carry off rituals – ceremonies, traditions and routines which symbolized, presumably, a vital order for the child. They use the term 'deliberate family process' to describe the pattern. The message for those in a child-focused family support role would seem to be to value and emphasize opportunities for family members to mark and celebrate their identity as 'family'.

In this review of the underlying core ideas in family support, attention has been drawn to the concepts of developmental pathways, key turning points and of opportunities in people's development. The importance of recognizing protective factors and trying to maximize them in attempts to balance out the effects of risk factors have also been stressed. Specific ideas relevant to practice which were considered were: the range of potential sources of support within a social network; the protective value of maximizing for parents and young people the number of role identities they have; the significance of taking time and effort to build trust and common ground – a therapeutic alliance – between worker and family; the importance of working with schools and of building neighbourhood resources; and the value of reinforcing family identity through rituals and celebrations.

Does family support work?

To ask whether family support actually does work is a reasonable question which families, communities, professionals, agency managers and politicians are entitled to put. To answer the question, it is necessary to unpack the question 'does it work?' into a number of more focused questions. To start with, it is important to know whether consumers are satisfied with intervention. The best way to find out is to ask them: something which Smith (1996) did in her British study of family centres. The overwhelming majority (97%) of the sample of 125 centre users said they would recommend the projects to someone else; 86 per cent said the projects had made a difference to them; and 84 per cent to their children. In addition to consumers, a key set of stakeholders is that of referring professionals. They gave favourable views of the impact of Homestart on families known to them when asked by Frost and his colleagues in a British study (1996), and of the impact of the Swedish contact person and contact family scheme in a study by Andersson (1993).

Opinions about a service may be useful, but they are relatively 'soft' in terms of answering the hard question 'does it work?'. Increasingly the 'gold standard' for answering this question is considered to be the randomized control trial (Oakley 1992). In this approach, a carefully drawn sample population is divided randomly between an intervention group and a non-intervention control group. Key baseline information is gathered about the functioning of the two sets of people, the intervention is made and the populations are measured again. In this technique, any differences measured can be attributed to the intervention because of the close similarity in every other respect of the two groups.

An Irish example of a randomized control trial of a family support intervention is the study of the Community Mothers Programme undertaken by Johnson et al. (1993). They found considerable gains for those in the intervention group. The children in the intervention group were more likely than the control group children: to have received all of their primary immunizations; to be read to daily; to have played more cognitive games; to be more exposed to nursery rhymes; to be less likely to begin cows' milk before 26 weeks; and less likely to have inappropriate types or amounts of food in their diet. Similarly, the mothers in the intervention group when compared to the control group mothers: had better diet; had more positive feelings; were less likely to be tired; were less likely to feel miserable; were less likely to want to stay indoors; and were less likely to display negative feelings.

A key problem in studying any intervention which appears to work is whether any positive effect found lasts or does it 'wash out'? To try to answer this question, it is necessary to use randomized controlled trials, but with the addition of a long-term follow-up (divide target population into two groups randomly, one receives special service, the other does not, measure differences and follow up over time). Four studies are selected here which demonstrate enduring gains for family support intervention over periods from 7 to 23 years. This is quite remarkable when it is considered that in some instances the extent or duration of the original intervention might have been quite modest. Oakley *et al.* (1996) found that offering socially disadvantaged 'at risk' mothers additional support during pregnancy had a positive impact on measures of children's health status and family well-being seven years later. As part of a research project which was an experimental versus control study rather than a randomized controlled trial, Kellaghan and Greaney (1993) carried out an eight-year follow-up. Young people who had been through a preschool programme in inner city Dublin when compared to controls who had not were found at 16 years old to have stayed on longer at school with a greater proportion taking public examinations; thus acquiring important qualifications on entering the labour market. Olds and his colleagues (1997) found that home visits during pregnancy and 23 visits until second birthday by a nurse can reduce the number of subsequent pregnancies, the use of welfare, child abuse and neglect and criminal behaviour on the part of low-income, unmarried mothers for up to 15 years after the birth of the first child (from Pubmed abstract on World Wide Web). In a 24-year follow-up, Schweinart, Barnes and Weikart (1993) found that an intervention group who received a quality preschool programme had a better chance by age 27 than a comparison group of: being employed; of being a high school graduate; of having vocational or college training; of not ever having been arrested; of not having had a teenage pregnancy (females only); and of having spent less time in special education.

Durlak and Wells (1997) conducted a meta-analysis of 177 evaluative research studies of programmes to prevent behavioural and social problems in children and adolescents. For inclusion in their meta-analaysis, studies had to have a control group report by the end of 1991 and be targeted mainly at young people aged 18 or under. They found that most categories of programmes produced positive outcomes. They also found that the degree of positive outcome was similar or better to levels achieved in interventions in the medical and wider social science field. The findings of Durlak and Wells are at least supportive of a new optimism about the potential of primary prevention and the value of research into it (Sandler 1997).

Looking to the specifics of what might work best, it may be helpful to note the findings of three major literature reviews. The first reviews the evidence on impact of social support on families manifesting child neglect (DePanfilis 1996). The review found that modest improvements in the parenting behaviour of neglectful parents can be achieved through the following:

- specific assessment – special focus on availability and helpfulness of social network
- multi-service approach (including concrete help)
- intensive social contact with volunteer, lay therapist or parent aide
- use of modelling, coaching, rehearsing and feedback, both on a one-to-one basis and in support group, to improve social interactional skills
- development of personal networks, mutual aid groups and connections to neighbourhood helpers
- structured parenting and support groups for socializing, support and social and parental skill building.

It also finds that individual support, at least initially, may be more appropriate for neglectful families because they lack the social skills necessary to get along well in groups. It also stresses the significance of professional supervision and service, concrete help and long-term intervention to help sustain change over time.

A second review examined the evidence on effective early prevention of physical child abuse and neglect (Guterman 1997). Key preventive measures were found to be education and support to help parents learn to care for the new child and linking families with necessary formal and/or informal supports. Both long- and short-term programmes had shown some success. While the issue of whether long- or short-term intervention is better remains unclear, long term with moderately frequent contact showed better success than long term with less frequent contact. Programmes using para-professionals do not show inferior outcomes, but are most effective when coupled with more service-intensive approaches. Universal intake is better than screened intake.

The third review concerned the prevention of delinquency and highlights the significance of multi-faceted intervention. Yoshikawa (1994) proposed that the evaluative evidence supports a programme with the following features: an intervention of at least two years duration; high-quality educational infant day care or preschool provision; informational and emotional support on development and childrearing for parents; pre-natal and post-natal care for the mother; and educational and vocational counselling and training if not otherwise available. Thus in the three reviews, in the meta-analysis of 177 studies and in the four selected studies, the message seems to be the same: family support can work and it can make a difference.

Issues facing family support

A major issue for the further development of family support is getting the necessary political support. Within Ireland it is very welcome that the Commission on the Family in its recent recommendations calls for family support to families living in adverse circumstances to 'be prioritized and a mechanism developed to ring-fence resources, money and professional time for family support work at this level' (Commission on the Family 1998, p.7). This may help, among other things, to give more life to the provisions of the Child Care Act 1991 (Ireland 1991) which mandate and require family support provision under the child welfare functions of the health boards.

One constituency which it might be hoped would support higher priority for family support work is that of the professionals working in the broad child welfare field. Yet at times there is an ambivalence or scepticism among at least some of those professionals. Some may be sceptical about the effectiveness of family support and yet the evidence cited above certainly challenges such an attitude. Ann Oakley (1992) reminds us that the findings of controlled social support interventions may threaten professionals' claims to expertise insofar as they demonstrate the health-promoting importance of what may often be essentially non-professional activities. When one looks at the pay and conditions of many who do the front-line work in family support – the family support workers, the workers in child care centres, day nurseries, and so on – one must be appalled by the low value put on their important work. Is this again part of the ambivalence towards family support? A clear policy challenge for this field is to raise the status of people who deliver support and the work they do.

The second major area to be addressed is ensuring that future programme design incorporates a number of key features. The first of these to note is increasing naturally occurring social support in the long term. Intervention may make a difference while it is available, but Lakey and Lutz (1996) are pessimistic about the evidence that it can mobilize longer term informal support, which endures beyond the initial intervention. This is certainly an issue that deserves further investigation and attention. Family support programmes also need to be multi-faceted and integrated (Commission on the Family 1998). The complexity of many family stresses and difficulties means that multiple solutions are often needed to tackle the multiple problems of the most disadvantaged families (Utting 1995). In many instances what may be needed is imaginative customized responses to need, not unlike the American concept of a 'wraparound' service (Eber and Nelson 1997). As part of these family support packages, much greater attention needs to be given to mobilizing the potential of schools and the education system (Commission on the Family 1998).

Programme design must provide realistic parenting support. There is a danger of over-simplistic prescriptions for tackling shortcomings in parenting. For example, reducing the idea of improving parenting to a short course does a grave disservice to parents under stress. It greatly underestimates the complexity of the parenting task and the array of pressures affecting a parent. It is also important not to forget that it is not just young parents who need help, or the parents of young children. A facility such as a 'parents of teenagers circle' may be a helpful forum where parents of adolescents can share experience and discuss their concerns (Smith, Gilford and O'Sullivan 1998). It is important to remember that a readiness to go public in this way with one's difficulties is very challenging for someone just beginning to come to terms with the scale of the problem facing them and the stigma and humiliation which they fear public disclosure may bring.

Family support programmes need to address gender issues and specifically the challenge of engaging men. A US study of children in female-headed households (63.9% of pre-schoolers and 38.2% of school-age children) found that fathers were part of their social networks. The researchers found from their data that father–child contact is usually positive for the child, although they concede that problems such as substance abuse or child abuse can be a risk for some. The researchers call for 'the presence of fathers as a potential asset' to be acknowledged. 'It is time to bring these men out of the shadows and back into their children's lives' (Perloff and Buckner 1996). Family support must also take men out of the shadows, since so much of its work is, in reality, transacted with women. Other necessary features to be included in a programme design are:

- listen to the voice of family members (Weick and Saleebey 1995)
- engage with major social problems such as drugs and domestic violence
- be culturally competent, taking account of ethnic and social class differences in an affirming fashion.

Conclusion

The challenges facing family support involve: securing a strong and diverse constituency of support; developing a strong technology of support; achieving effective dissemination of 'good practice' to professional and to lay audiences; and identifying models of evaluation and research appropriate to the complex agenda which family support sets itself. Experience within Ireland and elsewhere suggests that the most promising future for family support lies in an inclusive vision where elements from a diverse range of fields including community development, adult education, schools, social work, criminal justice, early childhood services, social employment and local area regeneration are joined in a common venture to promote family support.

The development of family support entails addressing issues raised by gender and cultural diversity and by complex social problems such as domestic violence and the needs of neighbourhoods ravaged by high density drug use. The research evidence to date on the impact of family support in its varied and developing forms, such as kinship care and family group conferences (Marsh and Crow 1998), suggests it is a sound investment for financial resources, policy attention and professional time. Family support is a key way of enhancing the development, welfare and safety of children and young people.

References

Andersson, G. (1993) 'Support and relief: The Swedish contact person and contact family program.' *Scandinavian Journal of Social Welfare 2*, 54–62.

Bennet, L., Wolin, S. and Reiss, D. (1988) 'Deliberate family process: A strategy for protecting children of alcoholics.' *British Journal of Addictions 8*, 3, 821–829.

Borge, A. (1996) 'Developmental pathways of behaviour problems in the young child: Factors associated with continuity and change.' *Scandinavian Journal of Psychology 37*, 195–204.

Briggs, F. (1997) 'The importance of schools and early childhood centres in child protection.' *Journal of Child Centred Practice 4*, 11–23.

Caya, M. and Liem, J. (1998) 'The role of sibling support in high-conflict families.' *American Journal of Orthopsychiatry 68*, 2, 385–395.

Clarke, B., Lahert, J. and McCabe, F. (1994) *The Neighbourhood Youth Projects – North Inner City Dublin 1979–1994*. Dublin: Eastern Health Board.

Clausen, J. (1995) 'Gender, contexts and turning points in adult lives.' In P. Moen, G. Elder and K. Lüscher (eds) *Examining Lives in Context – Perspectives on the Ecology of Human Development*. Washington DC: American Psychological Association.

Commission on the Family (1998) *Strengthening Families for Life: Final Report to the Minister for Social, Community and Family Affairs – Executive Summary*. Dublin: Commission on the Family.

DePanfilis, D. (1996) 'Social isolation of neglectful families: A review of social support assessment and intervention models.' *Child Maltreatment 1*, 1, 37–52.

Dolan, P. (1993) 'The challenge of family life in the Westside – A six week course for parents of young people attending the neighbourhood youth project.' Dissertation in partial fulfilment of the requirements for the Advanced Diploma in Child Protection and Welfare, Dept of Social Studies, University of Dublin, Trinity College.

Dolan, P. (1997) 'Perceived social networks and social support among parents of adolescents: A study of twenty-six cases in a disadvantaged community.' Unpublished Masters degree thesis for the Degree of M.Litt to the Dept of Social Studies, University of Dublin, Trinity College, Dublin.

Dryfoos, J. (1994) *Full Service Schools – A Revolution in Health and Social Services for Children, Youth, and Families*. San Francisco: Jossey-Bass.

Durlak, J. and Wells, A. (1997) 'Primary prevention mental health programs for children and adolescents: A meta-analytic review.' *American Journal of Community Psychology 25*, 2, 115–152.

Eber, L. and Nelson, M. (1997) 'School-based wraparound planning: Integrating services for students with emotional and behavioural needs.' *American Journal of Orthopsychiatry 67*, 3, 327–333.

Fortin, A. and Chamberland, C. (1995) 'Preventing the psychological maltreatment of children.' *Journal of Interpersonal Violence 10*, 3, 275–295.

Frost, N., Johnson, L., Stein, M. and Wallis, L. (1996) *Negotiated Friendship – Homestart and the Delivery of Family Support*. Leicester: Homestart.

Gilligan, R. (1995a) 'Family support and child welfare: Realising the promise of the Child Care Act 1991.' In H. Ferguson and P. Kenny (eds) *On Behalf of the Child: Professional Perspectives on the Child Care Act 1991*. Dublin: A. and A. Farmar.

Gilligan, R. (1995b) 'Making a success of fostering – What we want for the children, what we need for the adults.' In D. McTeigue (ed) *A Journey through Fostering: Proceedings of the Eighth International Conference of the International Foster Care Organisation, Dublin, July 1993*. Dublin: Irish Foster Care Association.

Gilligan, R. (1998) 'The importance of schools and teachers in child welfare.' *Child and Family Social Work 3*, 1, 13–25.

Gilligan, R. (2000) 'Adversity, resilience and young people: The protective value of positive school and spare time experiences.' *Children and Society 14*, 1.

Greif, G. (1994) 'Using family therapy ideas with parenting groups.' *Journal of Family Therapy 16*, 199–207.

Guterman, N. (1997) 'Early prevention of physical child abuse and neglect: Existing evidence and future directions.' *Child Maltreatment 2*, 1, 12–34.

Harris, T. (1993) 'Surviving childhood adversity: What can we learn from naturalistic studies?' In H. Ferguson, R. Gilligan and R. Torode (eds) *Surviving Childhood Adversity – Issues for Policy and Practice*. Dublin: Social Studies Press.

Hooper-Briar, K. and Lawson, H. (1994) *Serving Children, Youth and Families through Interprofessional Collaboration and Service Integration: A Framework for Action*. Oxford, OH: Danforth Foundation and Institute for Educational Renewal at Miami University.

Inglis, T. (1994) 'Women and the struggle for daytime adult education in Ireland.' *Studies in the Education of Adults 26*, 1, 50–66.

Ireland Child Care Act 1991 (1991). Dublin: Stationery Office.

Jacobs, F. (1988) 'The five-tiered approach to evaluation: Context and implementation.' In H. Weiss and F. Jacobs (eds) *Evaluating Family Programs*. New York: Aldine de Gruyter.

Johnson, Z. and Molloy, B. (1995) 'The Community Mothers Programme – Empowerment of parents by parents.' *Children and Society 9*, 2, 73–85.

Johnson, Z., Howell, F. and Molloy, B. (1993) 'Community Mothers Programme: Randomized controlled trial of non-professional intervention in parenting.' *British Medical Journal 306*, 1449–1452.

Kellaghan, T. and Greaney, B. (1993) *The Educational Development of Students Following Participation in a Pre-School Programme in a Disadvantaged Area of Ireland*. Studies and Evaluation Papers 12. The Hague: Bernard van Leer Foundation.

Lakey, B. and Lutz, C. (1996) 'Social support and preventive and therapeutic interventions.' In G. Pierce, B. Sarason and I. Sarason (eds) *Handbook of Social Support and the Family*. New York: Plenum Press.

McGlone, F., Park, A. and Smith, K. (1998) *Families and Kinship*. London: Family Policy Studies Centre.

McTeigue, D. (1998) 'The use of focus groups in exploring children's experiences of life in care.' In D. Hogan and R. Gilligan (eds) *Researching Children's Experience*. Dublin: Trinity College, Children's Research Centre.

Marsh, P. and Crow, G. (1998) *Family Group Conferences in Child Welfare*. Oxford: Blackwell.

Masten, A. and Coatsworth, D. (1998) 'The development of competence in favourable and unfavourable environments – Lessons from research on successful children.' *American Psychologist 53*, 2, 205–220.

Morrison Dore, M. and Alexander, L. (1996) 'Preserving families at risk of child abuse and neglect: The role of the helping alliance.' *Child Abuse and Neglect 20*, 4, 349–361.

Oakley, A. (1992) *Social Support and Motherhood.* Oxford: Blackwell.

Oakley, A., Hickey, D., Rajan, L. and Rigby, A. (1996) 'Social support in pregnancy: Does it have long-term effects?' *Journal of Reproductive and Infant Psychology 14*, 7–22.

O'Callaghan, J. (1993) *School-Based Collaboration with Families.* San Francisco: Jossey-Bass.

O'Flaherty, J. (1995) *Intervention in the Early Years: An Evaluation of the High/Scope Curriculum.* London: National Children's Bureau Enterprises.

Olds, D., Eckenrode, J., Henderson, C., Kitzman, H., Powers, J., Cole, R., Sidora, K., Morris, P., Pettit, L. and Luckey, D. (1997) 'Long-term effects of home visitation on maternal life course and child abuse and neglect: Fifteen-year follow-up of a randomized trial.' *Journal of American Medical Association 278*, 8, 637–643.

Opgenhafen, R. (1996) 'The family–family support worker relationship – A study of five cases based on perceptions of the family, family support worker and social worker.' Dissertation in partial fulfilment of the requirements for the MSc in child protection and welfare, Dept of Social Studies, University of Dublin, Trinity College.

Perloff, J. and Buckner, J. (1996) 'Fathers of children on welfare: Their impact on child well-being.' *American Journal of Orthopsychiatry 66*, 4, 557–571.

Romans, S., Martin, J., Anderson, J., O'Shea, M. and Mullen, P. (1995) 'Factors that mediate between child sexual abuse and adult psychological outcome.' *Psychological Medicine 25*, 127–142.

Runyan, D., Hunter, W., Socolar, R., Amaya-Jackson, L., English, D., Landsverk, J., Dubowitz, H., Browne, D., Bangdiwala, S. and Mathew, R. (1998) 'Children who prosper in unfavorable environments: The relationship to social capital.' *Paediatrics 101*, 1, 12–18.

Rutter, M., Champion, L., Quinton, D., Maughan, B. and Pickles, A. (1995) 'Understanding individual differences in environmental–risk exposure.' In P. Moen, G. Elder and K. Lüscher (eds) *Examining Lives in Context – Perspectives on the Ecology of Human Development.* Washington DC: American Psychological Association.

Sameroff, A., Seifer, R., Baldwin, A. and Baldwin, C. (1993) 'Stability of intelligence from preschool to adolescence: The influence of social and family risk factors.' *Child Development 64*, 80–97.

Sandler, I. (1997) 'Meta-analysis of primary prevention programs for children and adolescents: Introduction to the special issue.' *American Journal of Community Psychology 25*, 2, 111–113.

Schorr, L. (1991) 'Effective programs for children growing up in concentrated poverty.' In A. Huston (ed) *Children in Poverty.* Cambridge: Cambridge University Press.

Schweinart, L., Barnes, H. and Weikart, D. (1993) *Significant Benefits: The High/Scope Perry Preschool Study Through Age 27.* Ypsilanti, MI: High/Scope Press.

Simmons, R. and Blyth, D. (1987) *Moving into Adolescence: The Impact of Pubertal Change and School Context.* Hawthorne, NY: Aldine de Gruyter.

Smith, C. and Carlson, B. (1997) 'Stress, coping and resilience in children and youth.' *Social Service Review,* June, 231–255.

Smith, J., Gilford, S. and O'Sullivan, A. (1998) *The Family Background of Homeless Young People.* London: Family Policy Studies Centre.

Smith, T. (1996) *Family Centres and Bringing Up Your Children.* London: HMSO.

Sylva, K. (1989) 'Does early intervention "work"?' *Archives of Diseases in Childhood 64*, 1103–1104.

Thiede Call, K. (1996) 'Adolescent work as an "arena of comfort" under conditions of family discomfort.' In J. Mortimer and M. Finch (eds) *Adolescents, Work, and Family – An Intergenerational Developmental Analysis.* Thousand Oaks, CA: Sage.

Thoits, P. (1983) 'Multiple identities and psychological well being: A reformulation and test of the social isolation hypothesis.' *American Sociological Review 48*, 174–187.

Thompson, R. (1995) *Preventing Child Maltreatment through Social Support – A Critical Analysis.* Thousand Oaks, CA: Sage.

Toynbee, P. (1998) 'Children of despair.' *The Guardian,* 3 June, 22.

Utting, D. (1995) *Family and Parenthood – Supporting Families, Preventing Breakdown.* London: Family Policy Studies Centre.

Weick, A. and Saleebey, D. (1995) 'Supporting family strengths: Orienting policy and practice towards the 21st century.' *Families in Society: The Journal of Contemporary Human Services 76*, 3, 141–149.

Werner, E. and Smith, R. (1992) *Overcoming the Odds – High Risk Children from Birth to Adulthood.* Ithaca: Cornell University.

Wills, T.A. and Cleary, S. (1996) 'How are social support effects mediated? A test with parental support and adolescent substance misuse.' *Journal of Personality and Social Psychology 371*, 5, 937–952.

Wilson, W.J. (1995) 'Jobless ghettos and the social outcomes of youngsters.' In P. Moen, G. Elder and K. Lüscher (eds) *Examining Lives in Context – Perspectives on the Ecology of Human Development.* Washington DC: American Psychological Association.

Wilson, W.J. (1996) *When Work Disappears – The World of the New Urban Poor.* New York: Vintage Books.

Yoshikawa, H. (1994) 'Prevention as cumulative protection: Effects of early family support and education on chronic delinquency and its risks.' *Psychological Bulletin 115*, 1, 28–54.

CHAPTER 2

Communities, Family Support and Social Change

Graham Crow and Graham Allan

Introduction

The importance of understanding family relationships in their broader community contexts is a well-established theme in the social science literature. However, the relationship between community and family support is complex. The aim of this chapter is to examine the nature of that complexity, drawing on data from different empirical studies of both supportive and unsupportive contexts. In so doing it is first important to distinguish between kin-based and other elements of community. Support for families which comes from wider kin networks within communities is founded on principles different from those arising out of non-kin community ties (such as between unrelated neighbours). As a result it is possible to identify two broad types of social support which vary both qualitatively and in their extent. Second, though, the conditional nature of social support needs to be recognized. Not only does the amount and quality of support given to families by members of wider communities vary significantly, but also the nature of the terms and conditions on which that support is provided has an important bearing on how the outcomes are shaped. The current vogue among researchers of approaching supportive relationships as 'negotiated' between those giving and receiving support has highlighted the diversity of norms on which it is possible to draw. Other recent research has also drawn attention to the historical and geographical variability of how the notions of 'good neighbourliness' and 'community mindedness' are interpreted and acted upon.

Understanding community

A common theme in many community studies, whether based in rural or urban areas, concerns the intricate connections which exist between 'community' and 'family':

> The problem of the influence of family structure and kinship early forced itself into the center of the stage. The form of the community and the lives of its members could not be understood apart from the kind of relations among persons bound by blood and marriage. (Arensberg and Kimball 1940/1968, p.xxvi)

This quotation might have appeared in any number of studies, though it happens to be from one of the first and most significant community studies conducted – Arensberg and Kimball's 1930s study of social and economic ties in County Clare, *Family and Community in Ireland* (1940/1968). Later writers have developed this theme of the interconnectedness of family and community. For example, Rees's (1951) account of 1940s rural Welsh community life in which most households were linked by kinship ties is memorable for its description of local people being woven together 'like a pig's entrails' (p.74) as the local saying had it. Other studies, too, such as Young and Willmott's (1957/1986) influential *Family and Kinship in East London*, remind us of the merits of this close identification of family and community (Morgan 1996, p.5).

Frequently, heightened levels of geographical mobility have been taken to be destructive of overlap between family and community, yet study after study continues to illustrate the significance of kin ties in people's everyday living. To take some recent examples, Wight (1993) cites estimates of two-thirds of the population of the former mining village of 'Cauldmoss' in central Scotland being related to each other, while 40 per cent of Warwick and Littlejohn's (1992) respondents in West Yorkshire each had ten or more relatives living locally. Jordan and his co-researchers, looking at a deprived housing estate in Exeter, found comparable instances of how people in their domestic lives are socialized and sustained by kin and community, not least because the majority had close kin living nearby (Jordan *et al.* 1992, pp.255–256). Similarly, in our own research in the small seaside resort of 'Steeptown' on the Isle of Wight, 22 (55%) of our 40 respondents had kin (beyond their immediate household) living in the town, with 8 (20%) having kin in the same street as themselves, providing further evidence of the continuing interconnection between 'family' and 'community'.

Yet while the enduring character of the family–community connection is not difficult to demonstrate, other aspects of functionalist models of 'community' have survived less well. In particular, the inherent limitations and contradictions of a perspective of community as a stable and integrated entity are now widely recognized. Change is driven by many factors, of which economic dynamics and contact with other cultural forms, especially those associated with urban industrial centres, are among the most powerful. Brody's (1973) study of 'Inishkillane' in the west of Ireland, for example, indicated how difficult it was for many rural communities to reproduce themselves economically, socially or culturally in the context of a dominant urban industrialism delivering wider economic opportunities and greater lifestyle choice.

In the wake of reassessments like Brody's, it is no longer possible to agree with Williams's judgement that the word 'community' seems never to be used unfavourably (1976/1983, p.76). The thrust of much recent scholarship has been to challenge the uncritical acceptance of 'community' as a phenomenon which is inevitably regarded positively by its members. Numerous studies have highlighted the restrictive character of those community ties which are experienced as constraining; that is, as bonds of involuntary obligation. Feminist writers have been prominent among those who have pointed out that a 'community' can be oppressive to at least some of its members, either by imposing demands on them to contribute (frequently in an unpaid capacity) to the welfare of others, or by setting restrictive terms and conditions on the behaviour of those in receipt of support. The general point being made by such writers is that patterns of involvement in community relationships are by no means always freely chosen (Crow and Allan 1994). Against the background of such arguments, it is important to re-examine the bases of people's involvement in community relationships, since such involvement cannot be taken for granted, either as a 'natural' phenomenon or as something prompted by individual self-interest.

The tendency in many of the earlier community studies was to see community solidarity as based upon the balanced reciprocities flowing between kin and friends. Importantly, the exchanges involved were rarely interpreted in a narrow economic fashion. Instead they were understood against the background of a wider, long-established local framework in which moral and social, as well as financial, considerations played their part. More recent writers have accepted this but questioned the extent to which relations between community members are fully reciprocal, since it is by no means clear that what is given and what is received in exchange does balance out for all individuals, even in the long term (Cheal 1988; Finch and Mason 1993). Concern not to become involved in relationships of significantly unequal exchange – either by becoming over-committed and giving more than one gets in return, or by compromising one's independence by being unable to repay other people for help provided – is an important factor which sets limits to people's involvement in neighbourly relations (Crow, Allan and Summers 1998). This point ties in with the frequently made observation that there are limits to the caring capacities of communities. The related point that exchanges between kin are less governed by reciprocity than are exchanges between friends and neighbours further highlights the need to avoid unwarranted generalizations about the nature of community relationships.

The attempt to paint a broad picture of family–community connections is thus complicated in several respects. To begin with, the basis of relationships between friends and neighbours is distinct from the basis on which relationships with kin are founded. Willmott (1986) has used the term 'friendly distance' to describe the norm of contemporary neighbourliness, arguing that a delicate balance needs to be struck between supportiveness on the one hand and respect for privacy and independence on the other, while different sets of norms underpin friendships on the one hand and kin relations on the other. Second, it is important to recognize that the norms governing these different types of community relationships are abstract and general rather than specific, and that as a result, negotiation over the details of the relationships is not only possible but inevitable (Finch 1989). This negotiation of the terms and conditions of social support has been the subject of extensive and detailed investigation in recent years, and one of the principal conclusions which can be drawn from this literature is that a great deal depends on context. Rural and urban differences matter, as do the gender, age, race and ethnicity compositions of the populations in question, along with the variable which has particular significance to the consideration of disadvantaged communities, the social class composition of the groups being investigated. Time also matters to how community support is expressed, and consideration of patterns of social change is an integral part of any overview of the links between families and communities.

Kin and other elements of community

Although they serve the useful purpose of providing a benchmark against which patterns of change can be assessed, conventional models of the traditional community need to be treated with caution when analysing contemporary and future patterns of community life. Leaving aside their tendency to exaggerate the extent to which everybody knew everybody else, such models have rightly been criticized for romanticizing the supportiveness of traditional communities and overlooking their less attractive insular, restrictive and violent sides (Crow and Allan 1994, Ch.2). In some people's hands, notions of the traditional community carry the further danger of suggesting that the supportiveness which undoubtedly did characterize many community relations in times past can be easily re-established. It is this concern which lies behind Gray's (1997) comment that communitarianism 'often operates with an idea of community which is unworkable and dangerous in our historical conditions' (p.81). Contemporary communities are necessarily more fluid and heterogeneous than were (for example) the more socially homogeneous occupational communities of a century ago that grew up around factories, mines, ports and other industries which held working-class people together through the bonds of shared employment and vulnerability to poverty – what Hoggart referred to as 'common hardship' (1995, p.329).

The argument has frequently been made that the mutual supportiveness of people in poor communities in previous generations arose out of their recognition of their common plight, their awareness that they were all vulnerable to the vagaries of illness, accidents, unemployment and other adverse circumstances associated with deprivation. The option of standing together or falling as a result of division is, of course, a Hobson's choice. In this sense the solidarity of traditional communities had a forced, compulsory character to it, as (among others) Abrams has noted (Bulmer 1986). Roberts (1995) suggests that mutual supportiveness was necessitated by poverty through her observation of the mid-twentieth century period that 'neighbourliness and neighbourhoods were strongest in the poorest areas' (p.201), a pattern which continued traditions established in earlier decades of neighbours constituting 'a mutual support society' (Roberts 1984, p.192). Roberts notes that in cases where kin did not live in close proximity, unrelated neighbours could be just as important in the provision of support to poor families, but this point is quite consistent with Abrams's argument that 'when closely examined, the networks of traditional neighbourhood usually proved...not to be primarily networks of neighbours, not territorially based networks at all, but, rather, either kinship networks or networks rooted in religion, occupation or race' (Bulmer 1986, pp.93–94). While the neighbours of poor families in traditional communities could generally be trusted and relied upon, reliance on kin was a preferred option. Broadly similar conclusions are drawn by Liebow (1967) and Stack (1974) in their widely cited studies of kinship and neighbourhood solidarities in US urban ghettos.

Roberts recognizes the special role of kin in her observation that although working-class women valued support from neighbours, distinct rules applied to support from people connected by family ties:

> Help from relations was of a different kind; there gifts were more usual than loans and relatives knew that they could not expect to be repaid for some long-term service. Helping was part of the family's duty as understood in working-class mores and an enormous amount was given and received almost as a matter of course. (Roberts 1986, p.242)

By contrast to that provided by kin, support from unrelated neighbours was less extensive and more conditional. It normally involved a greater concern for reciprocity and repayment, entailing a strong desire to keep the relationship balanced rather than becoming indebted. Traditional communities were characterized by scarce resources, and in such conditions the claims of the extended family took precedence over those of neighbours and friends, even before considerations of the latter's reliability and eligibility for assistance as 'respectable' members of the community were entered into the calculation. As Rosser and Harris (1965, p.228) noted, kinship networks have a greater permanence about them, and as a result 'give a sense of stability and belonging' to their members which relations with neighbours cannot provide. Home and extended family were the cornerstones of the social structures of traditional communities, however much these needed to be supplemented by mutually supportive relationships with neighbours and friends.

In addition, tensions and conflicts emerged within even the most integrated communities, sometimes within families but more importantly between neighbouring households. Sometimes these tensions were the result of disputes over what we might term 'boundary problems' – too much shouting, rowing or other noise from neighbours, gardens maintained to different standards, children allowed to behave in ways seen as inappropriate – in which the lifestyle adopted by one group impinged on that of another. Connected with this is the significance of status differences generally sustained within even the apparently most close-knit communities. From the outside it may have appeared that most families within a neighbourhood occupied essentially similar positions materially and socially. From the inside things were frequently understood differently, with quite minor distinctions being seen as important. 'Respectability', contested in myriad subtle ways, was often fiercely protected. A key strategy for this was to maintain distance, and at times aloofness, from those families who were defined as 'rough', whatever in the context this was taken to mean. One 'kept oneself to oneself' from such families, neither offering them support nor engaging in mutual reciprocities.

Importantly, such status designations were generally not restricted to individuals or households. More frequently they were seen as family issues; a result of the family standards into which members were socialized. That is, within well-integrated communities family reputation mattered, as kin groups were often judged collectively. The behaviour of one individual came to be seen as a reflection of the standards of the kin group overall and not just the idiosyncrasies of the particular person. Of itself this encourages a strong familial solidarity and the exercise of family controls which constrain individual freedom. Family reputation needed to be upheld, indeed promoted, within the status order and this usually meant exercising a degree of social exclusion, particularly with regard to patterns of association and support. While being supportive of those who, through some misfortune, were in need was seen as laudable, to become involved in reciprocities with those perceived as 'rough' was to put at risk your own reputation. Moreover, because reputation was linked to kinship, family could be trusted more readily than neighbours and other non-kin. As their status was linked in some fashion to yours, family members had a stake in policing and maintaining your reputation. Others had no such stake and so were potentially less trustworthy. Frequently the consequence of these features of more close-knit communities was that efforts were made to limit access to the private domain of the home. The home became the preserve of 'family', for in this way what went on inside would be less likely to become the subject of damaging gossip elsewhere.

Contemporary support

This examination of traditional communities has a bearing on our consideration of contemporary patterns of family support in two important respects. To begin with, it illustrates the more general point that communities can be held together by several quite distinct forces. If 'community' is defined as people having something in common, this can be understood, analytically, as one of three things: common residence, common interests and common identity (Willmott 1986), even if in practice these three dimensions of community overlap (Crow and Allan 1995). Traditional communities like the mining villages studied by Bulmer (1975) were held together by the common interests of an occupational community as well as by the common culture of people living similar lives. Both were in turn reinforced by the geographical isolation of these settlements. Second, social historians' work on traditional communities corrects the impression sometimes given of a golden age of community mindedness which has subsequently been displaced by more selfish, privatized lifestyles. As Williams reminds us in his survey of laments for lost community, we should always be wary of the well-known habit of using the past, the 'good old days', as a stick to beat the present (1975, p.21). The explanation for changing patterns of community life is more likely to be found in altered patterns of residence, occupational change and the impact of welfare state agencies than in a retreat from community as a cultural ideal. This is because past ideals of community were not antithetical to the privacy of family life and because contemporary community life is far more buoyant than proponents of the idea of privatization would have us believe (Allan and Crow 1991; Devine 1992).

Propositions about the decline of community are at odds with the findings of a range of social scientific investigations which point to the continuing importance of community networks in everyday life, especially in poorer areas. Morris (1988) drew on many studies of the impact of unemployment in support of her conclusion that networks not only carry information and influence in connection with employment, but also provide a source of support, both moral and material, in unemployment. Support networks can provide the child-care or domestic services which free many married women to take up employment (1988, pp.397–398). McKee's (1987) study of unemployment found similar networks of support:

> Examples of goods and assistance flowing into households from non-kin were fairly numerous…neighbours were variously described as providing help with household goods, furniture, child-minding or children's clothes. Women's networks were often the key to these exchanges… For the men, household repairs or mechanical assistance with cars were two examples of services which could be interchanged. (McKee 1987, p.113)

Similarly, Warwick and Littlejohn's (1992) research into four Yorkshire mining communities which have undergone considerable restructuring in recent years discovered the continued existence of strong connections linking individuals and households to wider social networks, with men being equally involved with friends and neighbours as they were with kin, while kin ties predominated in the social networks of the women whom they interviewed.

In Wheelock's (1990) study of unemployed men in North-East England who were *Husbands at Home*, she argues that it 'is worth distinguishing the voluntary economy work involving relatives from that involving neighbours, friends or others' (p.129) since the former was more extensive than the latter and founded on different principles. Caring for children and disabled and elderly people, food preparation, shopping and help with repairs could occur in both sets of relationships but, as in the historical research we have discussed, it was more likely to take place between relatives and, Wheelock reports, more likely to entail notions of exchange and reciprocity where non-kin were involved. Another study conducted in North-East England, Allatt and Yeandle's *Youth Unemployment and the Family*, found strong attachment to the idea of families having priority over non-kin, understood to mean that 'in a poor labour market "you first look after your own"' (1992, p.2), even though this was recognized to be in tension with broader notions of 'fairness' about what to do, for example, with knowledge of forthcoming job opportunities. In the less depressed labour market of Luton, Devine found a similar picture of family coming before neighbours: '…neighbours are not as significant a source of companionship and support as kin' (1992, p.91). The significance of the kin and non-kin distinction also emerges from studies of minority ethnic communities, such as Warrier's (1994) research into Gujarati Prajapatis in London. She found that, 'in general, individuals and families expect to be able to draw both material assistance and emotional support from their immediate kin when they need it, and therefore great value is attached to making kinship networks as strong as possible' (Warrier 1994, p.206). Similar findings to these can also be found in some of the recent US research into family and neighbourhood; see, for example, Campbell and Lee (1992) and Logan and Spitze (1994).

The increased levels of geographical mobility characteristic of late modernity clearly have a bearing on the character of solidarity and support that exists between kin, just as they alter patterns of neighbourhood cohesion. Yet the extent to which such mobility is built upon and supportive rather then undermining of kinship ties is often understated in accounts of contemporary change. If, as we argue, Willmott is correct in his claim that 'kinship remains a major force in the lives of most people' (1986, p.19), this is partly because people are often reluctant to move far from relatives and may sometimes move to be closer to kin (Ribbens 1994). Thus while geographical relocation does cause disruption to social networks, studies of migration like Warrier's indicate that people frequently choose to move to areas where kin are located so as to use their knowledge and contacts as a resource in settling into a new locality. Thus Grieco's (1987) research into recruitment to the Corby steelworks in the English Midlands revealed that kin connections were prominent in the extensive relocation of family members from Peterhead in the north of Scotland, while Wenger's (1984) study of older people found moving closer to children and/or siblings to be an established pattern, particularly among widowed elderly people. Similar conclusions can be drawn from Qureshi and Walker's (1989) study of elderly people and their families in Sheffield and Warnes and Ford's (1995) review of migration and later life.

It also needs to be recognized that, in the developed world especially, geographical mobility no longer has the force it once did. Developments in transport and communication mean that people do not need to live close to one another to sustain their relationships. Equally, for many though by no means all, patterns of social incorporation are not based around locality. Wellman's research into the development of social networks in Toronto in the latter part of the twentieth century demonstrates both the general tendency for friend and neighbour ties to dissipate with geographical mobility, but also for locality to play a smaller part in many people's personal networks (Wellman, Carrington and Hall 1988; Wellman and Wortley 1990). In particular, as well as some long-distance ties, many relationships are sustained with others who live in the same conurbation but not in the same locality. In this respect, the locality does not provide as many people with significant 'foci of activity' (Feld and Carter 1998) as it once did. Many people, though by no means all, are less engaged with activity-based networks of others and consequently less integrated into the locality as a social and economic system.

These and related findings may be taken to bear out the broad argument that relations with kin have a greater depth to them than relations with neighbours and friends; 'depth' being understood here in terms of the length of time over which they have operated, the degree to which the relationships may be considered to be intimate and the extent to which they can survive the principle of reciprocity being breached. However, while such an argument is convincing up to a point, it is too general, since there are wide variations in the extent to which different people mobilize (or, conversely, neglect to nurture) either type of relationship. Individuals and families draw more or less on the social support which is available to them from others in their personal networks, whether these others be kin, neighbours or friends. It is possible to find degrees of selectivity even among those whose range of options is quite limited (Jamieson 1998). Moreover, supportive 'family' ties are a subset of the full range of kin connections, with many kin ties being comparatively insignificant. Those that matter most, where there is most involvement and between whom most support is exchanged, are normally ties with primary kin – parents, children and siblings, augmented by grandparents and grandchildren. Other specific kin relationships may be important for idiosyncratic reasons (including geographical proximity and mutual bonds with genealogically intermediary kin), but the majority of recognized secondary kin ties are of limited consequence (Allan 1996).

So, too, the majority of neighbour ties are of comparatively little significance in people's lives; a theme that was evident in our small-scale study of neighbouring in Steeptown, a town of some 6000 population in the south of England. We interviewed 40 respondents from three different streets in the town, each representing a different socio-economic status. In the main we were concerned with the character and management of neighbour relationships and 'in particular' definitions of good neighbouring and aspects of 'balance' and reciprocity between neighbours. While 16 of the 40 respondents reported having had serious difficulties at some time in their lives with neighbours, only 3 said that they did not get along well with a majority of their current neighbours, compared with 29 who reported having positive relations with most or all of them. As might be expected, what conflict there was typically arose over issues of noise – from children playing, dogs barking or music on too loudly – and less frequently over aloofness or intrusiveness.

A key concern for our respondents was maintaining the 'delicate balance' encapsulated by the term 'friendly distance' (Willmott 1986, p.55) which studies have consistently shown to lie at the heart of contemporary neighbouring. The ambiguities in this were apparent; on the one hand respondents applied what Bourke (1994, p. 142) terms 'distancing mechanisms' to protect their privacy, but at the same time they wanted to signal a friendly disposition. Good neighbours were seen as people who are 'not intrusive, they don't pry into your business, which is what I like... I don't like people interfering' (R31, M, aged 38); 'Not being obtrusive, letting you live your life. Being friendly but not imposing. Not hanging over the garden fence to see what people are up to' (R11, F, aged 57). But at the same time such neighbours show a 'willingness to help in an emergency' (R10, M, aged 77); 'talking to them, noticing that they are there, especially the older ones. Offering help' (R8, F, aged 40). Bad neighbours were the converse of this, people who did interfere or whose lifestyle imposed unduly on others living nearby.

Our interviewees also emphasized the significance of reciprocity within neighbouring, both in terms of the need to 'live and let live' and in terms of active exchanges. Thus, in response to a hypothetical question about new, noisy neighbours, some respondents would 'let them know straightaway, obviously starting off the nice way. I'd have to let them know' (R39, M, aged 28). Most, though, would tread more gently: 'I wouldn't barge in' (R40, M, aged 64); 'There would come a time when I'd say something' (R23, M, aged 49); 'I'd put up with it for a little while but if it went on and on I'd probably...it depends on the people' (R35, F, aged 65). Throughout there was an emphasis on the 'give and take' of neighbouring, on being accepting, at least up to a point. There was also a recognition that neighbours should be willing to assist one another, especially in an emergency or time of crisis, but also at other times through exchanging minor services: 'The neighbour next door, I get her shopping and if it's a wet day I'll go and get her paper... She used to water our greenhouse for us, that sort of thing. And also she used to babysit my daughter when she was young' (R26, F, aged 52); 'I give the man next door eggs and he gives me vegetables. We swop whatever help we can to help each other' (R16, F, aged 75).

Yet while such exchanges are part of routine neighbouring, they are not extensive, in Steeptown at least. Only 16 of the 40 respondents identified three or more ways in which they helped their neighbours, and – in line with people's tendency to report higher incidences of giving rather than receiving – only 10 respondents identified three or more ways in which their neighbours helped them. Yet this did not mean they were poor neighbours, nor that Steeptown was an unfriendly place. The quality of neighbouring is defined as much by a willingness to help as by actively being engaged in sustained helping. 'Looking out for each other', helping 'if called on', assisting 'in lots of little ways', these, together with an emphasis on balanced exchange and reciprocity, are the hallmarks of 'good' neighbouring.

Despite, or perhaps because of, their limited content, the exchange basis of neighbouring is not always easy to manage. Perceptions of what is reasonable to ask or to give do not necessarily overlap, nor do people necessarily share the same notions as to what counts as equivalence. Respondents were conscious of not becoming 'over-involved', not only because of the desire to be seen as not interfering but also because the demands made by neighbours can become too great. There is no problem giving a little help, but those we interviewed did not wish to become 'trapped' into providing extensive support. 'They might not be big things but they might be sort of time consuming' (R30, F, aged 46); 'I'm trying not to get too involved [in providing elderly neighbours with transport] because it does get rather out of hand' (R35, F, aged 65). Similarly there are tensions over whether to ask for help or wait for it to be offered and over whether to offer or wait to be asked.

Conditions, negotiation and control in social support

Clear in these views about reciprocity is a recognition that social support is rarely unconditional, a point that has force for kin and friend relationships as well as neighbour ones. Yet the nature of the reciprocities, and consequently the forms of social support, which can be routinely derived from these relationships differs. Thus we can agree with St Leger and Gillespie's (1991) analysis in which they posit that 'friendship is sustained, not by "external" obligation, but by mutual enjoyment of one another's company, by affection and respect… Neighbours are not chosen voluntarily, and the obligations of the role are typically diffuse and limited… The level of commitment is low and reciprocation short-term.' What is more contentious is their characterization of kinship obligations as 'to a large extent unconditional, irrespective of any return, material or psychological, from the person helped, or the worth of the recipient' (pp.35–36). Such an approach is at odds with the growing body of evidence which suggests that, while kinship support may be less conditional than social support from neighbours and friends, it is by no means unconditional.

The issue here is whether support networks can ever be understood as simply supportive. The answer, of course, is that they cannot. Just as community involves 'outsiders' to those who are 'insiders', so 'support networks' also need to be viewed as 'control networks'. In analysing this, one also needs to be aware that 'support' can take many forms. As Oakley noted in her study of the health of mothers, 'support both given and received may be experienced more as a burden than a benefit' (1992, pp.26–27). Oakley was particularly concerned here not to take social support as a good thing by definition: 'Whereas most social support may be good…for health, it is easy to think of instances where the opposite may be the case' (1992, p.40). She went on to argue that it is necessary to allow at least the possibility of some of the things conventionally treated as social support being regarded as unhelpful.

Examples of constraining aspects of informal social support are not difficult to find. Indeed a great deal of the literature on informal caring is concerned with the costs of such caring for those providing it. In particular, many accounts of daughters and daughters-in-law tending parents (in-law) emphasize the different costs that arise for the carer with this mode of kinship solidarity. But it is equally the case that being the recipient of care also has its costs. Consider here three related issues pertinent to the conditional character of informal social support: reciprocity, network structure and familial ideology. We have already emphasized the importance of reciprocity in informal relations, particularly those of friendship and neighbouring. Within such relationships, receiving unilateral rather than reciprocal support usually leaves the recipient indebted, however carefully the support is conferred. It fosters a sense of dependence that threatens individual autonomy and allows for informal controlling pressure to be exercised in more or less subtle ways.

Second, we can recognize that it is difficult to be fully integrated into any set of relationships without their also constraining patterns of behaviour, whether or not it is experienced in this way. Moreover, the configuration of the relationships within a social network will also have an independent impact on the degree to which those relationships are experienced as constraining; a point on which Bott built her pioneering analysis and which other network theorists have since developed (Scott 1991; Wellman and Berkowitz 1988). Put simply, where network structures are loose-knit (that is, where people in an individual's social network do not have many significant ties with one another) the control there can be over an individual's actions is likely to be less than when the network structure is more dense (that is, where many of those in the network also have relationships with one another). In the former case, the 'pull' that those in the network can exert over behaviour is likely to be less effective than when, whether through economic considerations, gossip or subcultural tradition, they are able to act in concert. Social networks in 'traditional' communities did tend to be more dense, so it is not surprising that high levels of social control were operative. The issue is not one of locality or geography per se, but of the degree to which those involved in a network, however dispersed, can monitor and respond collectively to one another's behaviour.

The third issue to raise here concerns familial ideology. We saw earlier that status in 'traditional' communities was a family affair, not just an in-dividual matter. This characteristic of kinship – its shared moral basis – no longer impacts on local status issues in the way it did because kinship and residence are now rarely linked to the extent they were in these communities. However, it is undoubtedly true that kinship retains its moral basis in other regards. Most people accept that 'family' ties should be sustained at some level and that close family members have a 'natural' right to be involved in each other's lives (Allan 1996; Finch 1989; Finch and Mason 1993). This does not mean that all aspects of life are freely revealed or shared with kin: family members may work hard to ensure that some aspects of their lives remain outside family agendas. But it does result in a broad acceptance that close family members are seen as having a greater right to 'interfere' in one's life than others, even if such interference often needs to be managed delicately. In Schneider's (1968) term, there is a 'diffuse enduring solidarity' about kinship ties which is not found to the same degree in non-kin ties.

It is because of this that family relationships are not premised on reciprocity in the ways in which other ties are. In turn, of course, the absence of reciprocity as a normative principle within kinship means that receiving support from family members opens up possibilities of their attempting to influence and control behaviour, though this may nonetheless be resisted in subtle or other ways. As discussed above, reciprocity acts to limit the obligation and debt one feels to those providing support. In its absence, those offering support may attempt to exert influence over behaviour and those receiving support may feel more obliged to heed that influence. To put this differently, negotiation still occurs, as in other kinship matters (Finch and Mason 1993), but the balance of negotiating strength is altered by the principal direction in which support flows.

Thus our point here is that while family support is not governed by the same principles of short- and middle-term reciprocation concerning friend and neighbour ties, this does not mean it is unconditional. Examples of the conditional character of family support are evident in the research literature. Two recent examples will suffice as illustrations here. The first is provided by Duncan and Edwards's (1997) research into single mothers and the labour market. It is widely recognized that practical aid with child care is one of the most pressing needs of single mothers if they are to take up paid work, but such support from kin is by no means automatically forthcoming. In research conducted in inner London and Brighton, Duncan and Edwards found that there were significant differences in the norms which prevailed in the local social networks of the areas they studied, and that transgressing such norms would not be undertaken lightly as it 'can result in any available familial or friendship support, including child care, being withdrawn' (1997, p.73).

Duncan and Edwards give the following example:

> Sylvia, one of the lone mothers who lived on the peripheral Brighton council estate, said she would love to have paid work as she thought she would be better off than living on benefits... Her own mother, who lived nearby, was not in employment and offered Sylvia child care and other support when she needed it. However, her mother would not look after Sylvia's children to enable her to work because her mother believed that mothers should stay at home and look after their children. Thus if Sylvia took up paid work it would cause problems in her relationship with her mother. (Duncan and Edwards 1997, p.73)

Duncan and Edwards go on to argue that the higher rates of employment which are reported for African-Caribbean lone mothers may be due to the availability of child care from members of their communities which allows them to go out to work, whereas the social support available to white working-class lone mothers from their kin is more likely to have the condition attached that they do not combine motherhood and employment.

Different communities operate with distinct notions of what constitutes a 'good' mother, and the social support available within communities will vary accordingly.

The research by Dicks, Waddington and Critcher (1998) into the role of service providers such as health visitors and welfare workers in mining or former mining communities provides a second example of the conditional nature of family support. These professionals acknowledged the close-knit and supportive nature of the traditional community networks which endured among the people whom they served, but identified this as a potential problem for them in their work where community members' patterns of informal social support had the effect of 'obstructing the interventions of formal services'. Thus one health visitor complained of local people's unreceptiveness to advice and education:

> In a community that have lived here for the last I don't know how many generations, they're very resistant to change. I mean, you talk about the health divide, and trying to encourage healthy eating, it's very difficult here. It's because the power of grandparents and the extended family over child-rearing practice is incredible, and it's really hard to sort of replace granny. (Dicks *et al.* 1998, p.305)

Such findings echo those of an earlier generation of researchers who examined the tensions between families and professionals as sources of knowledge about health (Blaxter and Paterson 1983).

Thus, as in Duncan and Edwards's (1997) study, the informal social support provided to families comes with certain cultural assumptions attached which make its acceptance conditional. Even though important elements in the situation of the communities studied by Dicks *et al.* (1998) had been altered by the increased unemployment which has accompanied the contraction of the mining industry, the traditional culture has been slower to change, with social support still structured around women despite their reduced capacity to provide care. Dicks and her colleagues argue that

> women may well be actively involved in extended support networks, but...these can be considerable sources of strain for them as well as sources of support. It is women who are both needing and providing help, in a context where they are also often expending considerable energy in paid employment. In this context, where the male cultural 'taboo' on caring continues, female-sustained support networks can become vulnerable. (Dicks *et al.* 1998, p.306)

Conclusion

We have been concerned in this chapter with examining some key aspects of family and community support. In essence the argument has been that community and family support frequently overlap, particularly because kin often still live quite close to one another. What appears to be community support, in other words, often actually turns out to be inter-household family support, but of a form which in part – but only in part – is premised on living in the same locality. Where others than kin provide support within a community, the nature of that support tends to be different to support between kin. The former is typically more conditional than the latter and generally based on a more explicit sense of reciprocity. As numerous studies have shown, familial and kinship solidarities tend to be more enduring than non-kin ones, and to require less balance. A second major theme has been that support cannot be understood simply as a gift without strings. Receiving support potentially involves one in a matrix of obligation and control, particularly when that support is based on kinship. Here there is usually a tacit element of normative constraint experienced; to be helped is to permit others to have some say over the ordering of your life. Equally, though, to give help can also lead to becoming enmeshed in a pattern of activities from which it is hard to extricate oneself.

But if family and kinship relationships lie at the heart of much community support, it also needs to be recognized that the characteristics of family life, and in particular its demographic features, are altering in very significant ways which are likely to influence patterns of solidarity and integration. In Britain, for example, since the 1970s there have been major shifts occurring in patterns of family formation and dissolution (Allan and Crow 2000). Increases in births outside marriage, together with higher levels of divorce and re-marriage, have meant that the more traditional solidarities within and across generations cannot be assumed. For example, the number of men and women entering old age without a partner has been rising, as has the number of children reaching adulthood with poor or non-existent ties to one of their parents, usually their father. The growth of cohabitation is also relevant. Where this is a substitute for marriage, the relationships generated may in the long run be less stable. These and other changes in the demography of family life may well have an impact on the forms of support which members of kin networks require and the possibilities there are of that support being provided. Nonetheless, there also appears to be a robustness about close kin relationships which suggests that support will continue to be given, despite changed circumstances.

However, these changes will not only affect individuals and households. They are also likely to have a bearing on the configurations of support occurring within communities, though so far there has been little research on the details of how these implications are being worked out. Just as other changes affecting the structure of localities and the personal relationships which develop within them – for example, economic restructuring, changes in national and local state welfare provision, the development of new communication technologies – will influence the forms of support and solidarity generated in different places, so too changes in dominant patterns of family formation, commitment and dissolution will also shape the availability of different types of informal support. More contemporary studies focusing on how those familial decisions which individuals and couples make can have a profound impact on the patterns of social support occurring in communities would surely prove fruitful. However, as we have argued above, such research will need to be mindful of the historical and geographical variability of 'community'. Given the increasing diversity there is in the family, domestic and personal lives that people are constructing, the configurations of support in which they are involved, both as recipients and as providers, are also likely to be increasingly diverse, across the life course as well as between individuals. The challenge for social policy may well lie in developing appropriate initiatives which fully reflect this greater diversity, without stigmatizing those who require higher levels of service provision or making unwarranted assumptions about the support that an individual's different network members are willing to provide.

References

Allan, G. (1996) *Kinship and Friendship in Modern Britain.* Oxford: Oxford University Press.

Allan, G. and Crow, G. (1991) 'Privatisation, home-centredness and leisure.' *Leisure Studies 10,* 19–32.

Allan, G. and Crow, G. (2000) *Families, Household and Social Change.* London: Macmillan.

Allatt, P. and Yeandle, S. (1992) *Youth Unemployment and the Family: Voices of Disordered Times.* London: Routledge.

Arensberg, C. and Kimball, S. (1940/1968) *Family and Community in Ireland.* Cambridge, MA: Harvard University Press.

Blaxter, M. and Paterson, E. (1983) 'The health behaviour of mothers and daughters.' In N. Madge (ed) *Families at Risk.* London: Heinemann.

Brody, H. (1973) *Inishkillane: Change and Decline in the West of Ireland.* London: Allen Lane.

Bourke, J. (1994) *Working Class Cultures in Britain 1890–1960: Gender, Class and Ethnicity.* London: Routledge.

Bulmer, M. (1975) 'Sociological models of the mining community.' *Sociological Review 23*, 61–92.

Bulmer, M. (1986) *Neighbours: The Work of Philip Abrams.* Cambridge: Cambridge University Press.

Campbell, K. and Lee, B. (1992) 'Sources of personal neighbour networks: Social integration, need or time?' *Social Forces 70*, 1077–1100.

Cheal, D. (1988) *The Gift Economy.* London: Routledge.

Crow, G. and Allan, G. (1994) *Community Life: An Introduction to Local Social Relations.* Hemel Hempstead: Harvester Wheatsheaf.

Crow, G. and Allan, G. (1995) 'Community types, community typologies and community time.' *Time and Society 4*, 147–166.

Crow, G., Allan, G. and Summers, M. (1998) 'Neither busybodies nor nobodies: Managing proximity and distance in neighbourly relations.' Paper presented to the annual conference of the British Sociological Association, Edinburgh, April.

Devine, F. (1992) *Affluent Workers Revisited: Privatism and the Working Class.* Edinburgh: Edinburgh University Press.

Dicks, B., Waddington, D. and Critcher, C. (1998) 'Redundant men and over-burdened women: Local service providers and the construction of gender in ex-mining communities.' In J. Popay, J. Hearn and J. Edwards (eds) *Men, Gender Divisions and Welfare.* London: Routledge.

Duncan, S. and Edwards, R. (1997) 'Single mothers in Britain: Unsupported workers or mothers?' In S. Duncan and R. Edwards (eds) *Single Mothers in an International Context: Mothers or Workers?* London: UCL Press.

Feld, S. and Carter, W. (1998) 'Foci of activity as changing contexts for friendship.' In R. Adams and G. Allan (eds) *Placing Friendship in Context.* Cambridge: Cambridge University Press.

Finch, J. (1989) *Family Obligations and Social Change.* Cambridge: Polity Press.

Finch, J. and Mason, J. (1993) *Negotiating Family Responsibilities.* London: Routledge.

Gray, J. (1997) *Endgames: Questions in Late Modern Political Thought.* Cambridge: Polity Press.

Grieco, M. (1987) *Keeping it in the Family: Social Networks and Employment Chance.* London: Tavistock.

Hoggart, R. (1995) *The Way We Live Now.* London: Pimlico.

Jamieson, L. (1998) *Intimacy: Personal Relationships in Modern Societies.* Cambridge: Polity Press.

Jordan, B., James, S., Kay, H. and Redley, M. (1992) *Trapped in Poverty? Labour-Market Decisions in Low-Income Households.* London: Routledge.

Liebow, E. (1967) *Tally's Corner: A Study of Negro Street-Corner Men.* Boston: Little, Brown.

Logan, J. and Spitze, G. (1994) 'Family neighbours.' *American Journal of Sociology 100*, 453–476.

McKee, L. (1987) 'Households during unemployment: The resourcefulness of the unemployed.' In J. Brannen and G. Wilson (eds) *Give and Take in Families: Studies in Resource Distribution.* London: Allen and Unwin.

Morgan, D. (1996) *Family Connections: An Introduction to Family Studies.* Cambridge: Polity Press.

Morris, L. (1988) 'Employment, the household and social networks.' In D. Gallie (ed) *Employment in Britain.* Oxford: Blackwell.

Oakley, A. (1992) *Social Support and Motherhood: The Natural History of a Research Project.* Oxford: Blackwell.

Qureshi, H. and Walker, A. (1989) *The Caring Relationship: Elderly People and Their Families.* Basingstoke: Macmillan.

Rees, A. (1951) *Life in a Welsh Countryside: A Social Study of Llanfihangel yng Ngwynfa.* Cardiff: University of Wales Press.

Ribbens, J. (1994) *Mothers and Their Children: A Feminist Sociology of Childrearing.* London: Sage.

Roberts, E. (1984) *A Woman's Place: An Oral History of Working-Class Women, 1890–1940.* Oxford: Blackwell.

Roberts, E. (1986) 'Women's strategies, 1890–1940.' In J. Lewis (ed) *Labour and Love: Women's Experience of Home and Family, 1850–1940.* Oxford: Blackwell.

Roberts, E. (1995) *Women and Families: An Oral History, 1940–1970.* Oxford: Blackwell.

Rosser, C. and Harris, C. (1965) *The Family and Social Change: A Study of Family and Kinship in a South Wales Town.* London: Routledge and Kegan Paul.

Schneider, D. (1968) *American Kinship: A Cultural Account.* Englewood Cliffs, NJ: Prentice Hall.

Scott, J. (1991) *Social Network Analysis.* London: Sage.

Stack, C. (1974) *All Our Kin: Strategies for Survival in a Black Community.* New York: Harper and Row.

St Leger, F. and Gillespie, N. (1991) *Informal Welfare in Belfast: Caring Communities?* Aldershot: Avebury.

Warnes, A. and Ford, R. (1995) 'Migration and family care.' In I. Allen and E. Perkins (eds) *The Future of Family Care for Older People.* London: HMSO.

Warrier, S. (1994) 'Gujarati Prajapatis in London: Family roles and sociability networks.' In R. Ballard (ed) *Desh Pardesh: The South Asian Presence in Britain.* London: Hurst.

Warwick, D. and Littlejohn, G. (1992) *Coal, Capital and Culture: A Sociological Analysis of Mining Communities in West Yorkshire.* London: Routledge.

Wellman, B. and Berkowitz, S. (eds) (1988) *Social Structures: A Network Approach.* Cambridge: Cambridge University Press.

Wellman, B. and Wortley, S. (1990) 'Different strokes by different folks: Community ties and social support.' *American Journal of Sociology 93,* 558–588.

Wellman, B., Carrington, P. and Hall A. (1988) 'Networks as personal communities.' In B.Wellman and S. Berkowitz (eds) *Social Structures: A Network Approach.* Cambridge: Cambridge University Press.

Wenger, G. Clare (1984) *The Supportive Network: Coping with Old Age.* London: George Allen and Unwin.

Wheelock, J. (1990) *Husbands at Home: The Domestic Economy in a Post-Industrial Society.* London: Routledge.

Wight, D. (1993) *Workers not Wasters: Masculine Respectability, Consumption and Employment in Central Scotland.* Edinburgh: Edinburgh University Press.

Williams, R. (1975) *The Country and the City.* Frogmore: Paladin.

Williams, R. (1976/1983) *Keywords: A Vocabulary of Culture and Society.* London: Fontana.

Willmott, M. (1986) *Social Networks, Informal Care and Public Policy.* London: Policy Studies Institute.

Young, M. and Willmott, P. (1957/1986) *Family and Kinship in East London.* London: Routledge and Kegan Paul.

CHAPTER 3

Social Pedagogical Family Help in Germany

New Wine in Old Vessels or New Vessels for Old Wine?

Joachim Wieler

Introduction

It is being realized increasingly that Europe is not just a single community but part of a global village, to use Marshall McLuhan's apt phrase. Even so it is important to be cautious with global generalizations. Saloman, an internationally recognized pioneer of social work, conducted the first worldwide survey of social work education:

> An international comparison cannot attempt to set up standards by which to gauge the quality of various systems. It remains doubtful whether it can ever be measured. For the only test of quality and value of…social work is its usefulness and adaptation to the specific needs it has to serve and these needs are national. (Salomon 1937, p.3)

However, this statement was written in 1937, at a critical time in world history when national interests and competitiveness were all too apparent. In today's world the opportunities for developing mutual interests and sharing learning are much improved. There is a growing sense of interdependence and agreement that would seem to justify at least tentative identification of trends and tendencies beyond national and even continental boundaries. The family, despite the differences and relativities apparent in cross-national and cross-cultural comparison, has become a focal point for international concern and intervention as evidenced in the themes of international social work conferences during the Year of the Family in 1994. At the same time, there seems to be a growing awareness of the contribution that social work has made in the development of conceptual as well as practical advances in the area of family work.

There is a view among some specialists on family matters in Germany that the idea and implementation of family-centred work is probably the most important contribution which social work has made to the helping professions. Therefore, the purpose of this chapter is to delineate a conceptual framework of social work and a clarification of how family support fits into this framework. To achieve this, it will be necessary to look at the development of both social work and the family focus before describing the current state and future trends. There are important lessons that history teaches for current and future practice. Family-focused social work has an interesting and intriguing past, and a better future is possible only if that past is recognized and understood. To cover all these areas the chapter is built around four main headings:

- Defining social work with a family focus
- Origins of family-centred social work in Germany
- Social pedagogical family help (SPFH)
- Trends in social work with families.

When German and English terms do not clearly match (translations are often only approximations), the German term or phrase is added.

Defining social work with a family focus

Before coming to the more central themes of social work with families, who are generally living in disadvantaged communities, it is important to touch on some basic value positions (such as commitment and concern for disadvantaged and marginalized populations), controversies (such as individual versus collective approaches) and questions and ambivalences (such as the focus and forms of intervention). It is these which determine the nature of social work and through which social workers will determine their future. An examination of these issues will go some way towards illuminating the particular social work characteristics that are different from other perspectives, such as general medicine, psychiatry, psychology, sociology, economy, law, education or pedagogy. These are all established and acknowledged scientific disciplines that are very important to social work theory and practice. Yet social work is not the mere sum of them all, but a combination or a constellation weighed according to the tasks at hand. Despite that, social workers, particularly in Europe, still tend to be trained by representatives of those other disciplines rather than by social workers themselves. This can easily lead to lack of professional identity, a difficulty in the definition of social work and what in German is called *Fremdbestimmung* – being defined or determined by outside rather than inside forces. So it is important to define some of the core features of social work.

Who are the people with whom social work is mostly concerned?

Traditionally and predominantly, social workers are working with the most marginalized people; those with very low or no income depending on a minimal life standard provided through social welfare provisions. They are people with various kinds of handicaps who cannot afford or cannot make use of the many specialized expert services that seem to be increasingly available. In the report by the International Federation of Social Workers (1997) on *Social Exclusion and Social Work in Europe – Facilitating Inclusion*, disadvantaged families are explicitly listed as one of the frequently excluded groups with which social work is particularly concerned (p.26).

What are the settings in which social work takes place?

Within the service structure in Germany, social work takes place in both public and non-profit (semi-) private organizations on a scale ranging from the very large (such as general welfare offices) to the rather small (such as neighbourhood counselling bureaus), and increasingly in the growing profit sector of social services (such as hospitals and senior citizens' homes). However, typical social work clients are often excluded from the private services because they cannot afford them. This leads to the question of who social workers identify with, who they serve and how they serve them. For as long as social work has existed, this has been one of the largest controversies. Sooner or later the question is raised as to which practice methods are applied in these various organizations – traditional social work methods or newly developed clinical methods? Some of the social work labour force is absorbed in private practice and in the growing number of private and partly profit-oriented social services. It seems to be the goal of an increasing number of social work students to follow the trend of privatization which is so apparent in the development of contemporary social policy and is structuring the job market.

If setting is defined as the place where clients live, then social workers are more often to be found in neglected neighbourhoods than the representatives of the more established social science professions. The time seems to have passed when physicians made home calls. Schoolteachers appear to visit the families of their pupils much less frequently. It is unusual for clinical psychologists or psychiatrists to make home visits. There are, of course, exceptions in those professions that insist on 'meeting clients in their natural habitat', but unlike social workers they are the exceptions rather than the rule.

What is the focus or level for concrete intervention?

Social work is mainly concerned with interaction between human beings or, in more technical terms, between social systems, small and large. There is an ongoing debate over what should have preference – the focus on individual interaction and support or the focus on networking, structural or societal change, so as to accommodate individual needs. For a long time this has been conceived as a dichotomy. When special social work methods were developed, many schools of social work were established around specialized programmes with particular focuses on social case work, social group work and on community organization, almost as if they were separate entities. This changed with the introduction of the integrated or generic approach which originated mainly in the USA. Like the classical or traditional methods earlier, this integrated approach seemed to be rather reluctantly appreciated in Europe and elsewhere outside North America. A very important resource in spreading understanding of integrated methods was the English-language text by Anne Vickery from Europe and Harry Specht from the USA. The German edition (Specht and Vickery 1980) was soon out of print.

It is unfortunate that the ongoing controversy on individual adjustment versus structural and societal change (sometimes scorned as 'putting band-aids on effects' versus 'building castles in the air') seems to create a lot of misunderstanding or even tension among professionals. The opponents are usually identified with the behavioural and clinical disciplines on the one side and the societal and structural disciplines on the other. In spite of one of the main postulates in social work theory and practice, namely the reciprocity or interdependence of the individual and his/her social environment, much has been written and even 'preached' on where the real social work must or should take place. The answer to 'what do we concentrate on: the family, the disadvantaged community or both?' is that both should be addressed, perhaps to differing degrees at different times.

Common terminology for the different levels and methods of intervention

There seems to be agreement, at least theoretically, on some of the terms that have been used to describe the different levels of concern and intervention in social work. When the focus is on the individual or on a family, terms used include 'micro level', 'small systems', 'social case work' and, more recently, 'clinical social work'. When the focus is on agency structure or groups of up to around fifteen people, and some people include families here too, the terms are 'mezzo level', 'intermediate systems', 'the institutional level' and 'social group work'. With the focus on the community and larger social structures, the following terms are commonly used: 'macro level', 'larger systems' and 'community organization'. This differentiation is helpful in building a conceptual framework, but for family work the terminology is rather expansive and loose. Within the different approaches to family therapy, family counselling and family care there is now a range of inter-esting and promising terms: 'systemic', 'contextual', 'structural', 'integrated', 'multi-dimensional', 'multi-factorial', 'comprehensive', 'holistic', 'strategic'. On the one hand this stream of words is confusing or even irritating, but on the other they all reinforce a crucial theme: the need to work with families as families or with individuals in their family context. It can be argued that it is logical to take the theme further and involve the extended family, friends, neighbours, co-workers and where, for example, alcoholism is involved, bar keepers or even co-dependent friends from the pub.

Family-focused work within the spectrum of traditional social work methods

Within the classical or traditional social work methods of case work, group work and community organization, family work is usually considered part of social case work, but the lines between these methods are fluid. In social case work with individuals whose families are not available, for instance, in one-to-one probation work, the clients usually have some sort of family network in the background that needs to be taken into consideration (and there are techniques for working with such individuals on their family backgrounds). But since the family as a 'natural group' also presents group characteristics, it is sometimes seen as a target for social group work. Vice versa, in typical group activities, for example, with teenagers, mothers, parents and leisure groups, the family can be one or the central theme in one or more sessions (and there are also many ways to work with groups on their respective family issues). Good community organization, if money and other means are available, can and should encompass various provisions for family-centred work, such as the Irish Community After School Project (International Federation of Social Workers 1997, pp.26–27).

Origins of family-centred social work in Germany

Now, coming to the central theme of family support, how can it be described in order to substantiate the importance of the family focus, in an international and intercultural context? There are many similarities but there are also distinct differences in how social work developed and how the profession responded to family needs in different countries. The focus here is Germany, but, where appropriate, international parallels will be drawn, always recognizing that direct comparisons can seldom be made.

Family-focused work has deep roots and goes back to the very early stages in the development of professional social work, even before formal training began at the turn of the century. The work of the friendly visitors in the Anglo-Saxon countries and their colleagues in other parts of mainland Europe was, very generally speaking, organized in such a way that they visited their clients in their 'natural habitat' and had first-hand insight into the real life of those with whom they worked. It was outreach work, but, of course, burdened with control functions that constitute the so-called double mandate: on the one hand for and in the interest of our clients, but, on the other hand to ensure norms and conformity of society ('sitting between the chairs').

This dilemma still exists, more or less, depending on the kind of work being undertaken. Probation work, for instance, is more closely regulated than would be the case for an independent support group, a community project or even in clinical work. There is much talk about advocacy and the wish to side with clients, but in practice this is greatly constrained to avoid coming into conflict with designated tasks and hierarchies. Nonetheless, the outreach character of most social work has prevailed and along with home visits keeps social workers close to family's own concerns.

Physicians or family doctors and sometimes nurses, teachers and perhaps kindergarten teachers visited the homes of their patients or clients and looked at the families from the point of view of their particular expertise and not necessarily in a comprehensive way. The pioneers of social work, however, not representing a particular and narrowly defined discipline, were then, as is often the case now, confronted with a multitude of problems: ethnic, economic, housing, educational, medical, psychological and judicial. As public and private social services increased, the lack of co-ordination among the different kinds of services became the key stimulus to finding better ways to serve families.

First comprehensive scheme for family social work (Familienfürsorge)

In Germany, Marie Baum (1874–1964) was the initiator and Alice Salomon (1872–1948) probably the strongest promoter of family social work – Familienfürsorge or FA-FÜ for short. Later, they were to be called the 'great-grandmothers' of family social work (Urmütter der Familienfürsorge) (Preusser 1983, p.100). Marie Baum, experienced in public welfare, co-director of the school of social work in Hamburg and later member of the National

Assembly of the Weimar Republic, had gathered materials on these issues. Alice Salomon, honoured as 'founder of social work as a women's profession in Germany' (Deutscher Verein für öffentliche und private Fürsorge 1958), had translated and modified Mary Richmond's *Social Diagnosis* (1917) for the German situation (Salomon 1926) and supplemented it with early ideas on social therapy and with concrete family histories (Salomon and Wronsky 1926). They gathered material at home and in other countries, drafted plans and began with the implementation of programmes before a more comprehensive book on family social work was published (Baum 1928).

Innovation through cross-cultural comparison

While it is still common today for professionals to develop their strategies and concrete plans 'at home', without drawing on experiences elsewhere, these women were not operating on a strategy of trial and error but were looking around for other experiences along similar problem lines in other countries. They sent observers to countries such as the USA, England and Holland and included these findings in their overall planning. One aspect illuminates the different perception in welfare matters between Europe and the USA at that time. It is especially interesting because it explains why different national backgrounds and particular (mis)understandings may create different methods. Here are notes for a German audience on family case work in the USA in 1926:

> Because there is no proletariat as we understand it and not the large population living under the subsistence level in America (to these observers the poverty of a significant minority seemed not to be apparent, J.W.), the problems of correct behaviour and adjustment to societal norms were more in the foreground of social work intervention and not the issues of poverty as such. It is interesting that in a research report on Vocational Aspects of Family-Social-Work there are assumed to be 50 per cent of cases in which counselling and advice (Aufklärung, J.W.) are necessary but no direct material or financial support. (Baum 1928, p.164)

Within this cross-national comparison it was also noted that the triad of social case work, social group work and community organization was a clear and differentiated feature of US social work. Family social work was included under general social case work, but according to observers in other countries the unified approach to family work, calling for one social worker to be the co-ordinator of the services involved, did not exist in the USA, UK or Holland.

In *Familienfürsorge*, which was first published in 1927 with a second edition in 1928, Marie Baum described in detail the historical developments before the end of World War I and the reasons and steps for the integration of family social work in the public services structure during the Weimar Republic. In her introductory remarks she wrote:

> The term Family Social Work can be interpreted as:
>
> 1. A social-political goal. All social work activities have the purpose of strengthening the family and of enhancing the caring and educational capacities in accordance with paragraph 119 of the constitution.
>
> 2. A method. In the application of social work, not the individual need, neither destiny nor guilt of the individual, but principally the situation of the entire family will be the starting point for the assessment and the treatment plan.
>
> 3. An organisational form. The specialised branches of financial support, health care and educational provisions (and other aspects not listed here, J.W.) should be coordinated in such a way that parallel and overlapping services can be avoided, especially in the interest of the families. Their contact can be limited to only one person or office and the unified treatment plan for help can be offered and coordinated from only one side. (Baum 1928, p.5)

These quotes seem to mark the beginning of an early systems approach that grew out of very practical necessities observed in families and in the existing services structure. From the point of view of the different helping professions involved, these early colleagues were confronted with multiple problems that could not be solved in separate work relationships with different helpers from different institutions. Most important then, as now, the family was thought of as the centre of concern:

> ...because it could happen in families where health, financial and educational problems accumulated, that members had to reveal the agonizing stories of their lives again and again in front of strangers...and also that no one among the different agencies felt responsible for the entire situation. (Baum 1927, cited in Müller 1988, p.178)

By about 1925, before the first and second editions of the book were published, the new family approach and institutional reforms were implemented in many German municipalities. But as is often the case with new inventions and reforms, they were not accepted without controversy. Prior to the move towards family work, many welfare workers felt that upgrading of their functions had been too dependent on their superiors and institutional regulations. Others accepted the institutional reforms because at that time new rules were usually not challenged. On the whole, there seems to have been much enthusiasm about this reform. The professional associations had conferences on family social work and disseminated leaflets, and there is much evidence of this in the literature of the profession. But there were some who felt that too much was being asked of them:

> Slowly but surely, family social work will be implemented... The social workers, it seems to me, will have to be multi-headed creatures from fairy tales who will have to be experts in all areas. It will get increasingly more difficult to work with individuals, I don't see how this work can be superseded by a unified organizational concept. The colourful variety of life will be organized to death. (Stieve 1925/1983, pp.8–9)

Social workers involved in the workers' movement feared too much institutional centralization and adherence to conservative family traditions and philosophy. There were also representatives from other disciplines who, for reasons of professional politics, were reluctant to loosen their earlier control.

Very generally speaking, the family as an institution seemed to be in question and views about it were then, as they still are today, extremely varied. What functions does the family have for its members and what does society expect from families? Which social problems can the family absorb and where are the limits? What roles do children have in their families for learning and taking responsibility without being exploited? What are the possibilities and necessities for parents to fulfil their responsibility as key persons for the socialization of their children? What are the tasks of a community or larger social system in order to ensure the family's function in cases of unusual circumstances? Is there a special responsibility to high-risk families such as single parent families, or those living in urban and rural areas of housing blight? The list of questions and the possible answers are almost unlimited. Those who were most directly confronted with the daily problems of the most marginalized populations and who wanted to react to them seem to have recognized one thing: the need to put a solid foundation of knowledge under the daily work with their specific families. This went hand in hand with the need for professional development.

Social work research on family life and its curtailment in 1933

The new focus on family work, together with institutional reform and the pressure to improve the situation, were among the impetuses for the creation of the German Academy for Social and Educational Women's Work in 1925 (Deutsche Akademie für soziale und pädagogische Frauenarbeit), with Alice

Salomon as president. One of the most important purposes of this academy, as an early prototype of scientific social work training in Germany, was to initiate and co-ordinate specific research activities in the area of social work.

By 1933, when the Nazis seized power and brought the German Women's Academy to an early end, 13 volumes of research on various aspects of family life had been published and more were projected. The title of the series was 'Research about durability versus instability of the family in the present' (*Forschung über Bestand und Erschütterung der Familie in der Gegenwart*). The first volume *Das Familienleben in der Gegenwart. 182 Familien – Monographien* (Family life in the present, 182 family monographs) was co-edited by Alice Salomon and Marie Baum (1930). Other volumes, to name a few, dealt with: 'Structure of the family'; 'Family situations of divorced or abandoned women'; 'Working women in fatherless families'; 'Youth and families in large cities'; 'Life circumstances of unmarried mothers in rural areas'; 'Rhythms in family life, the daily workload'; and 'On the matrix of family income' (Salomon 1983, p.215).

Since Salomon and other teachers of the 'Women's Academy' were of Jewish descent, as were many of the students (it has been suggested that the proportion was more than one-third), the Academy came under attack and was closed. Many of the avant-garde of family work who had started the programmes were silenced or expelled from Germany, together with the prospects of innovative family work. The research was soon forgotten for a long period or repressed and an update has never been attempted. Many of the students took their knowledge as refugees to other countries. The so-called Frankfurt School which included Horkheimer, Fromm, Adorno and others who had worked on family issues from their particular points of view ('the authoritarian personality' is probably the best known) also had to leave Germany. Some were able to continue their work in institutions in other countries such as the 'New School of Social Research in New York', but the two strands seemingly never combined or fused in exile.

The breakdown of the rather promising developments regarding family-centred work is one indicator of the losses that German social work suffered through the interruption of the so-called 'Regime of a Thousand Years' (*Tausendjähriges Reich*) which lasted from 1933 to 1945. Certainly much has changed in social work since then. Even if the beginnings were recognized and acknowledged, one could not simply pick up the lost threads. But there is a break in the awareness and continuity and in the experience, good or bad, that could have been built on. Instead, more recent developments tend to be portrayed as if something completely new is happening.

Family social work or *Familienfürsorge* was kept alive during the Nazi period and beyond but was subjugated to the doctrines of eugenics; family support was promoted only for those who fitted the Germanic mould. This tainted continuity and its inherently conservative control functions are probably at the root of growing criticism of the entire concept of *Familienfürsorge* in Germany after World War II.

Post-war developments

The reconstruction of Germany and re-establishment of the social welfare system under democratic conditions were strongly influenced by the re-education processes imposed by the allied forces. Social case work, social group work and community organization were introduced by North American colleagues, among them many of the refugees who had to leave Germany, Austria and other Nazi-occupied countries after 1933. Some of them had become rather influential social workers in the USA; for example, Anne Fischer, Sophie Freud, Gisela Konopka, Louis Lowy, Henry Maier, Hertha Kraus, Walter Friedländer, Curt Bondy, Kurt Reichert, Hans Falck, Werner Boehm, Marianne Welter and many others (Wieler and Zeller 1995). The reconnection with lost colleagues was welcome, but there was resistance to foreign methods. They were seen as originally North American inventions and were eventually adapted, but more or less as exotic imports. Social work with families was partly included in social case work. It also reappeared as a separate method; the reasons for which are still rather unclear. In the recent literature, the early research on family social work and its application through *Familienfürsorge* have hardly been mentioned and only insiders seem aware of those early efforts. It may be that these accomplishments were forgotten and are still not popular because the Nazis seem to have done a thorough job of silencing some of the most innovative social workers. With more historical migration research in social work, these dark spots might be illuminated and will eventually lead to the recognition of the cross-fertilization processes as one of the positive results in forced migration.

Certainly family issues did not disappear and working with families became very popular again in the 1960s and 1970s. However, this was more clinically oriented family work and much of it came from North America. Virginia Satir, with her workshops and books on family therapy, became very popular. She was one of the relatively few social workers who became famous in this area. But there were many others from different psychological and therapeutic schools who refined family work into very differentiated treatment concepts; for instance, different psychoanalytic models, communication-focused and structural family work, the strategic and growth model, the behaviourist approach and the Milan school of family work (Beck 1985). This was indeed therapy – clinical social work in a clinical setting, but not social work with clients in their own homes and not in their communities.

In dividing up the work with other colleagues, there was a tendency for social workers to be assigned to the so-called welfare families. Outspoken arguments and unspoken resistances were in the air: lack of client motivation and verbal skills; too many problems; too many children; help cannot be given with financial and legal problems. The notorious argument that sophisticated clinical work does not fit the capabilities of these clients was very obviously correct. Typical welfare clients, referred as the last resort, did have something in common: many longstanding involvements with various public social services and sometimes even more loose contacts with private or volunteer services. These situations were indeed complex and complicated and very much like similar counselling situations in Germany. One of the biggest challenges in the beginning phase of working with these families was to find out who else was involved with them and who had the best rapport. There were situations where more than ten professionals from different services worked with the same family. Usually the workers did not know about each other. It was important to work carefully with the clients as well as with the engaged workers from other agencies and plan involvement to-gether. It is also clear why the early social work writers insisted that there should be one constant and reliable contact person – the *Bezugsperson* in German. While social workers in clinical settings were happy with the development of new family treatment modalities, the others, and that was the majority in more typical social work settings, did not find them as useful in their practice fields, or only to a limited degree.

New wine in old vessels or new vessels for old wine?

Sozialpädagogische Familienhilfe is the formal German term for family help through social pedagogics, but the underlying ideas and content are similar to what has been described earlier as the intended family social work of the 1920s. It is not tragic but certainly unfortunate that there is hardly any recognition of earlier developments. In some of the recent literature, the only references are to Mary Richmond and her book on *Social Diagnosis* (1917) in the USA. Probably one of the reasons for this is that social pedagogics and social work have long been treated as different disciplines, perhaps similar to youth care work and community work in the UK (this, of course, would be a theme for another book or two). But whatever the difference in terms, family help through social pedagogics began in the late 1960s in Berlin. It has developed into a very effective instrument in assisting the most disadvantaged and high-risk families. Since unification, it has also rapidly taken hold in the eastern part of Germany. To some extent it is similar to the US concept of family preservation.

Social pedagogical family help (SPFH)

Social pedagogical family help (SPFH) was, as the terminology indicates, strongly influenced by the university departments of education and/or social pedagogics. It began as a result of the dramatically rising costs of institutional care for children and youth and in response to criticisms of the quality of that care. It also coincided with critical voices during the student movement (*StudentInnen-Bewegung und ausserparlamentarische Opposition*) that stressed the need for societal change and change in the political structure. Slowly but steadily, the ideas spread and concrete programmes were implemented in most regions of West Germany. After unification, under the influence of the west, expansion continued in conjunction with the amended youth and general welfare policy (*Kinder- und Jugendhilfegesetz*, KJHG and *Bundessozial- hilfegesetz*, BSHG). These policies were part of the unification contract and it is important to recognize the place of social welfare within the former GDR as part of this history and contemporary developments.

Beside the similarities to the earlier concept in terms of the continued family focus, there are some distinguishing features that make the new approach more variable and thus more flexible for the clients and also for the service delivery. At the same time it does not have the unifying and centralized function that family social work (*Familienfürsorge*) had in earlier years. In 1997 the Federal Ministry for the Family, Senior Citizens, Women and Youth published a very thorough account of the conceptual and practical aspects of SPFH, including concrete guidelines and helpful suggestions. Its weakness lies in the history of family support in social work (Bundesminis- terium für Familie, Senioren, Frauen und Jugend 1997).

Who delivers the service and who pays for it?

SPFH can be delivered by the public youth agency (*Jugendamt*) as a specialized service or delegated to semi/private agencies. The situations in which it is used are diverse. It is usually associated with acute family crisis: for instance, in cases where there is danger of violence in the family; situations in which there is a need for placement of children outside the family; and situations where attempts to work with a family through the usual services have proved fruitless. It is also useful to note the proportion of foreign families needing SPFH. In 1995 the figure was 9 per cent, which included 2 per cent of mixed nationalities (Bundesministerium für Familie, Senioren, Frauen und Jugend 1997, p.71).

The availability of services in cities and rural areas varies greatly. Some clients may prefer public services over private or church-based services when they have a choice. The provision of different services is also in tune with a commitment to being client centred and to the principle of plurality. As in the early approaches, the support provided by SPFH is based on the specific needs with which clients are faced in their particular life situations (Thiersch 1992).

Some differences between services in western and eastern Germany are apparent from statistics on public and private provision shown in Table 3.1. Private services could not offer SPFH in the GDR, but following unification in 1991 they increased rapidly.

Table 3.1 Differences between services in western and eastern Germany					
No. of cases in western Germany					
	1991	1992	1993	1994	1995
Public services	4,543	4,768	4,333	4,723	5,093
Private service	1,602	1,707	1,954	2,170	2,541
Total	6,145	6,485	6,287	6,893	7,634
No. of cases in eastern Germany					
	1991	1992	1993	1994	1995
Public services	2,865	2,990	3,149	1,672	1,342
Private service	79	493	1,111	1,386	2,270
Total	2,944	3,483	4,260	3,058	3,612
Total in Germany	9,089	9,968	10,547	9,951	11,246

Source: Bundesministerium für Familie, Senioren, Frauen und Jugend 1997, p.12

SPFH is delivered by a number of different professional groups, but mostly by social workers. However, here again there are interesting differences between the two parts of Germany. As the figures in Table 3.2 demonstrate, the predominance of social work is much less marked in the east.

Table 3.2 Delivery of SPFH by different professional groups in western and eastern Germany

Professional Group	Western Germany		Eastern Germany	
	1990 %	1994 %	1991 %	1994 %
Social worker	57.9	63.1	21.4	23.5
Kindergarten teachers (*ErzieherInnen*)	11.4	11.4	35.4	35.8
Pedagogues (*Dipl. PadagogInnen*)	3.3	5.8	3.7	3.3
Psychologists	3.2	3.9	3.4	2.7
Teachers (for different subjects)	2.4	2.1	9.5	10.2
Worker with special skills	0.2	0.2	8.2	6.7
Nurses	1.6	1.1	7.5	5.0

Source: Bundesministerium für Familie, Senioren, Frauen und Jugend 1997, p.13

SPFH is mainly financed through public community budgets because the community is obliged to offer the service when individuals and families need help and have not sufficient private resources. Families do not have to pay for the SPFH service as such, but they are sometimes expected to cover minor costs in connection with activities (such as trips and entrance fees for swimming pools). Financial support for families in need is regulated in two of the most basic social policies: the general Social Welfare Law (*Bundessozial-hilfe-Gesetz*, BSHG) and the Youth Welfare Law (*Bundesjugendhilfe-Gesetz*, KJHG). According to a fundamental principle in German social welfare, the so-called 'principle of subsidiarity of public services', private providers of social services are the preferred option. They carry out the actual work and are eligible to receive public funds for their service. This may sound clear and reasonable, but the negotiations between the public and private sector seem to be an unending challenge.

SPFH between social case work and community organization

Depending on the population group, the orientation of social services and infra-structural circumstances, SPFH can be flexibly organized in conjunction with different methodological approaches. When practised in a disadvantaged community, there may well be a strong accent on methodological linkage with community organization in order to improve the general circumstances (somewhat at the cost of clinical priorities which some clients may not favour anyway). In an economically and social infrastructurally more balanced community, with only pockets of a few disadvantaged families, the methodological emphasis is likely to be more on regular social case work or even clinical work. The sophisticated practice concepts of different schools of family work are certainly not to be underestimated, but they need to stand the test of applicability for people in disadvantaged circumstances. As Bertold Brecht bluntly put it: 'First a full stomach and then morals.' But whatever the particular emphasis, the first critical evaluation of SPFH in West Germany by Wolfgang Elger showed that the programmes seemed to be guided by a number of subtle basic assumptions. He divided these into several categories based on aim and method (Elger 1990, pp.73–78):

- as a way of restoring the classical role structure in families (perpetuating the traditional roles of women and men in the families)

- as support for the weaker family members (focus on children and perhaps women, often combined with social group work)

- as practical support and enhancement of material existence (placing more emphasis on material and household skills than on social interaction)

- combined with the emphasis on community organization

- as a therapeutic service.

The particular orientation or any programme is more or less determined by the professional helpers and needs to be addressed in the planning and reflection processes (i.e. supervision). Elger seems to recommend the model of SPFH combined with community organization and social group work – and not predominantly with social case work (Elger 1990, p.73). This is not to underestimate the clinical aspects of working with families. Very direct and supportive work can often mark the beginning of the process of change. It is essential to start with the clients' presenting needs. In the ongoing process, however, not only do clients need to be won over to participate in more comprehensive schemes on their own and others' behalf (according to the concept of empowerment), but also practitioners need to involve themselves at the structural level.

Referrals and length of involvement

Referrals for SPFH come from a range of sources, but the statistics (Bundes-ministerium für Familie, Senioren, Frauen und Jugend 1997, p.11) show that almost two-thirds (63%) come from public welfare offices and youth agencies (ASD/Jugendamt) whose responsibility it is to provide services when everything else has failed. Almost one in five referrals (19%) come as self-referrals by parents (often single), one in ten (10%) of the families are referred by other public institutions such as schools and the health department and some (5%) come from private services and other sourcers (3%).

When cases for SPFH are suggested or selected, the SPFH contract is negotiated between the referred family and the agency that delivers SPFH and also between the delivering service and the public agency that carries the financial responsibility (this usually happens first). Before the actual treatment and at agreed intervals, staff meetings take place between the agencies and detailed action plans are developed in an ongoing process. The length of SPFH involvement differs, as can be seen in figures for 1994 shown in Table 3.3.

Table 3.3 Length of SPFH involvement	
Time	Percentage
Less than 6 months	19.9
6–12 months	26.6
12–18 months	17.9
18–24 months	14.0
24–30 months	8.6
30 months and more	12.9

Source: Bundesministerium für Familie, Senioren, Frauen und Jugend 1997, p.10

Growth and support for SPFH

All available studies indicate that SPFH is on the increase, particularly in eastern Germany. The reason for this steady rise is not clearly visible and can only be speculated upon. It is rather difficult to measure success and more longitudinal studies are necessary to verify the results. However, according to clinical evidence it does appear that the identified families benefit from this intensive service. The growth is also linked to a general decline in residential care for children and youth which has resulted in relative financial savings of public expenditure and support for SPFH as a preventive alternative. Services other than traditional residential care, such as day care and counselling services, are all developing at the local level to varying degrees. Institutional reform of the public youth services at local and regional levels also serves to reinforce interest in SPFH. They put more emphasis on co-ordination than 'parallelization' of separate services, though this does vary from region to region. The authors of the *Handbuch Sozialpädagogische Familienhilfe* (Handbook on SPFH) suggest the integrated use of methods, but are not explicitly indicating that community organization should be given a priority as in Elger's evaluation (Bundesministerium für Familie, Senioren, Frauen und Jugend 1997).

Trends in social work with families

Whatever happens in family work will largely depend on the family itself as an institution. The family has been praised and criticized and alternatives to the traditional family have been found and experimented with, but it seems that the institution, variations included, as a very fundamental or basic human system has survived throughout the centuries.

In 1994 the German Minister for Family Affairs and the President of the German National Commission for the International Year of the Family, Hannelore Rönsch, proclaimed in the final report: 'Those who want to create the future will have to support the family, because the family is the foundation of our society' (Deutsche Nationalkommision für das Internationale Jahr der Familie 1994, p.9). In the same report, the European Council of Ministers developed recommendations for congruent and interdisciplinary family politics:

> On the threshold to the next century family politics will have to support families and provide protection and assistance so that they can fulfil their tasks in society. The full potential of each family, particularly the most needy, must be supported so that they can carry out the responsibility and achieve independence with the dignity that is inherent in each human being. (Deutsche Nationalkommission für das Internationale Jahr der Familie 1994, p.95)

But what images do we have of the family if we do not hang on to the ideal constellation of mother, father and two children? It is this constellation that still seems to be the base for understanding good family life, for generalizations and the development of strategies and concepts for family support. Reality presents a different picture in different countries.

In Germany, about one-third of the population lives in the kind of model family – 'father, mother, child'. The number of one-person households is increasing (for instance, more than 50 per cent in Frankfurt). There is a drastic decrease in marriages, 20 per cent of marriages are childless and the wish for children is falling drastically in the eastern part of the country. Almost every third marriage ends with divorce and 18 per cent of the children live with only one parent. If we look at the families with whom social workers are concerned, it is even more difficult to draw conclusions for an easy plan of action.

At the present time, family researchers talk about an erosion process regarding the capability of families: normative powers and the model function of parents deteriorate in the wake of values and increasing individualization. On the other hand, hope is invested in the integrating power of the family and these hopes go higher the more diffuse the situation becomes and the narrower the social political possibilities. The family is idealized as a steady rock in a wild sea.

Much of the controversy is commonly reduced to the material aspects: to the problem of the gulf between the 'haves' and the 'have nots' and consequently on how to close this gap. However, as important as the financial and material aspects are, it is sometimes difficult to say if we should be primarily concerned with these or with the social aspects, the human relational challenges. We cannot reduce our human existence to money, but we cannot exist without it. To a large extent, the quality of life depends on it. What is our position in view of the fact that the financial gap is widening dangerously, not only between individuals, families, communities and countries, but between the industrial and less industrial world regions as well? If material and social problems are interlinked, how can we distinguish between the two and yet simultaneously pay attention to both? The widening repertoire of integrated social work methods provides a variety of options that are designed to respond to the needs of people in different social systems. As a tendency, the emphasis is on diversity and flexible application of practical tools, depending on what seems appropriate for the kind of social system, the problem at hand, the specific time and the available resources.

I have tried to demonstrate that the family system has traditionally been at the centre of social work concern. It must be obvious that this is not a shortlived idea, but a long-term developmental trend. Perhaps the main problem, if not the largest, is (as it always has been) a value or moral question that is tied to the double mandate: 'On whose side do we stand?'

Social workers around the world have been challenged, and some angered, by the book *Unfaithful Angels: How Social Work has Abandoned its*

Mission; perhaps a last public pronouncement from Henry Specht (1995), one of the pioneers of integrated social work methods. In short, he argues that social work has abandoned its earlier concern with the poorest people and has shifted attention to clinical or therapeutic methods for the elite, whereas what is required are reasonable checks and balances between individual and collective approaches and not just concentration on one. At this time in history, however, even the terms 'collectivity' and 'collective responsibility' seem to have lost credibility. The pendulum is swinging towards individualism, hopefully not for too long or too far.

References

Baum, M. (1928) *Familienfürsorge. Schriften des Deutschen Vereins für Öffentliche und Private Fürsorge*, 2nd edn. Karlsruhe: G. Braun.

Beck, R. (1985) *Familientherapie, Modelle zur Veränderung familialer Beziehungsmuster.* Bad Heilbrunn: Verlag Julius Klinkhardt.

Bundesministerium für Familie, Senioren, Frauen und Jugend (1997) *Handbuch Sozialpädagogische Familienhilfe.* E. Helming, H. Schattner and H. Blüml (eds). Stuttgart, Berlin, Köln: Kohlhammer Verlag.

Deutsche Nationalkommission für das Internationale Jahr der Familie (1994) *Abschlussbericht zum Internationalen Jahr der Familie 1994.* Bonn: Geschäftstelle der Kommission.

Deutscher Verein für öffentliche und private Fürsorge (1958) *Alice Salomon, die Begründerin des Sozialen Frauenberufs in Deutschland, ihr Leben und ihrWerk.* H. Muthesius (ed). Köln, Berlin: Carl Heymanns Verlag.

Elger, W. (1990) *Sozialpädagogische Familienhilfe.* Neuwied: Luchterhand Verlag.

International Federation of Social Workers (1997) *Social Exclusion and Social Work in Europe – Facilitating Inclusion. Executive Summary and Full Report on the IFSW Europe Project 1996–1997.* Olso: General Secretariat.

Müller, C. Wolfgang (1998) *Wie Helfen zum Beruf Wurde. Eine Methodengeschichte der Sozialarbeit.* Weinheim, Basel: Beltz Verlag.

Preusser, N. (1983) 'Fürsorge zwischen Massennot und Opfergang.' In H. Stieve *Tagebuch einer Fürsorgerin.* Weinheim, Basel: Beltz Verlag.

Richmond, M. (1917) *Social Diagnosis.* New York: Russell Sage Foundation.

Salomon, A. (1926) *Soziale Diagnose.* Berlin: Carl Heymanns Verlag.

Salomon, A. (1937) *Education for Social Work. A Sociological Interpretation Based on an International Survey.* International Committee of Schools of Social Work (ed). Zürich, Leipzig: Verlag für Recht und Gesellschaft.

Salomon, A. (1983) *Charakter ist Schicksal. Lebenserinnerungen.* (Finished approx. 1944 in English; an English version of the manuscript is available at the Leo Baeck Institute, New York.) R. Baron and R. Landwehr (eds) Weinheim, Basel: Beltz Verlag.

Salomon, A. and Baum, M. (eds) (1930) *Das Familienleben in der Gegenwart. 182 Familien – Monographien.* With co-operation of Annemarie Niemeyer and others. Berlin: Verlag F.A. Herbig.

Salomon, A. and Wronsky, S. (1926) *Soziale Therapie.* With co-operation of Eberhard Giese. Berlin: Carl Heymanns Verlag.

Specht, H. and Vickery, A. (eds) (1980) *Methodenintegration in der Sozialarbeit. Zur Entwicklung eines einheitlichen Praxismodells.* Freiburg: Lambertus-Verlag.

Specht, H. (1995) *Unfaithful Angels: How Social Work has Abandoned its Mission.* New York: Free Press.

Stieve, H. (1925/1983) *Tagebuch einer Fürsorgerin.* Weinheim, Basel: Beltz Verlag.

Thiersch, H. (1992) *Lebensweltorientierung in der Sozialen Arbeit.* Weinheim: Juventa Verlag.

Wieler, J. and Zeller, S. (1995) *Emigrierte Sozialarbeit. Portraits vertriebener Sozial-ArbeiterInnen.* Freiburg: Lambertus-Verlag.

CHAPTER 4

Children in Control

Helping Parents to Restore the Balance

Martin Herbert

There is a mounting tide of public concern about violence and disruptive behaviour in homes, classrooms and on the streets. The 1996 White Paper statistics for offenders convicted or cautioned for an indictable offence in England and Wales show that 10 to 15 year olds account for some 14 per cent of known offenders, and 10 to 17 year olds account for around 25 per cent. A small hard core of persistent offenders is responsible for a disproportionate amount of crime. Research indicates that about 3 per cent of young offenders commit 26 per cent of youth crime.

My first purpose in this chapter is to describe some of the features of these children, their early circumstances and developmental pathways on the way to delinquency. A sharply focused scientific look at these early years provides us with a counter to the gloom and nihilism of the apocalyptic view of juvenile crime. There is room for some optimism. A diverse range of risk factors has been identified in the empirical research literature on the causes of crime, a significant number of which 'may be offset by positive influences such as good parenting' (White Paper 1996).

My second purpose is to explore the meaning of good parenting in the context of finding a buffer against the drift into a criminal career and to explore how professionals can contribute to its emergence or enhancement by the provision of focused family and parental support. I believe that we now have the theoretical know-how and practical psycho-social technology to bring about more effective parenting during sensitive periods in child and adolescent development, such as to halt, perhaps even prevent, the downward slide of many potential criminals. To this end, I will review some of the empirical evidence on parental support, notably behavioural family interventions (including the parenting skills training component) and their success in improving childrearing in distressed families and families with children exhibiting high levels of disruptive, antisocial and aggressive behaviour.

The support that such interventions provide for parents also constitutes support for children. The empowerment of parents – the conceptual core of this work – is not at the expense of their offspring. The children I refer to as out of control (in one sense) and in control (in another) and the management issues to which they give rise are not happy children – in fact quite the opposite, as we shall see.

Conduct disorders

An examination of the criteria in the ICD-10 (World Health Organization 1992) classification of childhood disorder demonstrates the centrality of the antisocial, aggressive behaviours described above, in the conduct disorder classification. In the absence of early treatment, the long-term outlook for children with aggressive conduct disorders is particularly grave. Their scholastic underachievement and failure have debilitating short-term and long-term consequences – notably (in the latter case) in high rates of unemployment and dependency on state support (Rutter and Giller 1983). Hard-pressed parents (particularly mothers) are quite likely to manifest stress-related disorders such as anxiety states, depression and psycho-physiological disorders (Brody and Forehand 1986; Webster-Stratton and Hammond 1988). We require treatment programmes which can be widely available for purposes of remediation and prevention.

Unfortunately, the prevalence of disruptive behavioural disorders (which is increasing) has generated a need for services that far exceeds available resources and personnel (Hobbs 1982; Knitzer 1982). The consequences of such a mismatch are serious enough in the short term; one thinks of the distress that goes unalleviated for so many young people. But there is another concern: the possibility of blighted futures over the longer term. These 'aggressive', antisocial children are at increased risk of being rejected by their peers. They are also at risk of developing a veritable litany of problems later in life such as truancy, alcoholism, drug abuse, juvenile delinquency, adult crime and interpersonal problems (see Robins 1966; Robins and Price 1991). Paradoxically, children with less serious difficulties are more likely to receive the scarce resources of therapy than those with the more extreme disorders (Herbert 1994; Kazdin 1987).

Research (see Moffitt and Caspi 1998) indicates that maltreatment and witnessing parental aggression during early childhood are predictive of children developing conduct problems. Conduct problems, in turn, predict later partner violence, which first emerges during adolescent dating experiences. Rates of partner violence double among young couples who move from dating into cohabiting and who bear children at a young age. Thus, aggressive behaviour becomes highly stable across the life course of individuals and is transmitted from generation to generation within families.

Numerous studies have found associations between characteristics of the family, especially childrearing style, and aggressive behaviour in the young (Bandura 1973; Loeber and Dishion 1984; Patterson 1982). The consensus emerging from this work is that in children who exhibit higher than average levels of aggression, who bully others, whether inside or outside the home, there seems to be an association with cold, as opposed to warm, childrearing, intense levels of discord or violence in the home and a lack of clear rules about discipline or monitoring of aggressive behaviour (Herbert 1987a; Patterson 1982). Children growing up in such families have bullying behaviours to imitate, with little counteracting identification with caregivers who provide affection and/or training in self-restraint.

Location of control within the family

Oppositional defiant and conduct disorders are heterogeneous in their manifestations. The location of power within families and the direction of coercive influence and aggression within the home may vary and change over time. Many parents feel bruised and abused (literally and figuratively, physically and emotionally) by their children and teenagers. They tend to remain silent, too embarrassed to admit the harassment and fear they experience daily. My colleagues and I have worked with very young and older children whose hostility toward their parents spilled over regularly into verbal abuse (obscenities, humiliating criticism and threats) and physical assaults (ranging from slaps to serious violence). Researchers into family violence make the point that the very notion of children controlling, indeed assaulting, their parents is so alien to our ideas about the relationships between parents and offspring that it is difficult to believe such a reversal, especially one so subversive, can actually occur. Given the complexities of violence in children and families it is imperative that we look at causation, prevention and treatment in systemic terms and within a dynamic–developmental framework (Browne and Herbert 1997). Clinical observations of children and adolescents who exert continuing and extreme defiance of, or intimidation (including physical assaults) towards, parents indicate that most of these families have some disturbance in the authority structure within the family. The children in such families may develop a grandiose sense of self, feel omnipotent and expect everyone to respond to them accordingly

(Herbert 1987a). Not surprisingly, their siblings and peers also come within their line of fire (Gelles and Cornell 1990).

By the primary school years, individual differences in proneness to aggression are well established and these tend to remain stable into adolescence and beyond (Farrington 1991, 1995; Moffitt 1993). Aggression during middle childhood emerges as the best predictor of adolescent adjustment problems. Individuals who are aggressive in middle childhood tend as adults to have unhappy and conflict-ridden relations with their partners and their own children. The scope for aggression increases with age. Older individuals have bigger, stronger and better co-ordinated bodies and, in some cases, access to more dangerous weapons. They also have increasing competence in non-physical means of aggression, such as verbal abuse. What were merely difficult situations for parents can become menacing and, in some cases, dangerous – especially where their offspring have been granted too much control over decisions when young. Such a burden – being 'in control' when immature – is thought to cause the 'usurper of power' a mixture of anxiety and extreme frustration (Harbin and Madden 1979).

There is another dimension to the issue of children assuming too high a degree of control which underpins their coercive, aggressive actions: it has to do with their attitude to rules. Youngsters with oppositional conduct and (later) delinquent disorders demonstrate a fundamental inability or unwillingness to adhere to the rules and codes of conduct prescribed by society at its various levels. Such failures may be related to the lapse of poorly established learned controls, to the failure to learn these controls in the first place, or to the fact that the behavioural standards a child has absorbed do not coincide with the norms of that section of society which enacts and enforces the rules.

Socialization is a slow continuing process, involving countless 'lessons' from parents, siblings, peers and adults in authority over the child. The developmental literature provides some useful guidelines to supplement behavioural theory in parent consultation work (e.g. Baumrind 1971; Herbert 1974; Wright 1971). The desiderata for prosocial behaviour include the following: a rich supply of positive reinforcement for positive behaviour 'fuelled' by a strong attachment to a caregiver with whom a child can therefore identify; firm moral demands made by parents upon their offspring; the consistent use of sanctions; techniques of punishment that are psychological rather than physical (that is, methods which signify or threaten withdrawal of approval); and an intensive use of induction methods (reasoning and explanations).

A variety of social and family conditions preclude the operation of these factors in the lives of some children. Disharmonious, rejecting home backgrounds, the breakdown of discipline, parental loss and broken homes are examples of distal life variables that are linked aetiologically to conduct disorders (Herbert 1987a).

Of course, there is a sense in which very young children are asocial or antisocial. What happens, as the children mature, is that they have to learn to avoid certain behaviours and adopt others; that is to say, they must be trained to check certain impulses and to regulate their behaviour in terms of certain informal and formal rules of conduct. Most children are disobedient at times or go through disobedient phases; but some take to an extreme their antagonism to parental requests and commands. So intense is the resistance that at times it becomes quite clear that the child is not merely failing to comply, but is displaying a pattern of negativistic behaviour (a form of aggressive defiance) that is antipathetic to his/her ongoing social and moral development.

The perennial problem for the professional assessing the seriousness of disobedience is the ubiquity of non-compliance/defiance as a fact of childhood. It is, in a sense, a normal response to the rigours of socialization and one that peaks at certain stages in the child's development, notably during the striving for independence that takes place in toddlerhood and adolescence. Not for nothing do we talk about the 'terrible twos' and, indeed, the 'terrible teens'.

Up to a point, disobedience in the development of selfhood is undoubtedly adaptive; a manifestation of slavish conformity would be a matter of concern. But what is that 'point' at which non-compliance is thought to be excessive, counter-productive and thus dysfunctional?

The Diagnostic and Statistical Manual of Mental Disorders (4th edn, DSM-IV; American Psychiatric Association 1994), in its criteria for oppositional defiant disorder, requires the clinician to determine if a child 'often actively defies or refuses to comply with adult's requests or rules' (oppositional defiant disorder; Criterion 3, p.94). The DSM-IV does not provide an answer to the inevitable questions: What probability is implied by 'often', and with regard to what type of request, or style of instruction? In what social context and in relation to which rules does the defiance become clinically significant? Furthermore, the clinician is required to identify youngsters whose non-compliance 'occurs more frequently than is typically observed in individuals of comparable age and developmental level' (p.94). There is no objective psychometric device with which to accomplish this task validly. Clinicians must aggregate observational data, interview information, questionnaire results and clinic analogue measures (e.g. the Parent's Game, Forehand and McMahon 1981) with his or her own subjective standards. The difficulty is brought into sharp focus when a very young child displays repetitive, emotional non-compliance to simple chore-like tasks and the parent asks, 'Is that normal?' At age 2 years, divergence of opinion would flourish.

There is general agreement that the probability of obtaining compliant responses from children increases during normal socialization. This process is disrupted in emotionally disturbed and behaviourally deviant children – a pattern called 'arrested socialization'. Regrettably, no studies have adequate quantified normal levels of compliance for specific age and gender groups. Consequently, it is not possible to offer a scientifically based judgement about the normality of a specific child's reaction to parental instructions.

The children whom I think of as out of control (in one sense) and in control (in another) as in the title of this chapter, and the management issues to which they give rise, are those who fall mainly into the categories of oppositional and intermediate conduct problems.

Cost of conduct disorders

The terms 'oppositional behaviour' and 'conduct problem' share the common theme of a failure of the individual to conform his or her behaviour to expectations of some authority (e.g. parent or teacher) or to societal norms. Their definite rejection of rules is extreme, persistent and leads to significant impairment in a child's psychosocial functioning. Given the high cost of antisocial behaviour, society's concern is justified. Between one-half and two-thirds of all children and adolescents referred to mental health services are assessed as having so-called disruptive behaviour problems which include oppositional defiant and conduct disorders (Kazdin 1987). Of GP consultations involving children, 30 per cent are for behaviour problems; 45 per cent of community child health referrals are concerned with behavioural disorders; casualty departments have to cope with accidents and poisonings, which are particularly frequent in children who manifest antisocial behaviour and conduct disorder (see Herbert 1995). Social services departments devote most of their energies to child protection work, much of which arises from the harsh punishments meted out to children who are exceptionally difficult to manage. Residential care for children with disruptive behaviour disorders is extremely expensive (Knapp and Robertson 1989) and, sadly, not always caring or curative. The same can be said with regard to the cost of the various forms of provision in the educational system which are required to cope with classroom disruption and violence (e.g. bullying), in and out of the school grounds.

The conduct disorders represent one of the most intensively researched of all the categories of childhood psychopathology. Nevertheless, there is no consensus as yet with regard to 'how the accumulated facts should be interpreted, such as why anti-social trajectories develop, why they broaden and deepen with development in some children yet taper off in others, and why they are so difficult to deflect once stabilised' (Richters and Cicchetti 1993, p.2). Frick (1997) suggests that children with conduct disorders represent a very heterogeneous group in terms of the types of conduct problems being exhibited, the causal factors involved, the developmental course of the problems and the response to treatment (Farrington 1992). The implications of this assumption are that rather than seeking to find a single causal theory to explain the development of conduct problems in all children and adolescents, one should seek to delineate which causal theories might apply best to certain subgroups of children with conduct disorders.

Developmental progression of conduct problems

There seem to be certain subgroups of children with conduct disorders who show more stable patterns of antisocial behaviour than others. Indicators of stability include: the number of co-existing conduct problems in the child (multiple types of conduct problems, Loeber 1991); the diagnosis of comorbid ADHD (Farrington 1991); measuring at the lower levels of intelligence (Farrington 1991); and having a parent with an antisocial disorder (Lahey *et al.* 1992).

A developmental perspective is particularly relevant because conduct disorders, with their extreme antisocial, aggressive manifestations, also have age-related prognostic and treatment implications. There seems to be a typical developmental progression in which children start to show oppositional and argumentative behaviour early in life (e.g. between the ages of 3 and 8) and then gradually progress into increasingly more severe patterns of conduct problem behaviour (Loeber *et al.* 1992).

Although children who show the most severe conduct problems usually start by showing the less severe oppositional behaviours, a large number of children who show the less severe oppositional symptoms do not go on to show the more severe conduct problems (Lahey and Loeber 1994). This is why the figurative pyramid (from Paul Frick's writings) with the large base and the smaller peak is used to illustrate this asymmetrical relationship.

Most children who move on to display the more severe types of conduct problems do not change the types of behaviour they display, but instead add the more severe conduct problem behaviours (Lahey and Loeber 1994). That is to say, most children who show the more severe behaviours at the top of the pyramid continue to show conduct problems from the lower levels.

The antisocial, aggressive manifestations of conduct disorder have prognostic and treatment implications which are related to the two developmental pathways to the fully fledged condition: children who begin to show conduct problems well before adolescence (referred to as childhood onset conduct disorders) and a substantial number of young people who begin showing antisocial behaviour as they approach adolescence, with no history of oppositional behaviour during childhood (Hinshaw, Lahey and Hart 1993). The latter are referred to as 'adolescence-limited' conduct problems to reflect the findings from many longitudinal studies that young people who begin showing conduct problems in adolescence are much less likely to persist in their antisocial behaviour in adulthood (Farrington 1992, 1995; Robins and Price 1991). Additionally, boys revealing childhood onset conduct problems behaviour are more aggressive and have more neuro-psychological deficits than boys with the adolescent limited pattern.

Frick (1987) states that it would seem from these findings that onset in childhood (and often very early childhood) represents a much more severe pattern of dysfunction, whereas the adolescent limited pattern may be better considered an exaggeration of normal developmental process – a developmentally advanced form of oppositional defiant disorder. In the absence of early treatment a large percentage of the children are likely to remain circulating through the revolving door of the social services, mental health agencies and criminal justice systems. Clearly, there is an urgent need to develop and evaluate standardized therapeutic programmes which can be distributed widely for purposes of training practitioners who in turn train parents, who in turn (hopefully) train their children.

Intervening to help parents

Kazdin (1997) is adamant that treatment and training ought to have conceptual underpinnings – that is, explicit views about what an intervention is designed to accomplish and through what processes. How will the procedures used in treatment influence the processes implicated in the dysfunction, or counteract these influences by developing new repertoires? It may be that treatment directly addresses those processes considered to be involved in the development of the problem. I would wish to claim that this is the case for behavioural family therapy and parent management skills training, in dealing with oppositional and conduct disorders. They derive from social learning theory (at the strategic level) and cognitive behavioural techniques (at the tactical level). To take one example: inept discipline practices influence the development of oppositional and aggressive behaviour in children. Parent management training directly alters these practices and alters aggressive child behaviour. Of course, the focus may draw on change processes that do not directly address those processes involved in the development of the problem. For example, learning models may generate treatments that provide special learning experiences which are 'therapeutic', but not necessarily related to the aetiology of the problem.

The important question guiding the treatment conceptualization is: how does this treatment achieve change? In many cases, of course, the answer can involve basic psychological processes (e.g. learning and information processing). Kazdin (1997) says it is no longer sufficient to provide global conceptual views that foster a treatment approach. Rather, to ensure progress those processes that are considered to be responsible for therapeutic change ought to be assessed directly. He believes that this level of specificity would greatly improve the quality of research and advance our understanding.

Specification of treatment

In Kazdin's (1997) view, treatment ought to be operationalized and he particularly favours putting treatment into the form of a manual where possible, so that the integrity of treatment can be evaluated, the material learned from treatment trials codified and the treatment procedures replicated. The use of manuals in his view is essential so as to address all of those aspects of treatment that can be documented. Kazdin believes that their use in some form or other is essential in the light of the likely alternative: the kind of clinical practice in which there is improvisation and vast individual therapist differences in training, preferences for treatment and clinical judgement. Some of the information may seem relatively trivial, such as the materials used in a session, instructions to explain treatment and forms used to document the sessions. Of course, the effective application of treatments may not necessarily require slavish adherence to each of the points that are specified. At the same time, replication in research and clinical practice will require knowing precisely the essentials of what was done. Evaluation of the extent to which any particular practice is essential or optimal can then be teased out by research if there is doubt about the importance of this or that facet of treatment.

There has to be room for improvisation in treatment programmes. However, we need a balance of clear manual guidelines, possibilities for improvisation and space for individual therapist differences – a challenging task. Kazdin (1997) is of the opinion that, difficult though it may be, it would be a mistake to begin with the notion that critical facets of treatment and their implementation ought not (or cannot) be made explicit and codified. Carolyn Webster-Stratton's manuals and videotapes exemplify one such attempt (Webster-Stratton 1988); another is the author's (Herbert and Wookey 1997).

The family and parent consultation model

The outcomes of using behavioural family therapy (BFT) and parenting management skills programmes (PMSP) on an individual or parent/family group basis have proved to be encouraging (see Herbert 1987b, 1994; Webster-Stratton and Herbert 1993, 1994). Programmes address themselves to the fact that parents of children with behaviour problems tend to flounder because they issue so many commands, provide attention following deviant behaviour, are unlikely to perceive deviant behaviour as deviant, get frequently embroiled in extended coercive hostile interchanges, give vague commands and are generally ineffectual in bringing their children's deviant behaviour to a halt (Kazdin 1987, 1993; Patterson 1982). They also tend to suffer the kinds of socio-economic disadvantage which have an undermining influence on parenting and family life. At a systemic level, Patterson (1982) has demonstrated, by means of sequential analyses of family interactions (notably the working of negative reinforcers) in the home, the pervasiveness of a family pattern of escalating coercive interpersonal interactions. Parent training programmes therefore emphasize methods designed to reduce confrontations and antagonistic interactions among the family members, to increase the effectiveness of positive interactions and moderate the intensity of parental punishment.

The issue of parent training gives rise to a conceptual boundary problem. At what stage in childhood onset conduct disorders does one shift the therapy paradigm from the so-called triadic model that involves caregivers as primary mediators of change (notably in successful parenting skills programmes) to one that more appropriately deals with an individual in his/her own right (as in dyadic or group-based cognitive behaviour therapy)? Whatever the answer to this question, the involvement of the family (and, indeed, the school) remains crucial, as the conduct disorders have such a devastating impact on family life (Webster-Stratton and Herbert 1994), as well as life at school and in the wider community.

Social cognitive approaches to the study of aggression have come to the fore in recent years, pointing to the possibility that attributional biases may make some individual children and adolescents more vulnerable to provocation and more inclined to perceive aggressive responses as a means of dealing with conflicts. This work is theoretically attractive because it attempts to account for the links among cognition, affect and action. The view taken by cognitive theorists of the child's uncontrolled, rebellious and aggressive behaviour is that it is characterized by a range of social-cognitive distortions and ineffectual problem-solving skills (e.g. Hollin 1990; Kendall and Hollon 1994). Children and adolescents with conduct disorders tend to:

- have difficulty anticipating consequences of their behaviour

- recall high rates of hostile cues present in social stimuli

- attend to fear cues when interpreting the meaning of others' behaviour

- attribute others' behaviour in ambiguous situations to their hostile intentions

- underperceive their own level of aggressiveness

- underperceive their responsibility for early stages of dyadic conflict

- generate few verbal assertion solutions to social problems.

These distortions can be addressed in individual or group work with children and adolescents in their own right and are usefully discussed in relation to parents' offspring (and their own attributions) in parent management skills groups.

Experiential influences

In spite of the documented effectiveness of various types of parent training programmes, the literature contains comparatively little discussion of experiential and developmental issues as they affect individuals, or of the actual therapeutic processes utilized by therapists in order to deal with these and other matters in their intervention programmes. Behavioural techniques such as planned ignoring, time out, beta commands, praise, differential attention, response cost, logical consequences, and so on are detailed (e.g. Herbert 1987b, 1994). Describing the 'technology' alone, however, does not elucidate what happens when therapists try to change or influence parents' behaviours, attitudes, attributions and practices. How can they encourage regular attendance, persuade parents to keep records or ensure that homework is carried out? How do they help them, when well 'defended', to make connections between their own and their child's actions? Today, there is less emphasis on the contingency management of specific target behaviours and more on broad principles of child management, the interpersonal interactions of members of the family, the marital relationships (which are often poor in the parents of problematic children) and the perceived efficacy of parents (e.g. Bandura 1987). What we are talking about is a multimodal treatment and training package. While the content of such programmes is widely known and well researched, it is our contention (Webster-Stratton and Herbert 1994) that it is not sufficient to bring about success with a substantial proportion of cases (see Schmaling and Jacobson 1987).

Parents often complain that professionals simply do not understand, or attend to, their side of the story. An extensive qualitative analysis by Webster-Stratton of what parents say about these matters (Webster-Stratton and Herbert 1994) has begun to address this issue. When asked to name the dominant characteristics of their child's misbehaviour, parents specified (*inter alia*) aggression towards various victims (parents, animals, other children, siblings). It was the unpredictability and volatility of the negative behaviours – and their tendency to escalate – that caused parents so much distress. They had to be increasingly vigilant as behaviour problems might occur at any time, in any place or in any situation.

Such repeated episodes of verbal and physical aggression towards other children led to their rejection and ridicule by others – adults and children. This was a key element in the tension between parents of children with conduct disorders and parents of 'normal' children, contributing to their own feelings of humiliation, rejection and isolation. Children's invariable refusal to comply with parental requests compounded the misery. They seemed to control not only the parents but the entire family by virtue of the power they commanded through their wilful and temperamentally powerful resistance.

The author and Carolyn Webster-Stratton of the University of Washington have described, in books and manuals, their programmes which have been carefully evaluated (Webster-Stratton 1991, 1996; Webster-Stratton and Herbert 1994; Herbert and Wookey 1997). The underlying helping process we advocate for working with parents of conduct-disordered children is a collaborative model. Collaboration implies a reciprocal relationship based on utilizing equally the therapist's knowledge and the parents' unique strengths and perspectives. Collaboration implies respect for each person's contribution, a non-blaming relationship based on trust and open communication. It implies that parents actively participate in the setting of goals and the therapy agenda. The Rogerian influence here is clear (Rogers 1951). More recently, collaboration in cognitive behavioural work has been emphasized by theorists such as Kendall and Hollon (1994). The perceptions of parents with seriously disruptive children have important implications for treatment because their learned helplessness and low self-efficacy beliefs can be reversed by experiences of success. The promotion of effective parenting skills undoubtedly starts such a reversal process, giving parents some expectation that they will eventually be able to control outcomes – notably, their children's behaviour and their own proactive and reactive strategies. An access (or return) of self-confidence and self-pride are the recurring and particularly dramatic benefits of the collaborative approach (Herbert and Wookey 1997).

The collaborative therapist's supportive role

There are several components to this role (see detailed account in Herbert and Wookey 1997; Webster-Stratton and Herbert 1994):

1. Empathy and advocacy

2. Empowering parents

3. Teaching

4. Interpreting.

Empathy and advocacy

In a collaborative relationship, the therapist does not present as the kind of 'expert' who has worked out all the answers to the parents' problems, someone who stands apart from the family problems by failing to acknowledge the difficulties of the parents' reality. He or she attempts to empathize with such difficulties but, at the same time, to establish positive expectations for change. Parents are often sceptical about their ability to change, especially if they see in their behaviour a family pattern; after all, such patterns often seem irreversible. The therapist points out how each small step towards change – even the step of coming to therapy in the first place – is evidence that the problem is not fixed or irreversible. There is a deliberate use of humour to help parents relax and to reduce anger, anxiety and cynicism. Parents need to be able to laugh at their mistakes; this is part of the process of self-acceptance. Some of the videotape vignettes and role-play scenarios are chosen more for their humour value than for their content value. The therapist actively supports parents by acting as an advocate for them in situations where communication with other professionals may be difficult. In the role of advocate, the therapist brings relevant persons, programmes and resources to the family, or brings the family to them.

Empowering parents

The essential goal of the collaborative approach is to 'empower' parents by building on their strengths and experience so that they feel confident about their parenting skills and about their ability to respond to new situations that may arise when the therapist is not there to help them. Bandura (1987) has called this strategy strengthening the client's 'efficacy expectations' – that is, parents' conviction that they can successfully change their behaviours. We use several strategies to empower parents (see Table 4.1).

Table 4.1 Sources of increased self-empowerment		
	Content	**Process**
Knowledge		
Child development	Developmental norms and tasks	Discussion
Behavioural management	Behavioural (learning) principles	Book/pamphlets to read
Individual and temperamental differences	Child management (disciplinary strategies Relationships (feelings)	Modelling (videotape, live role play, role reversal rehearsal)
	Self-awareness (self-talk, schema, attributions)	Metaphors/analogues Homework tasks
	Interactions (awareness of contingencies communications)	Networking Developmental counselling
	Resources (support, sources of assistance)	Videotaping viewing and discussion
	Appropriate expectations	Self-observation/recording at home
	Parent involvement with children	Discussing record of parents' own data teaching, persuading
Skills		
Communication	Self-restraint/anger management	Self-enforcement
Problem solving (including problem analysis)	Self-talk (depressive thoughts)	Group and therapist reinforcement
Tactical thinking (use of techniques/methods)	Attend–ignore Play–praise–encourage	Self-observations of interactions at home Rehearsal
Building social relationships	Contracts	Participant modelling

Table 4.1 (continued) Sources of increased self-empowerment		
Enhancing children's academic skills	Consistent consequences Sanction effectively (time out, loss of privileges, natural consequences) Monitoring Social/relationships skills Problem-solving skills Fostering good learning habits Self-assertion/confidence Empathy for child's perspective Ways to give and get support	Homework tasks and practice Video modelling and feedback Self-disclosure Therapist use of humour/optimism Relaxation training Stress management Self-instruction Visual cues at home
Values		
Strategic thinking (working out goals, philosophy of childrearing, beliefs)	Treatment/life goals Objectives (targeted child behaviours) Idealogies Rules Roles Relationships Emotional barriers Attributions Prejudices Past history	Discussion/debate Sharing Listening Respecting/accepting Negotiating Demystifying Explaining/interpreting Reframing Resolving conflict Clarifying Supporting Adapting

Parents are encouraged to explore different solutions to a problem situation, rather than settling for 'quick fixes' or the first solution that comes to mind. The therapist studiously avoids giving any pat answers, keeping the focus of the discussion on the parents' insights. When parents seek professional help for their problems they have usually experienced or are experiencing thoughts and feelings of powerlessness and mounting frustration with their children due to a history of unsuccessful attempts to discipline them. This powerlessness is often expressed in terms of feeling victimized by their children: the 'Why me?' question. The feeling of helplessness, typically, is accompanied by intense anger and a fear of losing control of themselves when trying to discipline their children. Attention is paid to the 'self-talk' of parents and attempts are encouraged to modify cognitions that are negative, distorted or illogical. We teach parents actively to formulate positive statements about themselves, e.g. 'I was able to stay in control, I stayed calm, I am doing well.'

Parents are encouraged to look at their strengths and think about how effectively they handled a difficult situation. We ask them to express their positive feelings about their relationship with their child and to remember good times. The therapist also helps the parent (or the parent and partner) to define ways in which they can support each other when feeling discouraged, tired, or unable to cope with a problem.

Teaching

Just as the parents have their own expertise concerning their child and have the ultimate responsibility for judging what will be workable in their particular family and community, the therapist does wear an 'expert' hat when providing information about children's developmental needs, child protection issues, behaviour management principles and communication skills; also for 'coaching' parents when they are practising/rehearsing management strategies.

Therapeutic change depends on persuasion, which means giving parents the rationale for each component of the programme. The treatment principles, objectives and methods should not be shrouded in mystery. It is important for the therapist to voice clear explanations based upon valid information and knowledge of the developmental literature and particularly to differentiate between matters of act and opinion. Research has indicated that parents' understanding of the social learning principles underlying the parent training programme leads to enhanced generalization or maintenance of treatment effects (Herbert 1998). However, it is also important that these ideas be presented in such a way that the parent can see their connection with his/her stated goals.

The process of collaborative teaching involves the therapist working with parents to interpret concepts and adapt skills to the particular circumstances of the parents and to the individual temperament of the child. Much use is made of analogies, images, metaphors, charts, cartoons, vignettes, quizzes, play acting, debates, rehearsal and video feedback to achieve these ends. The teacher role involves giving an assignment for every session. Parents do some observing and recording of behaviours, thoughts and feelings at home; also experimenting with a particular strategy. Assignments are critical because there is an important message that goes with them: namely, that participation in group therapy is not a passive exercise and certainly not 'magic'. Parents collaborate with the therapist by working at home to make changes. Home visits, for checking progress and providing assistance, may be crucial for some families. The assignments and experiments help transfer what is talked about in therapy/training sessions to real-life situations (old and new) at home or outside it. For instance, some parents learn how to manage their children effectively at home, but have great difficulty knowing how to handle misbehaviour when it occurs in public. They have difficulty seeing how principles such as ignore, time out and logical consequences can be applied at the supermarket, cinema, park or school. Role playing – modelling and rehearsing newly acquired methods – is particularly suited to that dilemma. There is evidence that it is effective in producing behavioural changes. In addition, self-management skill training for parents and the use of telephone contacts by therapists facilitate generalization and, indeed, maintenance of beneficial change (see reviews in Gill 1998; Herbert 1998; Kazdin 1993, 1994).

Therapeutic change depends on providing explanatory stories, alternative explanations which help clients to reshape their perceptions of, and their beliefs about, the nature of their problems. Reframing by the therapist (cognitive restructuring) is a powerful interpretive tool for helping clients understand their experiences, thereby promoting change in their attitudes and actions. It involves altering the emotional and/or conceptual viewpoint of the client in relation to an experience, by placing the experience in another 'frame' which fits the facts of the situation well, but alters its meaning. In our programmes, it is a common strategy to take a problem which a parent is having with a child and reframe it from the child's point of view rather than the parent's perspective. Role reversal is useful for this purpose.

Part of the teacher role is to ensure that each session is evaluated by the parents so as to obtain immediate feedback about how each parent is responding to the therapist's style, the quality of the group discussions and the information presented in the session. The evaluations bring problems to light – the parent who is dissatisfied with the group, the parent who is resisting a concept, the parent who fails to see the relevance of a particular approach to his/her own situation, the parent who wants more group discussion or individual attention.

It is often necessary to counter the myths and attributions that get in the way of therapeutic change. Here are a few typical examples of some myths and unhelpful attributions: it's my child's problem; s/he's the one who has to change; it's me who's to blame (i.e. sole ownership); give her/him an inch and s/he takes a mile (narrow limit setting); s/he won't love me if I insist; I feel so guilty if I say no (broad limit setting); there's a demon in her/him; I don't trust him; he has his father in him (unhelpful attributions); I'm a complete failure as a parent; I can't forgive myself for the mistakes I've made (catastrophizing); other parents all seem to cope (unrealistic assumptions). Another way to interpret the thinking, language and culture of the family is to help the parents see the connections between their own childhood experiences and those of their child. This is a powerful way of promoting empathy and bonding between the parent and child.

There are a number of techniques that can be helpful in facilitating the therapist's teaching role. The Webster-Stratton group training programme relies heavily on videotape modelling as a therapeutic method (Webster-Stratton 1988). She developed a series of 16 videotape programmes (over 300 vignettes) showing parents and children of different sexes, ages, cultures, socio-economic backgrounds and temperamental styles. Parents are shown in natural situations interacting with their children: during mealtimes, getting children dressed in the morning, toilet training, coping with disobedience, playing together, and so forth. Scenes depict parents 'doing it right' and 'doing it wrong'. The intent is to illustrate how parents can learn from their mistakes without feeling 'put down'. The videotapes are used in a collaborative way – as a catalyst to stimulate group discussion and debate (80 per cent of each session is devoted to just that).

The use of videotape modelling training methods for parents of young conduct problem children has been shown to be not only more effective in improving parent–child interactions (in comparison with group discussion approaches and one-to-one therapy with an individual therapist), but also highly cost effective as prevention (see Webster-Stratton 1991, 1996; Webster-Stratton and Herbert 1993, 1994). Furthermore, videotape modelling has the potential advantage of being accessible to illiterate parents and to those who simply have difficulties with reading assignments and verbal approaches in general. Videotape modelling has potential for mass dissemination and low individual training cost when used in groups or in self-administered programmes (Webster-Stratton 1998). In addition, videotapes provide a more feasible, flexible method of treatment because they can portray a wide variety of models in different settings and situations, which may help parents generalize the concepts.

Interpreting

The therapist 'translates' the language of cognitive, behavioural and developmental concepts into words, behaviours and images that the parents can apply and which children can comprehend and respond to. It is here that therapy shows itself as a craft – an amalgam of applied science and art. No matter how good the science (the theoretical framework and empirical findings), without the creative element of translating abstract and complex ideas into concrete, imaginative and thus attention-holding applications which are relevant to children and their family's circumstances, the science is not likely to achieve its full potential in therapeutic work.

This partnership between clients and therapist has the effect of giving back dignity, respect and self-control to parents who are often seeking help for their children's problems at a vulnerable time of low self-confidence and intense feelings of guilt and self-blame. It is our hypothesis that a collaborative model, which gives parents responsibility for developing solutions (alongside the therapist), is more likely to increase parents' confidence and perceived self-efficacy in treatment than are models which do not hold them responsible for solutions. Support for the value of this approach comes from the literature on self-efficacy, attribution, helplessness and locus of control (see Bandura 1987).

Bandura has suggested that self-efficacy is the mediating variable between knowledge and behaviour. Therefore, parents who are self-efficacious tend to persist at tasks until success is achieved. The literature also indicates that people who have determined their own priorities and goals are more likely to persist in the face of difficulties and less likely to show debilitating effects of stress. Moreover, there is some evidence that the collaborative process has the multiple advantage of reducing attrition rates, increasing motivation and commitments, reducing resistance, increasing temporal and situational generalization and giving both parents and therapist a stake in the outcome of the intervention efforts (Herbert 1998). All of this sounds very well, but it is not so easy to put into practice and certainly not easy to get the balance of replicable structure, spontaneity and creative innovation.

We have attempted (Webster-Stratton and Herbert 1994; Herbert and Wookey 1997) to categorize the operations defining the therapeutic processes that arise from adopting a collaborative style with clients. These operations or strategies are classified by us in terms of knowledge, skills and values, as detailed earlier (see Table 4.1).

Conclusion

One of the main difficulties in evaluating the large number of studies of parent management programmes is that they describe a confusing variety of different treatment packages. While these are all based upon the teaching of principles of learning, development and behaviour to parents, the common denominator ends there. Some studies have the psychologist or social worker working individually with a single set of parents, or all the members of the family ('behavioural family therapy'); others use a group format in which two persons work with a group of up to twelve parents.

With regard to comparison studies, programmes based on changes from Patterson's parent training approach have been shown to be superior to family-based psychotherapy, attention-placebo (discussion) and no-treatment conditions (Patterson 1982). Those from Forehand and McMahon's (1981) programme have been shown to be more effective than a family systems therapy and a group version of the programme was more effective than a parent discussion group based on the systematic training for effective parenting (STEP) programme (see Webster-Stratton 1991 for a review of the evidence). The consultation format, in which parents receive advice and reading material or have contact by phone, has had its successes, as has the individual training approach (see Herbert 1987a, 1987b). Parents have also been successfully and economically trained in groups (see Gill 1998; Webster-Stratton and Herbert 1993; Herbert and Wookey 1988).

It is important that this approach does not suffer the fate of social skills training and come to be thought of as a panacea. Not all clients benefit from this approach. Of course, negative findings may reflect an erroneous clinical formulation, or perhaps a lack of ability on the part of the therapist, or an inability of the parents to conceptualize learning principles, or a resistance to perceiving improvement in their children's behaviour. Some practitioners suggest that failure is sometimes a reflection of great stress (social and economic, marital and personal) undermining parents with exhaustion and despair (see Webster-Stratton and Herbert 1994). The disappointing results may relate to the parents' own previous experiences of parenting, to ideologies of child care that are rigid and to attributes that insist on giving children the sole 'ownership' of their difficulties. One of the research challenges for the future is to discover what it is and why it is that we fail in our supportive role with certain parents and certain children.

References

American Psychiatric Association (1994) *The Diagnostic and Statistical Manual of Mental Disorders*, 4th edn. Washington DC: APA.

Bandura, A. (1973) *Aggression: A Social Learning Analysis*. Englewood Cliffs, NJ: Prentice Hall.

Bandura, A. (1987) 'Regulation of cognitive processes through perceived self-efficacy.' *Developmental Psychology 25*, 729–735.

Baumrind, D. (1971) 'Current patterns of parental authority.' *Developmental Psychology Monograph 1*, 1–102.

Brody, G.H. and Forehand, R. (1986) 'Maternal perceptions of child maladjustment as function of child behaviour and maternal depression.' *Journal of Consulting and Clinical Psychology 54*, 237–240.

Browne, K. and Herbert, M. (1997) *Preventing Family Violence*. Chichester: Wiley.

Farrington, D.P. (1991) 'Childhood aggression and adult violence: Early precursors and later-life outcomes.' In D.J. Pepler and K.H. Rubin (eds) *The Development and Treatment of Childhood*. Hillsdale, NJ: Erlbaum.

Farrington D.P. (1992) 'Psychological contributions to the explanation, prevention and treatment of offending.' In F. Losel, D. Bender and T. Bliesender (eds) *Psychology and Law: International Perspectives.* Berlin: De Gruyter.

Farrington, D.P. (1995) 'The development of offending and anti-social behaviours from childhood: Key findings from the Cambridge study of delinquent development.' *Journal of Child Psychology and Psychiatry 36,* 929–1064.

Forehand, R. and McMahon, R. (1981) *Helping the Noncompliant Child: A Clinician's Guide to Parent Training.* New York: Guilford Press.

Frick, P.J. (1987) 'Conduct disorder.' In T. Ollendick and M. Hersen (eds) *Handbook of Child Psychopathology,* 3rd edn. New York: Plenum Press.

Gelles, R.J. and Cornell, C.P. (1990) *Intimate Violence in Families,* 2nd edn. Beverley Hills, CA: Sage.

Gill, A.N. (1998) 'What makes parent training groups effective? Promoting positive parenting through collaboration.' Unpublished PhD, University of Leicester.

Harbin, H. and Madden, D. (1979) 'Battered parents: A new syndrome.' *American Journal of Psychiatry 136,* 1288–1291.

Herbert, M. (1974) *Emotional Problems of Development in Children.* London: Academic Press.

Herbert, M. (1987a) *Conduct Disorders of Childhood and Adolescence,* 2nd edn. Chichester: Wiley.

Herbert, M. (1987b) *Behavioural Treatment of Children with Problems: A Practice Manual,* 2nd edn. London: Academic Press.

Herbert, M. (1994) 'Behavioural methods.' In M. Rutter, E. Taylor and L. Hersoy (eds) *Child and Adolescent Psychiatry: Modern Approaches,* 3rd edn. Oxford: Blackwell.

Herbert, M. (1995) 'A collaborative model of training for parents of children with disruptive behaviour disorders.' *British Journal of Clinical Psychology 34,* 325–342.

Herbert, M. (1998) *Clinical Child Psychology: Social Learning, Development and Behaviour,* 2nd edn. Chichester: Wiley.

Herbert, M. and Wookey, J. (1997) *Childwise Parenting Skills Manual.* Exeter: Impact Publications.

Herbert, M. and Wookey, J. (1998) *Childwise Parenting Skills Manual.* (Revised edition) Exeter: Impact Publications.

Hinshaw, S.P., Lahey, B.B. and Hart E.L. (1993) 'Issues of taxonomy and co-morbidity in the development of conduct disorder.' *Development and Psychopathology 5,* 31–50.

Hobbs, N. (1982) *The Troubled and the Troubling Child.* San Francisco, CA: Jossey-Bass.

Hollin, C.R. (1990) *Cognitive-Behavioural Interventions with Young Offenders.* Elmsford, NY: Pergamon.

Hollin, C.R. (1995) 'The meaning and implications of "programme integrity".' In J. McGuire (ed) *What Works: Effective Methods to Reduce Reoffending.* Chichester: Wiley.

Kazdin, A.E. (1987) 'Treatment of anti-social behaviour in children: Current status and future directions.' *Psychological Bulletin 102,* 1897–2203.

Kazdin, A.E. (1993) 'Treatment of conduct disorder: And directions in psychotherapy research.' *Development and Psychopathology 5,* 277–310.

Kazdin, A.E. (1994) 'Psychotherapy for children and adolescents.' In A.E. Bergin and S.L. Garfield (eds) *Handbook of Psychotherapy and Behaviour Change,* 4th edn. New York: Wiley.

Kazdin, A.E. (1997) 'A model for developing effective treatments: Progression and interplay of theory, research and practice.' *Journal of Clinical Child Psychology 26,* 114–129.

Kendall, P.C. and Hollon, S.D. (eds) (1994) *Cognitive-Behavioural Interventions: Theory, Research and Procedures.* New York: Academic Press.

Knapp, M.R.J. and Robertson, E. (1989) 'The costs of child care services.' In B. Kahan (ed) *Child Care Research, Policy and Practice.* Milton Keynes: Open University Press.

Knitzer, J. (1982) *Unclaimed Children: The Failure of Public Responsibility to Children and Adolescents in Need of Mental Health Services.* Washington DC: Children's Defense Fund.

Lahey, B.B. and Loeber, R. (1994) 'Framework for a developmental model of oppositional defiant disorder and conduct disorder.' In D.K. Routh (ed) *Disruptive Disorders in Childhood.* New York: Plenum Press.

Lahey, B.B., Loeber, R., Quay, H.C., Frick, P.J. and Grimm, J. (1992) 'Oppositional defiant and conduct disorders: Issues to be resolved for DSM-IV.' *Journal of the American Academy of Child and Adolescent Psychiatry 31,* 539–546.

Loeber, R. (1991) 'Antisocial behaviour: More enduring than changeable.' *Journal of the American Academy of Child and Adolescent Psychiatry 30,* 393–397.

Loeber, R. and Dishion, T.J. (1984) 'Boys who fight at home and at school: Family conditions influencing cross-setting consistency.' *Journal of Consulting and Clinical Psychology 52,* 759–768.

Loeber, R., Green, S.M., Lahey, B.B., Christ, M.A.G. and Frick, P.J. (1992) 'Developmental sequences in the age of onset of disruptive child behaviors.' *Journal of Child and Family Studies 1,* 21–41.

Moffitt, T.E. (1993) 'Adolescent-limited and life-course persistent antisocial behavior: A developmental taxonomy.' *Psychological Review 100,* 674–701.

Moffitt, T.E. and Caspi, A. (1998) 'Implications of violence between intimate partners for child psychologists and psychiatrists.' *Journal of Child Psychology and Psychiatry 39,* 137–144.

Patterson, G.R. (1982) *Coercive Family Process.* Eugene, OR: Castalia.

Richters, J.E. and Cicchetti, D. (1993) 'Toward a developmental perspective on conduct disorder.' *Development and Psychopathology 5*, 1–4.

Robins, L.N. (1966) *Deviant Children Grown Up.* Baltimore: Williams and Wilkins.

Robins, L.N. and Price, R.K. (1991) 'Adult disorders predicted by child epidemiologic catchment area project.' *Psychiatry 54*, 116–132.

Rogers, C.R. (1951) *Client-Centered Therapy.* New York: Houghton Mifflin.

Rutter, M. and Giller, H. (1983) *Juvenile Delinquency: Trends and Perspectives.* Harmondsworth: Penguin.

Schmaling, K.B. and Jacobson, N.S. (1987) 'The clinical significance of treatment gains resulting from parent training interventions for children with conduct problems.' Paper presented at meeting of Association for the Advancement of Behavior Therapy, Boston, MA, November.

Webster-Stratton, C. (1988) *Parents and Children Videotape Series: Basic and Advanced Programs 1 to 7.* 1411 8th Avenue West, Seattle, WA 98119, USA.

Webster-Stratton, C. (1991) 'Annotation: Strategies for helping families with conduct disordered children.' *Journal of Child Psychology and Psychiatry 32*, 1047–1062.

Webster-Stratton, C. (1996) 'Early intervention with videotape modelling: Programs for families with oppositional defiant disorder or conduct disorder.' In E.D. Hibbs and P. Jensen (eds) *Psychological Treatment Research of Child and Adolescent Disorders.* Washington DC: American Psychological Association.

Webster-Stratton, C. and Hammond, M. (1988) 'Maternal depression and its relationship to life stress, perceptions of child behavior problems, parenting behaviors, and child conduct problems.' *Journal of Abnormal Child Psychology 16*, 299–315.

Webster-Stratton, C. and Herbert, M. (1993) 'What really happens in parent training.' *Behavior Modification 17*, 407–456.

Webster-Stratton, C. and Herbert, M. (1994) *Troubled Families: Problem Children. Working with Parents: A Collaborative Process.* Chichester: Wiley.

White Paper (1996) 'No more excuses: A new approach to tackling youth crime in England and Wales.' London: Parliamentary (Home Office) Report.

World Health Organization (1992) *International Classification of Diseases 10th edition (ICD-10).* Geneva: WHO.

Wright, D.S. (1971) *The Psychology of Moral Behaviour.* Harmondsworth: Penguin.

CHAPTER 5

Social Support Principles for Strengthening Families

Messages from the USA

Carolyn E. Cutrona

These are difficult times for families. All over the world, families seem to be struggling to do their jobs of raising children and sheltering one another. Families receive little help from the larger society. In the words of psychologist Mary Pipher, 'We used to raise children to join the larger society. Now, we struggle to protect them from the larger society' (Pipher 1996, p.5). What can be done to lend a hand to today's families? How can we offer support to parents and their children?

In this chapter I will not recommend specific programmes, but instead will suggest a set of principles that I hope will be useful in guiding the design of specific programmes. These principles are based on research on social support processes and benefits. Most of this research was conducted in the USA, but I believe that the findings are relevant to other cultures as well. Social support can be defined as behaviours that assist persons who are undergoing stressful life circumstances to cope effectively with the problems they face. Social support can be directly relevant to solving the problem, such as giving advice, offering to drive the person to a doctor's appointment, or loaning needed resources. This kind of support is termed 'instrumental support'. Social support can also be relevant primarily to easing the negative emotions engendered by the problem situation rather than actually solving the problem. Examples of this kind of support include empathic listening, encouragement and expressions of caring and concern. This kind of social support is termed 'nurturant support'. Both kinds of social support are relevant to family support, ongoing programmes and policies that assist families in meeting their important goals of raising healthy children and fostering healthy adult functioning.

Although research on social support has been ongoing for approximately thirty years, we still know relatively little about how to increase the social support of those who do not have enough. For example, we do not know whether the best strategy is to provide new support providers or to work to improve the supportiveness of existing relationships. Efforts to provide new relationships encounter many barriers. We are highly selective in who we allow to give us emotional support. We may have large families and many friends, but those whose love provides true comfort, whose encouragement lifts our spirits and builds our resolve to carry on, whose advice is treasured and trusted – those people are few. Furthermore, it usually takes many years to build a relationship that provides meaningful support. This poses a problem for mental health professionals – most of whom are not able to commit years to building rapport and trust. Our interventions must be efficient and cost effective. Furthermore, the role of the mental health professional is not to become a member of the family, or even to become a friend.

These issues suggest that it is preferable to help those who lack support by improving the supportiveness of the individual's existing relationships. How can that be done? A woman's husband may be abusive; her mother may be alcoholic. An isolated single mother may have chosen to isolate herself from her family, knowing that they cause more hurt than help. A working woman with small children may not have time to participate in a neighbourhood group. A very shy child may be afraid to participate in activities in a community centre. It is not easy to change the nature of a person's social network. That does not mean that we should not try. It simply means that the task will be difficult and that we will only succeed with a certain percentage of those we try to help.

I will try to articulate some general principles that may help us increase the percentage of families for whom our support will make a genuine difference in their lives. It is hoped that these principles, derived from research with American families, will have broader applicability to efforts at increasing family support in other nations. After a brief overview of these principles, I will discuss each one in more depth.

The first principle is that the source of support is critically important. People are not interchangeable when it comes to providing support. The second is that some types of support are more beneficial than others. The timing of support is also critical. Early in a crisis, different kinds of assistance are needed to what is required six months later, when people have largely left the individual to cope on his or her own. Different kinds of support are most beneficial for different kinds of stressful events. Although a support effort may be well intentioned, if the wrong kind is offered it will not be as effective as more appropriate support. The context in which support is offered is important. People do not want to be labelled as 'social isolates' or 'in need of friends'. A context that avoids such labels, or even the implication of such labels, is important. People do not want to be indebted to others. Opportunities to reciprocate support are important. People are very sensitive to the reasons why others offer them support. If support is offered out of genuine concern, it will have a greater impact than if it is offered out of obligation. It is especially difficult for a mental health professional to offer support that is perceived as genuine, because people know that professionals are paid to give support. This may diminish the perceived value of support received from a mental health professional.

Another important principle is that people differ in the ways that they cope with stress in their lives. Support that does not match individuals' style of coping will not be as effective as support that bolsters their natural strengths. Men and women often cope quite differently, and helping couples to understand and accommodate their partner's coping style may be an important contribution to their ability to sustain one another through difficult times. Finally, clear communication is a vital part of providing support to another. Miscommunication can ruin a well-intentioned request for support or a well-intentioned attempt to provide it. There are specific communication skills that can increase the success with which support is requested and provided. If people are given the skills to obtain support from the people around them, there is no need for ongoing support from a mental health professional. The individual has been given the tools to take care of himself or herself.

Sources of support

Marital support

In times of duress, the most meaningful support is what we receive from the people closest to us. Among married individuals, the spouse is typically the first person from whom support is sought during crises (Beach *et al.* 1993). Evidence suggests that support from other sources cannot compensate for a lack of intimate or marital support (Brown and Harris 1978; Coyne and DeLongis 1986). Thus, in some cases, the best kind of family support that can be provided by a mental health professional is to facilitate the flow of support within the family. We are not born knowing how to be supportive marital partners. A number of skills are involved in the process of requesting and providing support. Like any other skills, they can be improved with 'coaching' and practice. Ideally, these skills should be taught early in the marital relationship, before resentments have built up that prevent people from wanting to provide support to one another.

In the USA, many churches require engaged couples to receive pre-marital counselling before they can be married. Howard Markman has developed a pre-marital intervention called PREP (Prevention and Relationship Enhancement Program) that is designed to teach skills that will prevent the development of marital distress (Renick, Blumberg and Markman 1992). Included in this prevention programme for couples are opportunities to learn skills relevant to communication, conflict management and social support. Such programmes may serve a valuable family support function in giving engaged couples and newly-weds the skills to provide support to one another throughout their married life. Research shows a reciprocal relation between conflict and support in marriage. The higher the spousal support level, the lower the conflict level. When people receive support from their partners, they fight less often and less bitterly. The less conflict couples engage in, the more support they provide to each other.

A second context in which social support skills could be presented is in the context of support groups for couples who are facing a specific crisis, such as the diagnosis of serious illness in a family member (e.g. breast cancer in the wife or leukaemia in a child). Hospitals often offer support groups to such families. An important component of these support groups should be a focus on how family members can help one another cope with the stress. Divorce rates increase following traumatic events in the family, such as the death of a child. However, not all relationships deteriorate following traumatic events. Instead, relationships tend to polarize (Lehman *et al.* 1989). Some become worse and some become even stronger. An important component of family support is to give people the tools to deal together, as a team, with tragedy and stress.

Finally, social support skills should be included in marital therapy programmes designed to help couples whose marriages are experiencing distress. Of course, if a couple comes to therapy filled with such anger that they cannot be in the same room without shouting, conflict management skills must come first. However, there is some research which suggests that marital therapy often changes angry marriages to empty marriages. As a well-known marital therapist said, 'People don't get married to manage conflict. They get married for companionship, intimacy, and support' (Markman, personal communication, cited in Cutrona 1996). To assist persons in recovering or discovering these treasures for the first time is a crucial component of family support.

Workplace stress and support

There are some circumstances where marital support is not sufficient. For example, there is evidence that when events or circumstances in the workplace are the cause of a person's distress, support from the spouse is not effective in preventing burn-out and distress. In such situations, the most important sources of support are in the workplace. Studies of teachers, nurses and counsellors all revealed that social support from the individual's supervisor is most critical in preventing demoralization and depression in the workplace. Thus, it may be beneficial to provide training to employers on how to promote a humane environment in the workplace, as part of a broad effort to provide family support.

Support for the unmarried

Many of the people who need support the most are not married. For example, many divorced or widowed women raise children on their own. Family support may be especially critical for single parent families. One strategy for assisting single parent families is to facilitate the strengthening of extended family ties. In the USA, grandmothers frequently play an active role in helping their daughters raise their children. Mental health professionals may help mother–daughter pairs negotiate and clarify their roles to facilitate smooth collaboration in the childrearing domain. Some family therapists request a session or two with the entire extended family to mobilize support when a member is in crisis (e.g. admitted to a hospital for psychiatric treatment). Such sessions may help the family to understand the nature of the family member's problems, clarify the best ways that family members can be helpful and avoid the common problem of fighting within the extended family over who to blame or how to react to the crisis.

Friends as providers of support

Family members are not the only source of potential support. There is evidence that for daily companionship, which is an important component of well-being, friendship is the crucial element. The importance of friendship for well-being persists across the life course, well into old age (Lee and Ishii-Kuntz 1988; Mullins and Dugan 1990). There are many people who feel alienated from their families and thus rely especially heavily on friends for functions that would more typically be served by family (e.g. assistance when ill). In a study of chronically mentally ill individuals, most of whom were not married, those who were the least lonely reported that they could count on friends for support. In this population, neither support from family nor support from their caseworker was associated with lower levels of loneliness. Thus, opportunities to develop friendship were an important component of providing support to these individuals. Support from their caseworker, whom most patients saw once a week, could not substitute for support from friends.

Building on the rather extensive research literature that documents the importance of friendship for well-being, Heller *et al.* (1991) attempted a community-based intervention to promote friendship among lonely elderly women. Women residing in three low-income areas in Indiana were screened and those who were lonely and/or reported little social support from friends were invited to participate. Because many elderly persons have physical limitations and/or difficulty obtaining transportation, the main goal of the intervention was to put each woman in regular telephone contact with another lonely woman. After an initial warm-up period, during which each woman became accustomed to receiving regular telephone contact from a research staff member, elderly women were randomly assigned either to initiate phone contact or to be the recipient of phone contact with another elderly woman. The women were instructed to speak to each other on the phone at least once a week for a period of ten weeks. At the end of that time, women were administered loneliness and social support questionnaires for a second time to see if the intervention was effective. Surprisingly, the intervention had no effect. There was no difference in loneliness or social support from friends between those who had engaged in the 10-week telephone intervention and a control group that had not been offered the telephone intervention. Even though some women continued the telephone contacts beyond the study period, when asked to list the people in their social network at the end of the study, very few women listed their telephone partner as a member of their social support network.

The difficulty of 'grafting' new relationships onto a person's social network is illustrated by this failed intervention. As I emphasized earlier, people are very selective in their choice of support providers. Heller and his colleagues randomly assigned women to their telephone partners, without regard to similarity of backgrounds or interests. Because a person is lonely does not mean that he or she will accept just anyone as a confidant and support provider. It appears that people need free choice in those whom they befriend. People are attracted to each other for many reasons. Although similarity in background and attitudes are known elements in interpersonal attraction, there are many others that we do not understand. Problems that may have prevented the intervention's success include the lack of opportunity for intimacy to develop in the absence of face-to-face meetings (since all contacts were over the telephone) and insufficient time for a meaningful supportive relationship to develop over the course of ten weeks. Finally, it may be that the women in the study were lonely because they wished for greater contact with their families, or were mourning following recent bereavement. Neither of these problems would be remedied by friendship.

Different kinds of support at different times

Life crises unfold over time and different kinds of support are most useful at different phases of the crisis. Robert Weiss (1976) has described the stages of crises and their requirements from support providers. When a person is first confronted with a crisis – a child in an automobile accident or a spouse with a serious heart attack – he or she needs assistance in simply managing the crisis – summoning an ambulance, driving to the hospital, gathering information about the patient's prognosis. A sympathetic presence is also needed in the long hours of waiting. A crisis ends in one of two ways: by a return to the previous situation (if the patient makes a full recovery) or by persisting disruption (the patient dies).

If the crisis leads to ongoing serious disruption in the individual's life, he or she enters into a period of transition. In addition to coping with new problems imposed by the loss of a loved one, the individual must deal with strong emotions, establish new routines, find new sources of security, feelings of worth and other components of well-being. During such a transition stage, a helper can be useful by providing the individual with a framework that helps make sense of the experience, makes overwhelming emotions understandable and assists in the exploration of the available options for reorganizing life. People in transition often feel socially isolated. It may benefit the person to be part of a temporary community of persons in the same situation, such as a support group. Others in the same situation can provide understanding and acceptance and offer ideas regarding how to cope with specific problems.

To assist people in the state of transition, Weiss (1976) suggests that three different kinds of support providers are important. One is the 'expert', an individual who has studied the problem with which individuals are dealing and can speak with authority about it. In the case of serious illness, a physician or nurse would serve this function and offer programmes to patients and their families about the causes, course and treatment of the disease from which they or their loved one suffers.

A second type of support provider is the 'veteran'. This is a person who has been through the stressor and is able to draw on his or her experiences in discussing issues. This person can also demonstrate that recovery is possible. Continuing the example of serious illness, an individual who has been successfully treated for cancer might be an excellent leader of an ongoing support group for newly diagnosed cancer patients.

Finally, Weiss describes the important role that can be played by fellow participants – others who are going through the same life transition. For example, other persons who are undergoing chemotherapy for cancer can offer the immediate empathy and understanding that comes from being in the same situation.

Weiss describes the third crisis phase as a 'deficit situation'. By this time the individual's life has stabilized again. Emotions are less intense. New routines have been established. Confusion and fear of the unknown have subsided. However, the ongoing loss remains. At this point, ongoing problem-focused support seems most useful. Financial counselling, information on how to find companionship and advice on how to obtain services required to maintain the family's health and well-being are most useful. Weiss has used this model of changing needs for support in community-based interventions for newly separated adults and for recently bereaved adults and has reported very promising results.

Type of stressor affects the type of support needed

Not only the amount of time since the crisis but the nature of the crisis affect the effectiveness of different approaches to family support. A vivid example is provided by Weiss's efforts to provide supportive interventions for persons undergoing marital separation and those recovering from the death of their spouse (Weiss 1976). At first, thinking that both were struggling with similar issues of loss, Weiss placed divorcing and bereaved people in the same support groups. He found that the needs and preferences of the two groups were very different. For the separated, discussion of their separation distress was very helpful. For the bereaved, discussion of their grief provoked considerable pain. Group leaders had to find ways to let them experience their pain in manageable doses. For the separated, they were confused by the distress they experienced, even if they had initiated the separation. They benefited from a discussion of why they were suffering – lectures and discussions of attachment theory helped them make sense of overwhelming and bewildering feelings. The bereaved had no need for explanation of their distress. The intensity of their grief was at times frightening, but they did not need to explore the roots of their sorrow. The separated wanted desperately to overcome their distress. They wanted their sorrow to end. The bereaved tended to be more ambivalent about their grief: they wanted to return to effective functioning, but they also felt that their grief testified to the depth of their feelings for their spouse. The separated had a number of ways of coping with their pain – by disparaging the spouse, saying that the separation was for the best, contacting the spouse if their loneliness became unbearable, fantasizing about reconciliation. The bereaved generally viewed their loss as without compensation and completely irrevocable. Distraction and keeping busy were their primary defences. Virtually every topic had to be approached differently for the separated and the bereaved. The separated viewed themselves as misunderstood, betrayed and personally flawed. Compared with the separated, the bereaved appeared less self-doubting, more hurt. They were more resentful of clumsy attempts at aid. They were less tolerant of group members who dominated discussions. Even the gender composition of the groups had to differ. In separation groups, it was helpful for both men and women to participate – to help understand the other gender's point of view. In bereavement groups, the widows and widowers reacted very differently. The widows talked among themselves and the widowers sat quietly on the outskirts of the group. Bereaved men and women differed in their ways of expressing and recovering from their grief. It worked better to have separate groups for bereaved women and men.

Experience is the only way to learn the fine points of helping those facing different kinds of crises in their lives. Learning to provide support to families in times of stress involves a certain amount of trial and error. However, it is important to share information regarding the strategies which are successful with others so that we do not make the same mistakes over and over. Furthermore, not all principles of family support must be learned through trial and error. In the following section, I will turn to information I have learned through research on how people react to different kinds of support. Although knowledge gained in research does not always generalize to real life, it can serve as a starting point for refinement and expansion when put into action in efforts to help people.

Optimal matching between stress and social support

People can offer many different kinds of support to another person who is facing hard times. It is important to ensure optimal matching between stress and social support. We can express our caring, empathy and concern. This is called 'emotional support'. We can encourage the person and express our belief in their ability to overcome their problems. This is called 'esteem support'. Neither of these types of support actually helps to solve the problem facing the troubled individuals. However, they provide comfort. They may lessen the intensity of the individual's emotions of depression and isolation. Together, emotional and esteem support can be conceptualized as 'nurturant support'. We can also offer support that more directly addresses the difficulty causing the individual to suffer. We may offer suggestions or advice on how to deal with the situation. This is termed 'information support'. We may even offer to do or provide something that the person needs to solve the problem, such as taking care of the children for a day or loaning the person money. This is termed 'tangible support'. Both informational support and tangible support are attempts to help the individual overcome the difficulties that are causing him or her distress. Together, they can be thought of as 'instrumental support'.

I developed a theory of optimal matching (Cutrona 1990; Cutrona and Russell 1990) in which I hypothesized that nurturant support and instrumental support would be most beneficial following different kinds of stressful life events. I predicted that when the crisis could be controlled, when something could be done to solve the problem or lessen its consequences, then instrumental support would be most beneficial. An example is someone's house burning down. The family needs a place to live. They need advice on how to replace what they have lost. They need money to obtain a new house. These are all examples of instrumental support. However, when the crisis is not controllable, when nothing can be done to solve the problem or lessen its consequences, then nurturant support would be most beneficial. An example is the death of a close friend. Nothing can bring back the friend. However, nurturant support may make the person's grief more manageable and decrease feelings of being alone.

I have tried to test the optimal matching hypothesis in three different studies. I will briefly summarize these and will then apply their findings to the topic of family support. In the first study (Cutrona and Suhr 1992), I invited married couples into my laboratory and asked them to take turns telling their spouse about something that was currently a problem in their life. We asked them to choose a problem for which they did not blame their spouse and about which they had not argued in the past. We asked the spouse simply to respond naturally and spontaneously. We videotaped these conversations. At the end of each conversation, we asked the persons who disclosed the problem to rate how supportive they thought their spouse had been and how satisfied they were with the interaction. We later analysed the videotapes. We counted how many times the listener had provided emotional support, esteem support, information support and tangible support. We also analysed the type of stress that was discussed. We made ratings of whether the stress was something controllable or uncontrollable. Then we analysed the data to see whether the optimal matching theory was consistent with the results.

First, we found that when events were high in controllability, spouses did give more information support – more advice and suggestions on how to solve their problem. How successful was this information support? Did it lead to feelings of satisfaction and being supported? Sometimes it did, but sometimes it made the person disclosing a problem feel worse. When spouses had control over the situation – when they had special knowledge or resources that could help – their advice was welcome and the stressed individuals felt better the more information support they received. However, when the stressed persons themselves had control over the situation – when they had the knowledge or resources needed to solve the problem – their spouse's advice was not welcome and the stressed individuals felt worse the more information support they received. When people know how to solve their difficulties and believe in their ability to do so, they resent being told what to do by their spouse.

By contrast, emotional support (expressions of caring, empathy and concern) were always viewed as helpful, regardless of the nature of the stressful event under discussion. It appears that informational support (advice, suggestions) is only welcome under very specific circumstances, when the support provider really has expertise in the area of the problem. Advice can actually make a person feel worse. However, emotional support seems to be appreciated regardless of the circumstances.

A second study (Swanson-Hyland 1996) produced similar results. In this study, individuals who suffered from type II diabetes mellitus kept daily records of the types of support they received from their spouse every day for a week. They also rated their satisfaction with their marriage every day. The diabetes patients were asked to rate how much control they felt they had over their diabetes (through diet and exercise, for example). Regardless of the amount of control they felt they had over their disease, all patients felt better about their marriages the more nurturant support they received (emotional and esteem support). Among those who felt capable of controlling their diabetes, instrumental support from their spouse actually made them feel worse. The more advice and tangible assistance these people received from their spouse, the less satisfied they were with their marriages. For people who perceived a low level of control over their diabetes, social support from their spouse did not affect their marital satisfaction significantly. Perhaps these people had given up, both on themselves and on their marriages.

A final study that I conducted directly compared the effectiveness of emotional versus instrumental support. In this study, study participants evaluated the types of support that they thought would be most beneficial in stressful circumstances (Cutrona, Cohen and Igram 1990). Even in situations where the stressed individual needed both tangible assistance and emotional support, people rated emotional support as more valuable. When the stressed person wanted emotional support, tangible support was viewed as a very poor and unacceptable substitute. However, even when the stressed person expressed a need for tangible assistance, emotional support was viewed as a valuable resource and was evaluated as an acceptable substitute for tangible assistance.

How do these findings relate to family support? Several conclusions can be drawn. First, people seem to have a general preference for emotional support. The one exception is when the support provider actually has control over the problem causing distress – for example, expertise or resources needed to solve the problem. When the support provider does not have special expertise or resources, advice or tangible aid actually make the person feel worse and damages the quality of the relationship between the support recipient and the support provider. Thus, mental health professionals who are trying to strengthen families must take special care to evaluate their actual expertise in a given situation before giving advice or offering to intervene. As professionals, we often do have resources that will aid people in solving their life problems, but not always. In many situations, the best thing we can do is offer empathy, understanding and encouragement as people struggle to find their own solutions to the problems in their lives. We do not necessarily know enough about the people and their life circumstances to give our clients advice about how to manage a specific situation. In most cases we do not have the tangible resources that the stressed person needs to solve his or her problem. However, the empathy and encouragement we provide may be critically important in helping the person to be proactive and work to solve his or her dilemma. Furthermore, fostering a sense of control is beneficial. People who feel a sense of control are most likely to take active steps and to benefit from empathy and encouragement. Thus, one goal of providing family support should be to foster a sense of control and empowerment.

Context in which support provision is important

Many different strategies have been tried to bolster the support resources of families who are socially isolated or lack social resources. Some of these strategies are more successful than others. People do not want to be labelled 'friendless' or 'in need of support'. Thus, interventions that are overtly focused on friendship formation may meet considerable resistance. For a variety of reasons, friendships appear to emerge more easily from shared activities and projects than from interventions whose purpose is to build new friendships (Rook 1991). Examples of shared activities may include organizing a neighbourhood clean-up effort, volunteer work with elderly neighbors, adult education classes, exercise classes, and so on. Shared activities and collaborative projects may facilitate friendship formation in a number of ways (Rook 1991). A common focus lends structure to participants' interactions. It gives them something to talk about and reduces ambiguity and social anxiety. Interacting with others in the course of work on a shared project gives participants the opportunity to make discrete assessments of each other's suitability as potential friends, with a minimum of self-consciousness. Personal interests and experiences can be disclosed in a non-contrived way, as a natural offshoot of conversations that develop in the context of shared activities. Joint activities provide a small sample of the person's dependability and other personal traits that are relevant to their qualifications as a potential friend (Rook 1984, 1991). Thus, even when the ultimate goal of a family support intervention is to reduce isolation and build relationships among people (e.g. low-income mothers), the best strategy may be to design programmes that focus on shared interests or goals rather than on building relationships and reducing isolation.

Importance of reciprocity

An important consideration when trying to build support resources for families is that people do not like to receive without the opportunity to repay or reciprocate assistance. We do not like to feel indebted to others. Receiving support, no matter how much it is needed, creates an emotional cost for recipients and damages their self-image as independent, self-sustaining persons (Williams 1995). If recipients feel that they are unable to return the support they receive, relationships can become strained. More importantly, those in need may become unwilling to seek help or accept support when it is offered (Williams 1995). There is evidence that it is not the receipt of support, but the experience of reciprocal give and take that is most strongly associated with psychological well-being. This has been found among widows (Rook 1987), co-workers (Buunk *et al.* 1993), married couples (Acitelli and Antonucci 1994), and participants in self-help groups (Maton 1988). Thus, in efforts to increase the flow of support within naturally occurring social groups, it is important to facilitate mutual assistance rather than one-way giving.

Even among severely stressed individuals, people are uncomfortable receiving aid from others if they cannot reciprocate. For example, among parents of children with cancer, 70 per cent expressed a need to reciprocate or pay back the support and help they received from others. At the time they received the support, they were typically in a crisis and could not reciprocate. However, Williams (1995) found that they could restore their self-concept later on by helping other families who faced the same problem. Thus, family support programmes that include the opportunity to help others are highly desirable. An excellent example of this kind of programme is Habitat for Humanity, which provides low-cost, decent housing to low-income families. Volunteers donate their time to build homes for poor families. The persons receiving the home must spend 500 hours working on their own house and must then spend a specified number of hours working on homes being built for other families. Receiving aid does not damage people's dignity if they can subsequently offer the same assistance to others. Opportunities for reciprocity are an important component of family support.

Reasons for support affect its effectiveness

People do not uncritically accept offers of assistance. They are very sensitive to the reasons why others offer them support. If support is offered out of genuine concern, it will have a greater impact than if it is offered out of obligation, politeness or social pressure. One way that people judge whether or not support is offered out of a genuine sense of caring is whether it is given spontaneously or only given in response to an explicit request for aid. In our research, we found that support from a friend or spouse was valued more highly if it was given spontaneously than after a request (Cutrona *et al.* 1990). This poses a dilemma for potential help providers because they are left in the position of having to guess when support is needed. It may be helpful to encourage people to overcome their dislike of asking for support. One advantage of asking for support is that it allows the person to ask for exactly the type of support he or she desires. ('I had a really hard day at work. Tell me it wasn't a mistake to accept that promotion and that eventually it will get easier.') Of course, explicit requests foster the belief that persons are providing support only out of obligation and that they do not really believe what they are saying.

It may also be helpful to teach family members to recognize the subtle ways in which people indirectly signal their need for support. The most frequently used method of communicating a desire for support is simply describing the facts of the situation causing stress. ('My mother criticized me again for the way I dress the children.') The second is to describe one's emotional state. ('After being with my mother all afternoon, I feel really frustrated.') Family and friends are expected to recognize these statements as requests for support. Of course, they must guess what kind of support the person wants.

Within some families, people seem to have great difficulty believing in the sincerity of the support they receive from others. Because of bad experiences they had in the past, they believe that support is given for all the wrong reasons – to get something in return, to fulfil an obligation, to look good in front of others. When such attributions are made, even the most generous act will have little effect (Fletcher and Fincham 1991). Thus, one task that may face mental health professionals is helping people to evaluate the reasons for support more benignly, to entertain the possibility that others may genuinely care about their well-being. Of course, it is not useful to encourage people to delude themselves, but if it appears that a person has difficulty trusting the sincerity of seemingly genuine support efforts, it may be useful to view this difficulty as a therapeutic issue to be addressed. In the context of a marriage, issues that led to the suspiciousness and mistrust must be dealt with before support can be effectively exchanged.

Mental health professionals face an especially difficult situation in that people know that they are paid for offering support. This casts doubt on the sincerity of support offered by professionals. It may not be fair, but mental health professionals are frequently not accepted as genuine support providers until they have demonstrated their willingness to go far beyond the requirements of their position in aiding the family, such as working extremely long hours, or other demonstrations of commitment that are 'above and beyond the call of duty'. In most cases, trust takes considerable time to develop and until it does the mental health care provider can expect to be met with varying degrees of cynicism and lack of appreciation.

People differ in ways of coping with stress

People have their own distinctive ways of coping with problems. It is important for those providing family support to be sensitive to these differences. A wide variety of factors may influence people's typical approach to difficulties, including their gender, personality and the way problems were dealt with in their childhood home. People also differ in the kinds of events that affect them emotionally. For example, women react more strongly than men to negative events that occur in the lives of the people they know; for example, a friend's diagnosis of breast cancer or their child's experiences of rejection by peers (Kessler and McLeod 1985). There is some evidence that men react more strongly than women to problems in the workplace (Folkman and Lazarus 1980). Thus, a husband may not realize or understand the distress that is experienced by his wife over a friend's misfortune and she may not comprehend the extent to which a perceived failure at work affects his well-being. Because a primary goal of family support is to promote adaptive coping within families, it is important to understand the differences that may be found between husbands and wives in their efforts to cope with stress and to facilitate understanding within couples of how these differences can be handled.

Men and women tend to use somewhat different strategies for dealing with their emotions. Men report efforts to control their emotions through exercise, sports, drinking and smoking (Rosario *et al.* 1988; Thoits 1991). They also report withdrawal from the situation more frequently than women (Repetti 1989; Rosario *et al.* 1988). Women more frequently report direct expression of their feelings, through talking to another person or writing about their emotions (Stone and Neale 1984; Thoits 1991). Perhaps the most consistent gender-related difference in coping behaviours is the greater tendency of women than men to seek social support from others. This pattern has been found among undergraduate students, community adults and workplace samples equated for status and access to resources (Ptacek, Smith and Zanas 1992; Rosario *et al.* 1988; Stone and Neale 1984; Thoits 1991). Women more frequently seek both counsel and comfort from others when they are stressed than do men. Men, by contrast, may feel that seeking or accepting support is a sign of weakness.

In the research summarized above, most differences between men and women in coping strategies are relatively small and many of the differences in coping do not emerge consistently across studies. However, differences between people may become more noticeable or significant in times of severe stress, whether the differences are associated with gender, personality or past experience. The consequences of such differences were illustrated in a study of the parents of seriously ill children conducted by Gottlieb and Wagner (1991). Marked differences emerged between the reactions of mothers and fathers to their child's illness. The greatest difference appeared in the domain of emotional expression. Mothers frequently expressed intense emotions connected with their child's suffering, perceived worsening of the condition and, above all, fears for their child's future. Fathers remained much more impassive. They rarely verbalized apprehensions about the child's future. They preferred to handle daily problems as they arose, without dwelling on potential catastrophes. Because women assumed most of the responsibility for caregiving, they were immersed in daily experiences that included home treatments, blood tests and insulin injections. They were responsible for preparing special foods, supervising the child's adherence to dietary restrictions and doctor visits and witnessed the pain associated with treatment and diagnostic procedures. By contrast, fathers were able to escape from these draining experiences to the workplace, where they reported relief from the strains of their child's illness. Fathers appeared to 'compartmentalize' their lives and were able to derive pleasure from sources of satisfaction outside of the family.

Couples in Gottlieb and Wagner's (1991) study described mounting tensions that resulted from these stylistic differences in coping. Husbands accused their wives of emotional over-involvement. They pressured their wives to behave more 'maturely', to engage in less self-pity, to over-dramatize less. They asked to be spared from hearing their wives' fears and apprehensions, since such self-disclosures were upsetting to their own equilibrium. Wives accused their husbands of not being involved enough, either emotionally or in the taxing routines of caring for the child. They exerted pressure on their husbands to express their emotions and urged them to assume a greater share of the responsibility for the child's home treatment regimens and general care. Women reported hiding their emotions from their husbands to gain their approval, but said they resented the strain this placed upon them and felt lonely and isolated as a result.

The way that couples deal with such stylistic differences can have a profound effect on the success with which they handle difficult life circumstances. Because of their interdependence, marital partners are affected not only by the impact of events on their own emotional well-being, but also by the impact of the stressor on their partner's adjustment and the methods their partner uses to cope with the strain. Each tries to cope using long-established patterns of stress management. However, the coping behaviours of one may be incompatible with the needs of the partner. Adjustments in coping behaviours may be made to win the other's approval and support. However, these adjustments may have negative consequences, as illustrated by the resentment and loneliness of mothers who hid emotions connected with their child's illness from their spouse.

Importance of clear communication

The importance of recognizing, understanding and communicating openly about differences cannot be emphasized enough. With effort and compassion, marriage partners can benefit from the balance provided by the other's approach to dealing with crises. Without such efforts, the other's differences may be evaluated as a personal threat and evidence of indifference to the relationship. An important contribution of those providing family support is to help couples learn to understand and respect each other's differences in coping styles. This may prevent couples from the added burden of conflict and resentment when they need each other most during times of crisis and stress.

Conclusion

Family support can be a critical resource for parents and children who are striving to overcome adverse circumstances. However, supportive interventions are not always effective. The source of support is critical. Support is most effective from those with whom we share close emotional bonds. Thus, the mental health professional's first priority should be facilitating the flow of support within existing social networks of family and friends, rather than trying to 'graft on' new sources of support. Good communication skills are a critical component of social support. Skills that allow people to ask for and receive the support they need should be incorporated into pre-marital counselling, prenatal counselling, and crisis-related support groups. Opportunities to reciprocate support are important to people. Different kinds of support are most beneficial, depending upon the recency of the traumatic event, the type of trauma and the preferred coping style of the stressed individual. In general, support that communicates genuine caring, yet encourages the individual to solve his or her own problems, is most effective.

References

Acitelli, L.K. and Antonucci, T.C. (1994) 'Gender differences in the link between marital support and satisfaction in older couples.' *Journal of Personality and Social Psychology 67*, 688–698.

Beach, S.R.H., Martin, J.K., Blum, T.C. and Roman, P.M. (1993) 'Effects of marital and co-worker relationships on negative affect: Testing the central role of marriage.' *American Journal of Family Therapy 21*, 313–323.

Brown, G.W. and Harris, T.O. (1978) *Social Origins of Depression: A Study of Psychiatric Disorder in Women.* New York: Free Press.

Buunk, B.P., Doosje, B.J., Jans, L.G.J. and Hopstaken, L.E.M. (1993) 'Perceived reciprocity, social support, and stress at work: The role of exchange and communal orientation.' *Journal of Personality and Social Psychology 65*, 801–811.

Coyne, J.C. and DeLongis, A. (1986) 'Going beyond social support: The role of social relationships in adaptation.' *Journal of Clinical and Counseling Psychology 54*, 454–460.

Cutrona, C.E. (1990) 'Stress and social support – In search of optimal matching.' *Journal of Social and Clinical Psychology 9*, 3–14.

Cutrona, C.E. (1996) *Social Support in Couples: Marriage as a Resource in Times of Stress.* Thousand Oaks, CA: Sage.

Cutrona, C.E. and Russell, D. (1990) 'Type of social support and specific stress: Toward a theory of optimal matching.' In I.G. Sarason, B.R. Sarason and G.R. Pierce (eds) *Social Support: An Interactional View.* New York: Wiley.

Cutrona, C.E. and Suhr, J.A. (1992) 'Controllability of stressful events and satisfaction with spouse support behaviors.' *Communication Research 19,* 154–176.

Cutrona, C.E., Cohen, B. and Igram, S. (1990) 'Contextual determinants of perceived social support.' *Journal of Personal and Social Relationships 7,* 553–562.

Fletcher, G.J.O. and Fincham, F.D. (1991) 'Attribution processes in close relationships.' In G.J.O. Fletcher and F.D. Fincham (eds) *Cognition and Close Relationships.* Hillsdale, NJ: Erlbaum.

Folkman, S. and Lazarus, R.S. (1980) 'An analysis of coping in a middle-aged community sample.' *Journal of Health and Social Behavior 21,* 219–239.

Gottlieb, G.H. and Wagner, F. (1991) 'Stress and support processes in close relationships.' In J. Eckenrode (ed) *The Social Context of Coping.* New York: Plenum Press.

Heller, K., Thompson, M.G., Trueba, P.E., Hogg, J.R. and Vlachos-Weber, I. (1991) 'Peer support telephone dyads for elderly women: Was this the wrong intervention?' *American Journal of Community Psychology 19,* 1, 53–74.

Kessler, R.C. and McLeod, J.D. (1985) 'Social support and mental health in community samples.' In S. Cohen and S.L. Syme (eds) *Social Support and Health.* New York: Academic Press.

Lee, G.R. and Ishii-Kuntz, M. (1988) 'Social interaction, loneliness, and emotional well being among the elderly.' *Research on Aging 9,* 459–482.

Lehman, D.R., Lang, E.L., Wortman, C.B. and Sorenson, S.B. (1989) 'Long-term effects of sudden bereavement: Marital and parent–child relationships and children's reactions.' *Journal of Family Psychology 2,* 344–367.

Maton, K.I. (1988) 'Social support, organizational characteristics, psychological well being, and group appraisal in three self-help group populations.' *American Journal of Community Psychology 16,* 53–77.

Mullins, L.C. and Dugan, E. (1990) 'The influence of depression and family friendship relations on residents' loneliness in congregate housing.' *The Gerontologist 30,* 377–384.

Pipher, M. (1996) *The Shelter of Each Other.* New York: G.P. Putnam and Sons.

Ptacek, J.T., Smith, R.E. and Zanas, J. (1992) 'Gender, appraisal, and coping: A longitudinal analysis.' *Journal of Personality 60,* 747–770.

Renick, M.J., Blumberg, S.L. and Markman, H.J. (1992) 'The Prevention and Relationship Enhancement Program (PREP): An empirically based preventive intervention program for couples.' *Family Relations 41,* 141–147.

Repetti, R.L. (1989) 'Effects of daily workload on subsequent behavior during marital interaction: The roles of social withdrawal and spouse support.' *Journal of Personality and Social Psychology 57,* 651–659.

Rook, K.S. (1984) 'Promoting social bonding: Strategies for helping the lonely and socially isolated.' *American Psychologist 39,* 1389–1407.

Rook, K.S. (1987) 'Reciprocity of social exchange and social satisfaction among older women.' *Journal of Personality and Social Psychology 52,* 145–154.

Rook, K.S. (1991) 'Facilitating friendship formation in late life: Puzzles and challenges.' *American Journal of Community Psychology 19,* 103–110.

Rosario, M., Shinn, M., Morch, H. and Huckabee, C.B. (1988) 'Gender differences in coping and social supports: Testing socialization and role constraint theories.' *Journal of Community Psychology 16,* 55–69.

Stone, A.A. and Neale, J.M. (1984) 'New measure of daily coping: Development and preliminary results.' *Journal of Personality and Social Psychology 46,* 219–239.

Swanson-Hyland, E.F. (1996) 'The influence of spousal social support on psychological and physical health among persons with type II diabetes mellitus: A test of the optimal matching model of social support.' Unpublished doctoral dissertation, University of Iowa, Iowa City, Iowa.

Thoits, P.A. (1991) 'Gender differences in coping with emotional distress.' In J. Eckenrode (ed) *The Social Context of Coping.* New York: Plenum Press.

Weiss, R.S. (1976) 'Transition states and other stressful situations: Their nature and programs for their management.' In G. Caplan and M. Killilea (eds) *Support Systems and Mutual Help: Multidisciplinary Explorations.* New York: Grune and Stratton.

Williams, H.A. (1995) 'There are no free gifts! Social support and the need for reciprocity.' *Human Organization 54,* 401–409.

CHAPTER 6

Refocusing Project Work with Adolescents towards a Family Support Paradigm

John Canavan and Pat Dolan

Whether residual or highly statist in nature, there is little doubt that one of the main challenges of all welfare state provision in the developed world is to cater more effectively to significant minorities of adolescents who face serious adversity in their daily lives. As Cornia and Danziger (1997) point out, in spite of remarkable improvement in the living standards and general well-being of children in the second half of this century, there has been a concurrent growth in what they call the new child morbidity: '...an umbrella term which covers environment-related ailments, psychological and behavioural problems, developmental dysfunctions, dyslexia and accidents' (p.59). A concomitant of this new term is the phrase 'at risk'. Although sometimes claimed by professionals from different sectors working with children as meaningful only in their area, the term can equally be applied to adolescents in a range of situations; for example, young people who have experienced early and credential-less exit from mainstream education or whose labour market transitions will ultimately lead to long-term unemployment or poorly paid employment. In addition, 'at risk' should also include those who are involved in crime, both petty and serious, and those who are on the threshold of entry into state care due to neglect and sexual, physical and emotional abuse.

The aim of this chapter is to outline the experience of the Neighbourhood Youth Project (NYP), a community-based intervention for young people which operates in the Republic of Ireland. Our particular emphasis is the evolution of the project from one which primarily targeted adolescents in isolation, through an evaluation process and subsequent research, to an intervention with a far greater family support orientation. In tracing this process, we believe a number of critical points emerge in relation to the development and ongoing management of family support services, of value to both front-line workers and policymakers. Two specific pieces of research underpin the chapter. The first is an evaluation study undertaken in 1991–92, while the second is some exploratory research on social networks of parents whose children attend the project, which was completed in 1997.

The core of the chapter is in four sections. The first two describe the NYP model and outline the evaluation of an NYP project in Galway and its key findings. The third and fourth sections focus on the shift within this project towards working with parents more effectively, as exemplified in the research study of their social support networks. However, before going on to look at this research in detail, the next part of the chapter considers the broader contexts within which these developments occurred. First, prevailing ideas on the nature of adolescence are briefly considered. This is followed by a commentary on the nature of the response of the Irish state to those 'at risk', with a particular emphasis on the development of community- based supports in the form of the NYP.

Context

Adolescence has only been studied as a topic in its own right in relatively recent times and to some extent our understanding of the process of adolescence may be limited (Modell and Goodman 1993). Traditionally, adolescence has often been referred to as a time of storm and stress or *sturm und drang* (Garbarino 1990; Hall 1904; Hauser and Bowlds 1993, p.391) during which both the adolescent and the parents must overcome trauma and difficulty in their relationship. However, this image of adolescence is not necessarily accurate and most adolescents and their parents seem to survive the 'teenage experience' unscathed (Offer and Schnort-Reichl 1992). Herbert (1988) also agrees that the occurrence of adversity in adolescence has been overstated. In this regard Herbert (1993, pp.71–75) has described adolescence as 'a sheep in wolf's clothing'. Winn (1983, p.14), similarly suggested that adolescence could be described as 'the myth of the teenage werewolf'.

In fact, as has been well established in American research, it may be that only 15 to 20 per cent of the adolescent population experience difficulties in their teenage years (Garbarino 1990; Offer and Schnort-Reichl 1992). Also, where adolescents experience difficulties, they can often be helped successfully. In many ways, the problems with which such adolescents present are no different to those of younger children or adults. In addition, not all adolescents experience difficulty at the same time, nor do teenage problems appear at the same rate, which also gives parents a better chance to deal with their adolescent's difficulties (Harter 1993). All in all, the experience of being a teenager and of being a parent to an adolescent may not be as difficult or overwhelming as is commonly perceived (Fenwick and Smith 1993; Santrock and Yussen 1992).

Until as recently as thirty years ago, the main state response in Ireland to adolescents at risk was institutional in nature. On the back of the trend of the time (and particular reflected in the neighbouring UK) an official committee was established in 1967 to examine provision in what were known as industrial and reformatory schools. The terms of reference were later expanded to include all residential care of children in Ireland. The 1970 Kennedy Report which followed heralded the beginning of a new age of children's care in Ireland (Committee on Reformatory and Industrial Schools 1970). At its heart was the key recommendation that policy and strategies should be developed which aimed to prevent family breakdown. Residential care should be the final option and then only operating on the basis of small units staffed by trained child-care workers.

The impetus of the Kennedy Report was galvanized in 1973 with the establishment of the Task Force on Child Care Services, which had the remit:

- to make recommendations on the extension and improvement of services for deprived children and children at risk

- to prepare a new Children's Bill, updating and modernizing the law in relation to children

- to make recommendations on the administrative reforms which may be necessary to give effect to the above proposals. (Task Force on Child Care Services 1980, p.26)

The relative importance of the issue of care of children in Irish public affairs is evidenced in the six years that it took to complete the work of the Task Force and the full 17-year gap between the initiation of the Committee and the enactment of the Child Care Act 1991. In spite of these negative considerations, the work of the Task Force has been fundamental to the modern day services.

Two principles underpinned the consideration of the Task Force, the first being that of minimum intervention arising from what was seen to be the norm and the ideal that a child should grow up within a caring family. Efforts should 'be directed towards enabling this to take place or, failing that, towards enabling the closest approximation to it to take place'. Balancing this principle was the second which proposes 'appropriate response to the needs of the child' (1980, p.100). Although policy tends to reflect a variety of perspectives, the broad thrust of the proposals of the Task Force falls into what Fox-Harding (1997, p.70) describes as the 'modern defence of birth family and parents' rights' perspective. This perspective accords neither a laissez-faire nor paternalistic role to state; rather, it suggests one which supports families to remain together. Poverty, class and deprivation figure in the key explanations in this perspective.

In the context of this chapter, a more central theme of the report was the clear statement of a shift in the underlying model or approach to care of children in need and at risk. While the former model had minimal or non-existent involvement of the families and communities of children, the new orientation advocated by the Task Force involved comprehensive locally based systems incorporating community involvement in decision making about services in their area (pp.142–143). Additionally, working in a non-stigmatizing way to prevent adverse outcomes for children – for example, their entry to residential care or justice systems – was a key strand of this overall orientation (p.151).

Although the Task Force proposals were very much founded on clinical principles about how best to work with children and families, there is no doubt that they were part of the wider move in health and social service delivery from institutional to community care. As is the case in many aspects of public policy development, post-colonial Ireland was heavily influenced by its UK neighbour in this area. In Britain, beginning with Poor Law legislation in 1834 and continuing until the end of World War II, state responses to needy groups in society were characterized by segregation (Pilgrim 1993, p.168). Beginning in the 1950s and through the next two decades, deinstitutionalization was the main trend, especially in respect of mentally ill and intellectually disabled people. Barnes regards this policy shift as being unbalanced, in that while it focused on removing people from inappropriate care settings, it did not involve the nurturing and support of communities into which clients were moving (1997, p.19). In contrast, another aspect of the shift towards community care, community-oriented social work was very much about prevention and capacity building. Deriving from a broad community development philosophy and embodied in the 1968 Seebohm Report, community as a network of social relationships was seen to be the natural setting for delivery of personal social services and also a key resource.

In the context of this paradigm shift and following from its guiding principles, the Task Force in its Interim Report (1975) recommended the establishment of a number of pilot Neighbourhood Youth Projects (NYPs).

These projects, at the time a major innovation in Irish social policy, were intended to have as their target group children:

- who have lacked stable adult models with whom they could identify and establish relationships of trust

- whose parents or parent substitutes have been inconsistently rejecting or disturbed

- whose parent or parents have become so dependent on their child emotionally or otherwise that they are inhibiting the natural growing up process

- who have severe personal, family, educational or social problems for which they need outside help

- who, while not experiencing emotional problems or lacking in stable adult relationships, have established or are likely to establish patterns of persistent and serious delinquency.

A number of points informed the Task Force's choice of target group. First, it was of the view that some of those children in residential care at that time would not have been if such provision had previously been available. Second, a 'significant number' of children living at home needed supervised care of a non-residential nature. Furthermore, it identified the fact that existing provision in the community for young people in youth and sports clubs was not in a position to meet the needs of the children that the Task Force wished to target.

A major influence on the development of the concept of the NYP and the strategy it embodied was research by the Task Force on the intermediate treatment (IT) approach which was used in the UK consequent on the Children and Young Person's Act 1969. While NYP practice was intended to be similar to that used in IT, their start points were quite different – IT was a tool of the judiciary, while NYPs were designed to have a preventive and family support ethos (Task Force 1975, p.17).

Given the Task Force emphasis on the model in both the interim and final reports, it is somewhat surprising that the development of the NYPs was quite limited. Projects were established in Cork, Limerick and Dublin in 1977 with a further four in the 1980s, three in Dublin and one in Cork. A number of possible explanatory factors might be proposed for this. First, although the general trend in policy in the UK was beginning to shift towards protection after the 'prevention decade' of the 1960s (Fox-Harding 1997, p.171), Ireland lagged behind this trend somewhat. However, in the years which followed until the Child Care Act 1991, protection issues dominated personal social services agendas as they did with counterparts in other countries. Neither did economic conditions favour expenditure on preventive interventions, as Ireland suffered a series of economic recessions resulting in severe unemployment and national debt crises. The most important factor, however, was the continuing absence of a supportive legislative context, one which was eventually created with the advent of the 1991 Child Care Act.

Westside Neighbourhood Youth Project

Coinciding with the Child Care Act 1991 and in response to its key sections was the establishment of an NYP in the 'Westside' of the city of Galway, the project which is the focus of this chapter. The Western Health Board funded the work of Westside Neighbourhood Youth Project (NYP) with adolescents (12 to 18 years) from a disadvantaged area of Galway known as the 'Westside' (Canavan 1993; Dolan 1997). The project operates from a purpose-built youth centre and has a staff of one project leader, three project staff, a part-time community artist and secretarial support. Project staff come from child care, teaching and psychology disciplines. The project has a board of management comprising representatives from the Western Health Board, local schools, community groups and parents living in Westside. Westside NYP staff strive to achieve the aims of the project through supplying adolescents and their families with a range of supports suitable to their needs, including individual and group counselling, self-esteem building projects, outdoor pursuits/leisure programmes and social support interventions.

Adolescents are referred to the NYP through a variety of sources, but most typically through Western Health Board social work services, schools or by self-referral. The inputs used with adolescents are aimed at addressing the primary reason for their referral to the project, as indicated by the referrer, parent and the adolescent him/herself. Typical problems experienced by adolescents attending the Westside NYP include school failure, homelessness, delinquency, family discord and social marginalization. The project is adolescent centred and non-stigmatizing in its approach to families. Adolescents who come to the project are not treated by staff as 'clients' but as 'members' or 'participants'. Equally, the adolescents who attend do not refer to their group work sessions as 'therapy' but rather as their 'club'.

Approximately fifty adolescents are served by the project at any one time. On average, they attend groups once or twice per week. In addition to those who formally attend the project, a further twenty to thirty attend weekly 'drop-in' groups on an informal basis. The Westside NYP runs 13 different groups (approximately) for adolescents each week. These include informal early evening open groups, a range of activity-based groups, e.g. photography, hill walking, pottery, arts and crafts, and sports groups. The project also hosts life and social skills groups as well as those focusing on adolescent health issues. For groups on specific issues such as assertiveness and social skills, video work and role play are sometimes used. Also, a work practice model known as the 'intensive discussion group' is a core part of the NYP work programme. Through discussion and group exercises serious issues that affect participants' well-being are discussed in the intensive group with the dual purpose of increasing the participant's ability to take responsibility and also providing them with an opportunity to consider potential solutions to their difficulties.

The Westside NYP collaborates closely with a variety of health professionals as well as other statutory and voluntary service providers. In this regard, the NYP works closely with each of the local primary and secondary schools. Many of the children in the local schools who are a cause of concern to their teachers, because of disruptive behaviour or truancy, are often also a cause of concern to health board services. NYP staff and home–school liaison teachers work together with this identified group through a range of inputs including school group work programmes.

Westside NYP evaluation

After one year in operation, it was decided to undertake an evaluation of the Westside NYP and a researcher was appointed from the local university. The main research was carried out in the second half of 1992, with the evaluation report finalized in June 1993. The overall aims of the evaluation were to assess the project's effectiveness and to establish what lessons had emerged from its early experiences. The relatively straightforward evaluation model used took its start as the existence of a problem which is assumed to be resolvable through the achievement of certain objectives. In order to set about pursuing these objectives, a project will follow particular strategies using a series of inputs; for example, staff skill and time. The result of the implementation of these strategies will be a series of outcomes.

If the assumptions about the nature of the problem are broadly correct and the strategies are implemented as initially intended, the outcomes should reflect the original objectives and resolution or at least amelioration of the problem should be achieved. While firmly in a rational planning approach to social interventions, the evaluation model adopted was used as an aid to clarity rather than a view of the world to be slavishly followed. In order to arrive at clear conclusions and recommendations for use within the project and by its funding agency, the regional health authority, a comprehensive set of data sources was used in the research. These fed into a series of substudies on four core areas: project management and implementation, project costs, attitudes towards the project and project outcomes. The findings from each are briefly reviewed below.

Evaluation findings

The main finding in relation to the management and implementation of the project were that the project was working in a structured way towards the achievement of all its objectives. In pursuit of its two core care objectives, group work and individual support work activities were in place for approximately 45 children. These concern direct intervention with children who are identified as having specific problems and those not receiving adequate support within their family situation. In evaluation terms, the main inputs involved in group and individual work are the skills that the staff bring and the activities they use. At the time, the project's resources included approximately 80 games and activities which fitted 5 categories: physical activities, board games, relationship-building games, crafts, health and personal well-being. As well as the implicit and explicit aims which the workers sought to achieve through their use, these were the supporting context for the development of relationships between the client and his or her peers and with the workers.

The second main set of inputs in group and individual work concern staff skills. At the time of the evaluation, the NYP was staffed by a small but experienced team, with the ongoing support of a number of volunteers. To an extent, the staff worked as they had done in other child/adolescent care settings, drawing on initial training and accumulated experience. However, because the staff had all come from a background in residential care work, they were very conscious of the different demands of community-based work. In particular, there was a sense that they had to work independently, on their own initiative, to a greater extent than would have been required in a residential setting. Related to this point was the extent to which the staff had to engage with a range of individuals other than their direct clients, the children. Dealing effectively with parents, health-care and other professional workers and with community representatives was a further new challenge to the staff at the time.

The evaluator found that the project's group work activities were carefully planned, implemented and reviewed. Underpinning this work was an openness to experiment and at the time of the research the project had begun more intensive group work with a small number of teenagers. At the other end of the scale, the project's 'open house' activities proved to be very successful in destigmatizing the project, by involving a mix of project clients and other young people from the community. The findings in relation to individual work within the project were less positive, with concern about the extent to which they were a residual activity and one lacking appropriate structure.

Two main approaches were used in establishing project outcomes. The first was the use of the Coopersmith Inventory for measuring self-esteem, while the second was the analysis of data generated in the less formal client review process undertaken by project staff and referring agents. In the case of the Coopersmith study, because the evaluator began his work some months after many of the children began participating on the project, a pre- and post-test design was not possible. Instead, the design attempted to relate self-esteem scores to time on the project and the amount of group and individual input that the child received. The results failed to indicate any relationship between the project and levels of self-esteem and involvement with the project. However, they showed that the average self-esteem of the client group was quite low and highlighted this as an important area in the project.

The findings from the analysis of client reviews were more positive from the perspective of the project. The review sessions involved a discussion of the initial reason for referral, the type of intervention undertaken with the child and perceptions of both referring agent and the project of change. In relation to outcomes, the main finding from this analysis was that in the view of those who initially referred children to the project, there was 'some improvement' in the case of 70 per cent of clients, with targets achieved in the case of two clients (5%). In the main, the referrers' judgements mirrored those of project staff. The central themes throughout the study of outcomes were the need for improvement in initial assessment, for setting targets for work with the children and for designing focused intervention programmes. The latter point was balanced by the desire to maintain the project's trademark informal style.

While the preceding paragraphs reflect the views of the project staff, referring agents and the researcher, the single most important set of views about the work of the project were those of the children involved and their parents. Because there are methodological difficulties in eliciting evaluative comments from children, it is generally advisable to be cautious in interpreting research undertaken with them. In the case of the NYP, using a structured interview format, the evaluator asked a series of simple questions of 29 clients. The overwhelming response was that the children enjoyed the club, got on well with their peers and availed of the opportunity to talk to staff members about specific issues that troubled them. A similar type of response emerged from interviews with parents of children attending the project. Of the 22 parents interviewed, 19 were of the view that it had a positive effect on their child and that it met the initial expectations they had for it; 20 felt that they had a good relationship with a NYP team member, while 16 said that the level of contact with staff was adequate. One less satisfactory aspect of their response from a project perspective was parents' limited knowledge of what the project was actually about.

Responding directly to the needs of identified children and their parents was the sine qua non of the NYP. However, both because of its location in the community from where it drew its clients and its explicit orientation as a community care service, an important establishment task for the project was to become accepted and rooted in the Westside. Based on the observations of the evaluator, specific indicators of community involvement and a series of interviews with key informants from the area, the evaluator concluded that this basic task had been achieved. As with similar projects, an issue was beginning to emerge about the possibly negative implications of community involvement for the project's core work with children and their parents.

As one of the evaluation's main stakeholders, the project's funding agency wished to incorporate an analysis of the project's cost effectiveness. This was done from two perspectives. First, the NYP per child costs were compared with the cost of residential care for children. At approximately £2000 per annum per child, NYP costs compared favourably with £17,500 for the latter. While residential care is a short-term outcome which NYP sought to prevent, its work also incorporates medium and longer term preventive aims. At the time of the research the cost of secure unit care for children involved in crime was £70,000 per annum per child, while the cost of keeping someone in one of Ireland's prisons was £36,500 per annum per prisoner. The research illustrated the potential savings to the state for a minimal initial investment, on the basis that the medium and longer term preventive aims of the NYP could be achieved.

Factors in success

Despite identifying some concerns, the evaluation concluded that the Westside NYP was highly successful. What it also established was that the project's success was not randomly occurring, but was based on a number of key factors. The foundation of the success of the project was laid in the interim Task Force report. What was suggested as the basis of an NYP in that document, while relatively simple in organizational and operational terms, proved to be implementable. Thus, from the outset, one Westside NYP had a clear set of guidelines regarding the underlying rationale and specific ethos and the target group and general objectives which it should follow.

However, if the NYP blueprint represented the foundations, the commitment to planning and review represented the cornerstone on which its success was built. Planning and review operated at three levels within the project. First, the project engaged in a planning session each term during which the previous term was reviewed and the activities and timetables decided for the term ahead. As well as helping the project to be clear about its general direction, the sessions were also an opportunity for individual support and team building. The support of an outside facilitator was a key factor ensuring that these were effective sessions. The second level of planning in the project was the weekly team meetings. Although these only became formalized during the evaluation process, they proved to be important for reviewing the previous week's work, discussing issues that arose and in allocating tasks for the forthcoming week. The third level of planning within the project was in relation to direct work with project clients. Although not as effective in the case of individual work, the project's commitment to planning and review of group sessions was instrumental in the smooth implementation of that part of the project's work.

Although less easy to quantify, or express, the role of experienced, skilled and committed staff to the success of the project was also highlighted in the evaluation report. The area of staffing is often taken for granted in the design of social interventions, but experience demonstrates that this area is no less immune from human failure in terms of meeting basic professional standards than others. The Westside NYP was characterized by good teamwork in the literal sense of people working well as a single team unit. The report also referred to the quality of leadership within the project, both in terms of the work of the project leader at the time and, more importantly, the willingness of individual team members to take on leadership roles when necessary.

As a pilot project, the notion of experimentation was central to its ethos. Since everything that was being attempted was experimental, at least in the sense of it being the first time that particular ideas were attempted in a city in the west of Ireland, an ethos of innovation characterized the project. One example of innovation during the time of the evaluation was the development of the discussion-based group, due to staff dissatisfaction with the impact of diversionary or activity-based approaches. That this was subsequently superseded by other approaches is indicative of the extent to which innovation continued to be a feature of the project's work.

Group work with parents

In many respects the evaluation of the NYP was a discrete event in its history. However, it was particularly timely in that it occurred during the project's infancy, when staff were still in the process of developing practice. Thus, at this stage what was good practice for community-based intervention in Ireland was still very much a fluid notion. In addition, the evaluation affirmed the experimental and flexible approaches which the staff had adopted and highlighted the central role for these attributes in the project's future. Coming from backgrounds in institutional care, one area in which innovation was not only appropriate for staff but also very necessary was the engagement of parents on the project. Both during and subsequent to the evaluation, the project began a process whereby informal, ongoing contact with parents evolved into more formal participation in project work programmes. Essential to this process was research.

Soon after it commenced operations, parents began coming to the project informally, usually regarding the attendance of their adolescent. Over time, parents then started sharing with staff the difficulties that they were experiencing in relation to parenting their teenagers. Soon it became clear to staff that parents needed a forum whereby they could share their experiences with other parents and learn better ways of parenting. However, parents stated that they were reticent of attending existing parenting courses because they feared that their faults as parents might be exposed. Therefore they needed a safe forum for learning. This gap in service provision led to the first pilot group for NYP parents which took place at the same time as the evaluation of the project (Canavan 1993). The pilot group ran for six weeks and was perceived by parents as very successful; a result which led to more formal and informal ongoing involvement of parents on the NYP (Dolan 1993).

Following this successful pilot group programme for parents of NYP participants (Dolan 1993), parent groups have now become a standard part of the NYP programme. These groups are usually of an eight- or ten-week duration and are held three times a year in spring, early summer and autumn–winter. Eight to ten parents are invited to attend any one forum. Parent groups cover a range of topics, including coping with bullying, assertiveness for parents, dealing with difficult behaviour from adolescents, building self-esteem. One issue regularly raised by parents is the lack of opportunity to spend positive time with their offspring; for example just playing games, relaxing or completing a fun task together. Parent and child pottery and arts groups are one outlet which the NYP has developed to counteract this problem. Parents have stated that they found this opportunity very useful and beneficial for them.

In addition to these formal groups for parents, the NYP has also hosted regular open 'drop-in' mornings. During this time, parents come for a cup of coffee and general chat in a relaxed informal atmosphere. This forum worked well for parents who have completed NYP groups and wished to stay in contact, as well as for parents who had not yet been using the programme. On a practical level, it also gave parents an opportunity to discuss parenting issues informally with project staff and other parents.

In the course of participating in the groups and drop-in mornings, parents on numerous occasions shared with staff their feelings of having a lack of support in their lives. This expressed need for support by parents was subsequently identified by the author and NYP staff alike as a gap in service provision which needed further consideration. This led to a study which focused on parents' perception of the nature and level of social support available to them (Dolan 1997). This research was completed on the assumption that if the NYP service became more aware of the support needs of parents, staff would be in a better position to help parents in supporting their adolescents.

NYP social network study

The social network study had a dual focus. First, it aimed to explore the perceived social networks of parents of adolescents attending the Westside NYP, including information regarding their perceptions of the source, type and quality of social support available to them. Second, it sought to examine a relationship between aspects of parents' perceived social support (types and qualities of social network support) and their general mental health status. Specifically, the researcher was interested in answering five questions in relation to NYP parents' perceptions regarding their social networks:

1. Who constitutes the membership of their social networks as perceived by parents?

2. What are the qualities of their network relationships as reported by parents?

3. How do the parents perceive their own mental health?

4. What relationship exists between the perceptions of parents of their social networks and their general mental health?

5. What, if any, are the possible policy and practice implications of the findings for those wishing to offer social support to parents of adolescents?

Methodology

Two instruments were used for the primary research in the study. The first was the social network map (Tracy and Whittaker 1990). The social network map (SNM) was developed for the self-assessment of informal and formal social network support. Pioneered by Tracy and Whittaker in the 1980s, the SNM has been widely used on a number of family preservation programmes in the USA, notably the 'Homebuilders Project' (Kinney *et al.* 1990). The SNM is both a research and social work practice tool which gathers information regarding one's perceived social network support. The map assists health professionals to identify a client's perceived sources of support and the type and quality of support available from these identified sources. Typical sources of support include informal supporters such as family, friends, neighbours and work colleagues or formal sources including professionals such as general practitioners or social workers and so on. (DePanfilis 1996). The social network map may be completed by a respondent in two parts. Part one involves completing the social network map in order to identify a person's perceived sources of support across a range of eight sources.

Having discovered a respondent's sources of support, the second part of completing the map focuses on looking at the level and types of support available as perceived by the respondent. Such types of support include concrete and tangible, emotional and advice and information support. Finally, having gathered data relating to the source and types of support available, the social network tool accesses information relating to four key qualities of social networks, including: closeness among network members; how critical they were to members; reciprocity of support; and durability of relationships (Cutrona 1996; Dolan 1997). Information regarding types and quality of support as perceived by the respondent are gathered by completion of the social network grid (Tracy and Whittaker 1990). The grid is completed by a respondent with the assistance of the interviewer by answering a range of questions and placing relevant scores and values onto the social network grid.

The second instrument used was the general health questionnaire (GHQ) (Goldberg and Williams 1991), a self-reporting question sheet which assesses respondents' perceived general mental health status. This is a commonly used tool which covers four areas of mental health: somatic symptoms; anxiety and insomnia; social dysfunction; depression. Both instruments were administered in one interview with each respondent, while field notes were kept as an additional source of data.

Twenty-six parents of adolescents referred to and attending the NYP in 1994 participated in the research. The parent chosen for interview was the one best known to project staff. This usually meant mothers, and therefore 25 of the 26 parents who participated in the study were mothers. Of the 26 parents, 16 were lone parents. Respondents were invited by the project leader to participate in the study and were subsequently interviewed by the project leader. Parents completed the SNM and GHQ on the same day, either in their home or at the NYP centre. Interviews with parents were completed over a six-week period.

Findings and implications

Although the research provided a range of important messages, for the purpose of this chapter there are four key findings which need highlighting: the importance of family and extended family; the strength of the adolescent–parent bond; the need by parents for instrumental support from professionals; and the link between social support and mental health.

IMPORTANCE OF FAMILY AND EXTENDED FAMILY

All 26 respondents nominated nuclear family members as part of their social network and no other network received a similar 100 per cent nomination. Over half of the total 277 network members nominated by the 26 respondents were nuclear or extended family members. Therefore, family constituted by far the largest network domain as nominated by respondents. In addition, family members were associated with providing strongest levels of emotional support. In particular, respondents tended to identify extended family members as offering a higher rate of all types of support. Finally, a majority of respondents had at least one extended family member who they perceived to be non-critical, very close and who also reciprocated support.

The fact that all 26 respondents nominated nuclear family members as part of their social network is not hugely surprising. However, this statistic, coupled with the fact that nuclear and extended family together outnumbered non-family network members, supports the assertion that family members are primary sources of support (Gilligan 1995; Tracy et al. 1994). However, having numerous family members present in one's network should not necessarily be seen as a feature of a perfect social network. The presence of family members in itself does not guarantee successful social support provision – not only can family members be non-supportive but they can also abuse and harm each other (Murphy 1996).

Allowing for the fact that not all family network members provide positive support, one of the key tasks for social workers is to assist effective family network members in their task of providing natural informal support (Thompson 1995). Levitt, Silver and Franco (1996) suggest that trouble-some relationships may be part of human experience and can occur both inside and outside the family. The function of professionals in supporting clients who suffer negative support from close family members may be either to exclude these family members from the network or, better still, help them resolve outstanding conflict and learn to be effective supporters. In the Galway study, family members were perceived by a substantial majority of parents as an important part or their social network. Additionally, extended family was seen as strong providers of all types of support, particularly emotional support. In a similar study in which the social network map was used, respondents also perceived extended family as 'strong supporters' (Tracy *et al.* 1990). This finding in favour of extended family as a primary source of emotional support may also be given extra weight as it is consistent with the findings by Cutrona, Cohen and Ingram (1990). Therefore, this study suggests that, despite the presence of any negative family members, professionals need to consider seriously the utilization of nuclear and extended family as the first option when pursuing social network support interventions for their client group.

THE ADOLESCENT–PARENT BOND

Overall, results from the study found that nuclear family members were perceived by parents as closest to them. However, nuclear family members were also rated to be the most likely source of criticism among respondents' network memberships. Specifically, within their family, some parents per-ceived their adolescents (attending the NYP) as among their severest critics. However, despite the presence of a perception of high rates of criticism from their adolescents, all parents still rated themselves as being very close to their teenagers.

Some parents stated that they felt very comforted in the fact that they were still able to nominate their teenage offspring as close network members despite current difficulties in their relationship. It should be noted that some of these same adolescents were perceived by their parents as a cause of extreme stress to them at the time of completing the SNM. As indicated by Garbarino (1990), this would seem to dispel the myth that parents of adolescents automatically become estranged and distant from their teenage offspring in times of adversity. Interestingly, another study on adoles-cent–parent attachment also carried out in the city of Galway (Walsh 1996) found that adolescents often perceive family members, particularly parents, as confidants and important to them even in times of confrontation and difficulty.

Results from this and other studies suggest that the parent–adolescent bond is strong, even in times of adversity. This would imply that, in order to help adolescents in difficulty, professionals should support their key supporters, i.e. their parents. We may need to consider it as given that adolescents cannot be worked with in isolation and, as Herbert (1988) suggests, working with a young person successfully inevitably means working with the family, particularly parents. Furthermore, given that the parent–adolescent relationship may be a durable one, rather than bypassing parents, effective community-based interventions may only be optimally successful where parents are engaged as key players.

PARENTAL NEED FOR INSTRUMENTAL SUPPORT FROM PROFESSIONALS

All in all, professionals were not seen by parents as providing strong network support. However, of the 20 respondents who chose a professional, 12 (60%) perceived at least one nominated professional as supplying strong advice and information support. Whereas 90 per cent of responding parents rated professionals as hardly ever critical of them, only a quarter rated themselves as being very close to the set of professionals in their network. However, many parents commented on their need for instrumental support from professionals. A notable number of respondents indicated that they valued the concrete support that professionals provided as equally, if not more, important than emotional or advice support. For example, some parents who nominated the NYP in their social network stated that having their adolescent attend the NYP for evenings and/or weekends freed them and allowed them time for themselves.

Although this appreciation of practical support from professionals (including NYP staff) was not apparent in respondents' corresponding social network maps, the researchers still considered this an important finding, albeit somewhat anecdotal. Professionals, rather than seeing it as being asked to provide an inappropriate 'babysitting service' to parents, might consider formalizing this type of support. Community services such as the NYP could specify times and schedules in offering parents a chance to pursue a parenting course, a night class or a hobby on the basis that their offspring attend the NYP for individual or group work at specific times and dates. This process may involve professionals just formalizing what may have been happening to some extent already. Obviously, due care needs to be taken to ensure that professionals and services are not taken advantage of in any such arrangements. However, if well organized, both the adolescent and the parents could benefit from this co-ordination of work practice on the part of professionals and services.

LINK BETWEEN PERCEIVED SOCIAL SUPPORT AND PERCEIVED MENTAL HEALTH

The 26 completed general health questionnaires (GHQs) were scored and analysed. A respondent who scores at or above a recognized threshold figure can be deemed at risk of developing or actually having a mental health problem (Goldberg and Williams 1991). In this recent study, 10 respondents (38.5%) scored above this threshold figure and therefore can be deemed as being GHQ cases. This group of 10 respondents will be referred to as GHQ cases while the remaining set of 16 respondents will be referred to as GHQ non-cases. Therefore, these 10 parents who are GHQ cases can be described as having a mental health problem with potential for experiencing serious mental health difficulty.

Comparison between GHQ cases and GHQ non-cases indicated that average network size was similar for both groups and that GHQ cases had, in fact, a perception of having slightly greater availability of support from network members. What is more important, perhaps, is that GHQ cases perceived themselves as having less variety of sources of support, less network members with whom they shared reciprocal support, more members who were very critical of them and more network members to whom they did not feel very close. Therefore, results regarding this present study suggest a possible link between respondents' perception of the quality of their social network relationships and their general mental health status.

Although the results of this study are suggestive of an association between social support and mental health, this finding in itself is nothing new (Brugha 1995; Millstein and Litt 1993) and in this regard one key question still remains unanswered. Does the existence of social network support affect one's mental health status, or alternatively does one's mental health condition affect one's ability to access and mobilize social support? Brugha (1995), in his discussion of the relationship between social support and psychiatric disorder, suggests that the dilemma is not as basic as whether social support reception is a cause or effect of psychiatric disorder. He also indicates that the relationship of cause and effect between social support and psychiatric disorder may be related differently at various levels depending on the typology and degree of the psychiatric disorders in question. Others have expressed a similar viewpoint (Sheppard 1994). Coyne, Wortman and Lehman (1988) suggest that at certain times insufficient social support can enhance symptomatology of mental ill health and at other times too much support can have the same effect, as it may put too much stress and attention on the support recipient.

To summarize, this finding confirms a link between respondents' perception of their general mental health and their perceived quality of network support. Although respondents who were GHQ cases tended to access more support from their network members than those who were GHQ non-cases, they tended to have less variety or sources of support available to them. Also, parents with poorer reported general mental health saw themselves as more criticized by, and not as close to, their network members. However, although this link was established, how social support affects, or is affected by, psychiatric disorder is in itself quite complex and unclear and requires further research and discussion. Overall, the implications of this research do confirm that work with parents and attempting to better understand their needs is appropriate for the NYP. The clear message is that the NYP should work towards supporting the social networks of parents as a means of supporting adolescents.

Conclusion

This chapter has traced the evolution of the Westside NYP from a community-based intervention project targeting at-risk adolescents to one which is now far more inclusive of parents. In doing so, it has demonstrated that the project is effective, and central to its ongoing development and success is a willingness to experiment. What has emerged from the project's experiments and research with parents is a shift in emphasis in its operation to one which is supportive of adolescents in their families rather than adolescents in isolation. At project level, this indicates a future direction which will encompass a greater focus on social networks, both of parents and adolescents, as a key practice tool.

In relation to broader policy questions, this chapter affirms not only the value of work in community settings, but also the importance of incorporating a research component in pilot and mainstream service provision. In doing so, this increases the possibility of dynamism and development in services, as opposed to their becoming stagnant and institutionalized. In the case of the Westside NYP, the early evaluation and later research on social networks opened up a new debate on how best to support adolescents and their families; ideas which were not on the policy agenda in Ireland at that time.

There is no one approach to working with adolescents that will be successful in all cases. Different contexts, even within regions within countries, will require specific responses. What this chapter proposes is that for successful family support intervention a new guiding principle of continuous innovation, evaluation and research should apply.

References

Barnes, M. (1997) *Care, Communities and Citizens.* London: Longman.

Brugha, T.S. (1995) 'Social support and psychiatric disorder: Recommendations for clinical practice and research.' In T.S. Brugha (ed) *Social Support and Psychiatric Disorder, Research Findings and Guidelines for Clinical Practice.* Cambridge: Cambridge University Press.

Canavan, J. (1993) 'Westside Neighbourhood Youth Project. Evaluation report.' Unpublished report. Western Health Board/UCG.

Committee on Reformatory and Industrial Schools (1970) *Report on the Reformatory and Industrial Schools System.* Dublin: Stationery Office.

Coopersmith, S. (1981) *Coopersmith Inventory (School Form).* Paolo Alto, CA: Consulting Psychologists Press.

Cornia, G.A. and Danziger, S. (1997) *Child Poverty and Deprivation in the Industrialised Countries, 1945–1995.* Oxford: Clarendon Press.

Coyne, J.C., Wortman, C.B. and Lehman, D.R. (1988) 'The other side of social support: Emotional over-involvement and miscarried helping.' In B.H. Gottlieb (ed) *Marshalling Social Support: Formats, Process and Effect.* Newbury Park, CA: Sage.

Cutrona, C.E. (1996) *Social Support in Couples – Marriage as a Resource in Times of Stress.* London: Sage.

Cutrona, C.E., Cohen, B.B. and Ingram, S. (1990) 'Contextual determinants of the perceived supportiveness of helping behaviours.' *Journal of Social and Personal Relationships 7,* 553–562.

DePanfilis, D. (1996) 'Social isolation of neglectful families: A review of social support assessment and intervention models.' *Child Maltreatment 1,* 35–72.

Dolan, P. (1993) 'The challenge of family life in the Westside – A six-week course for parents of young people attending the Westside Neighbourhood Youth Project.' Unpublished dissertation, Dept of Social Studies, University of Dublin, Trinity College, Dublin.

Dolan, P. (1997) 'Perceived social networks and social support among parents of adolescents: A study of twenty-six cases in a disadvantaged community.' Unpublished Masters degree thesis for the Degree of M.Litt to the Dept of Social Studies, University of Dublin, Trinity College, Dublin.

Fenwick, E. and Smith, T. (1993) *Adolescence – The Survival Guide for Parents and Teenagers.* London: Dorling Kindersley.

Fox-Harding, L. (1997) *Perspectives in Child Care Policy.* London: Longman.

Garbarino, J. (1990) 'Troubled youth, troubled families: The dynamics of adolescent maltreatment.' In D. Cichetti and V. Carlson (eds) *Child Maltreatment.* Cambridge: Cambridge University Press.

Gilligan, R. (1995) 'Family support and child welfare: Realising the promise of the Child Care Act 1991.' In H. Ferguson, and P. Kenny (eds) *On Behalf of the Child, Child Welfare, Child Protection and the Child Care Act 1991.* Dublin: Farmer.

Goldberg, D. and Williams, P. (1991) *A User's Guide to the General Health Questionnaire.* Basingstoke: Macmillan.

Government of Ireland (1991) *Child Care Act 1991.* Dublin: Stationery Office.

Hall, G.S. (1904) *Adolescence: Its Psychology and Its Relations to Physiology, Anthropology, Sociology, Sex, Crime, Religion and Education.* New York: Appleton.

Harter, S. (1993) 'Self and identity development.' In S.S. Feldman and G.R. Elliott (eds) *At the Threshold: The Developing Adolescent.* Cambridge, MA: Harvard University Press.

Hauser, S. and Bowlds, M. (1993) 'Stress coping and adaptation.' In S.S. Feldman, and G.R. Elliott (eds) *At the Threshold: The Developing Adolescent.* Cambridge, MA: Harvard University Press.

Herbert, M. (1988) *Working with Children and Their Families.* London: Routledge.

Herbert, M. (1993) *Working with Children and the Children Act: A Practical Guide for Helping Professions.* London: BPS Publications.

Kinney, J.D., Haapala, D., Booth, C. and Leavitt, S. (1990) 'The homebuilders model.' In J.K. Whittaker, J. Kinney, E.M. Tracy and C. Booth (eds) *Reaching High Risk Families: Intensive Family Preservation in Human Services.* Washington DC: Centre for Social Welfare Research, University of Washington, School of Social Work.

Levitt, M.J., Silver, M. and Franco, N. (1996) 'Troublesome relationships: A part of human experience.' *Journal of Social and Personal Relationships 13*, 4, 523–536.

Millstein, S.G. and Litt, I.F. (1993) 'Adolescent health.' In S.S. Feldman and G.R. Elliott (eds) *At the Threshold: The Developing Adolescent.* Cambridge, MA: Harvard University Press.

Modell, J. and Goodman, M. (1993) 'Historical perspectives.' In S.S. Feldman and G.R. Elliott (eds) *At the Threshold: The Developing Adolescent.* Cambridge, MA: Harvard University Press.

Murphy, M. (1996) 'From prevention to family support and beyond: Promoting the welfare of Irish children.' In H. Ferguson and T. McNamara (eds) 'Protecting Irish children, investigation, protection and welfare.' *Administration 44*, 2, 73–101.

Offer, D. and Schnort-Reichl, K. (1992) 'Debunking the myths of adolescence: Findings from recent research.' *Journal of Academic Child and Adolescent Psychiatry,* November, 1003–1014.

Pilgrim, D. (1993) 'Anthology: Policy.' In J. Bornat, C. Pereira, D. Pilgrim and F. Williams (eds) *Community Care: A Reader.* Basingstoke: Macmillan/Open University.

Santrock, J. And Yussen, S. (1992) *Child Development,* 5th edn. Dubuque, IA: W.C. Brown Publishers.

Seebohm, F. (1968) *Report of the Committee on Local Authority and Allied Personal Social Services.* London: HMSO.

Sheppard, M. (1994) 'Childcare, social support and maternal depression: A review and application of findings.' *British Journal of Social Work. 24,* 287–310.

Task Force on Child Care Services (1975) *Task Force on Child Care Services: Interim Report.* Dublin: Stationery Office.

Task Force on Child Care Services (1980) *Final Report to the Minister for Health.* Dublin: Stationery Office.

Task Force on Child Care Services (1981) *Task Force on Child Care Services Final Report.* Dublin: Stationery Office.

Thompson, R. (1995) *Preventing Child Maltreatment through Social Support – A Critical Analysis.* London: Sage.

Tracy, E.M. and Whittaker, J.K. (1990) 'The social network map: Assessing social support in clinical practice.' *Families in Society: The Journal of Contemporary Human Services,* October, 461–470.s

Tracy, E.M., Catalano, R., Whittaker, J.K. and Fine, D. (1990) 'Reliability of social network data.' *Social Work 26,* 2, 33–35.

Tracy, E.M., Whittaker, J.K., Pugh, A., Kapp, S. and Overstreet, E. (1994) 'Support networks of primary caregivers receiving family preservations services: An exploratory study.' *Families in Society, The Journal of Contemporary Human Services,* 481–489.

Walsh, P. (1996) 'Self-reported delinquency in relation to attachment and parental control: An empirical study.' Unpublished thesis. Dept of Psychology, University College, Galway.

Winn, M. (1983) *Children without Childhood.* New York: Penguin.

CHAPTER 7

Drug Prevention

Perspectives on Family and Community Support

Saoirse Nic Gabhainn and Fiona Walsh

Introduction

The use of psychoactive substances is widespread, particularly among young people (Friel, Nic Gabhainn and Kelleher 1999), and the west of Ireland is no exception to this emerging trend (Kiernan 1995; Nic Gabhainn and Comer 1996). Not unsurprisingly, alcohol remains the main drug of choice for young people but as the availability of other substances grows, illicit drug use is also likely to increase. Authors, especially from the USA, have traditionally addressed this issue from the perspective that all drugs are dangerous, any drug use is harmful and the ultimate objectives of any drug interventions must be to cease or avoid use at any level. As such, the concentration has been on epidemiological research and correlates or predictors of initiation into drug use or problematic use. Most interventions have been targeted at youth in general and located within schools. The primary prevention of drug use has a varied history, having been influenced by philosophical perspectives on drug use, popular conceptions of efficacy and a litany of ambivalent empirical reviews.

More recently and with the advent of greater interest in the issue from non-medical professionals, a wider picture is emerging of the role of drugs and drug use in culture (Grant and Johnstone 1991) and the social contexts of drug use for young people (Hirst and McCamley-Finney 1995; Plant 1994). Based on this more recent work there has developed a number of intervention approaches relevant to the family. Models of best practice and evidence for their effectiveness are accumulating around these basic approaches. The first of these focuses on how family processes impact on individual drug users. The second concentrates on working with families or parents in groups and the third approaches the family from a community

145

perspective. Such developments challenge professionals to make changes in their roles in addressing drug issues with families and communities. These include collaborating with one another and with outside bodies, the provision of accurate and appropriate knowledge, contributing to the creation of a supportive environment for non-use and early intervention and screening of high-risk individuals. All of these involve altering ways of working and depend on thinking more holistically about professional responsibilities towards supporting families.

Perspectives on drug use

Various factors, including the media, influence the perspective of a society on drugs, and research evidence can sometimes fly in the face of what is considered obvious, especially in aetiology, prevalence, trends and prevention (Hansen and O'Malley 1996). For example, use is declining in Afro-American youth in the USA (Bass and Kane-Williams 1993) and in many areas is below the rates for white youth. It is important to guard against stereotypes and be mindful of the source of information about drugs and drug use. The notion of peer group pressure as an important initiator of drug use among young people has been losing ground. Research findings suggest that young people who use drugs have friends who take drugs or obtain their drugs from friends. This has been often been interpreted as evidence of young people pressurizing each other. Where research participants have been asked in a qualitative fashion about this issue, they have indicated that they are more likely to be putting pressure on drug users to share their substances than the other way around (Hirst and McCamley-Finney 1995). It appears that they actively seek out other young people who will support their efforts to try drugs (Sheppard, Wright and Goodstadt 1985). Young people tend to share ideologies with their peer group and will gravitate towards others involved in activities they see as desirable (Coleman 1984; Lamarine 1993).

The popular idea of gateway drugs such as alcohol and cannabis and the perceived inevitability of their use leading to more dangerous patterns of consumption has come increasingly under attack in recent years (Swadi 1992a, b; Yu and Williford 1994). Although later 'hard' drug use is usually preceded by earlier 'soft' or legal drugs, this is not always the case and youth can and do stop at various stages along the way; the trajectory is not unidirectional (Coombs, Fawzy and Gerber 1986). Regular alcohol use usually precedes experimentation with illegal drugs, but for most young people drug use starts and finishes with experimentation. Research evidence suggests that most adolescents mature out of illegal substance use (Swadi 1992a, b). Indeed, Shedler and Block (1990) report on a prospective longitudinal study of young people and indicate that for their sample, experimentation (primarily with marijuana) was associated with higher levels of later psychological adjustment when compared with frequent users who were maladjusted and lifetime abstainers who were relatively anxious, emotionally constricted and lacking in social skills. None of this is to suggest that no peer pressure or gateway drugs exist, or indeed that experimental drug use should be encouraged; merely that it is important to look beyond the stereotypes or reliance on media-fed explanations of phenomena.

Blackman (1996) presents an interesting perspective on the issue of drugs in youth culture. He argues that the evidence he has collected suggests that drug use is supported by the ideology of consumer capitalism which validates immediate gratification. Drug use has been normalized in youth culture and is perceived and experienced as being largely unproblematic. Drug use, largely of drugs like cannabis and ecstasy, is identified with positive experiences for the individual user (Parker, Measham and Aldridge 1995; Plant 1994). Coffield and Gofton (1994) report that young people approach 'soft' drugs with the same rational, matter-of-fact way in which they approach other consumer products. They search for value for money and weigh up the potential benefits and risks of taking any particular drug in a particular situation. This interpretation is confirmed by Hirst and McCamley-Finney (1995) who report on a series of qualitative studies with young people in Sheffield. The dominant theme emerging from their work suggests that drugs are a part of many young people's lives, but are not a central issue even for drug users. They are surprised by the lack of understanding many adults have of the drug scene and drug using, and indeed focus on this ignorance of their social world in order to distance themselves further from adults in general and prevention efforts in particular.

Perspectives on primary prevention

Irrespective of the potential adaptivity of experimental drug use, most efforts at prevention have been at the primary stage. That is, they attempt to eliminate all use and first use in particular. The emphasis on this aspect of prevention is clear from the literature, but it must be considered that most of the available literature stems from the USA, which has taken a very strict approach to drug use (Newcomb 1992; Peele 1986).

Providing information

Early approaches to interventions were based on the idea that people were rational and that the provision of good-quality information would allow them to garner the consequences of drug use, that they would decide not to use drugs and therefore would not. This approach often involved a description of the pharmacology of various drugs and the effects they had on the body, as well as the use of scare tactics which involved giving the public frightening stories about what would happen if they took drugs. Although intuitive, these types of initiative failed at almost every hurdle and sometimes even increased use (Blum 1976). Not until further information became available from a variety of social science disciplines and theories were developed about predictors of behaviour (Azjen and Fishbein 1980; Becker and Rosenstock 1984), and how to influence them, did the science of prevention become research led. Prior to that, attempts were premised largely on untested or incomplete theories.

Enhancing social behaviours

Subsequent interventions were based on the notion of enhancing social competencies with the underlying rationale that stable, well-adjusted people would not want to use drugs (Montagne and Scott 1993). While many affective programmes based on such perspectives did succeed in enhancing skills, the expected impact on the level of individual drug use rarely materialized (National Institute on Drug Abuse 1986). During the 1980s two separate approaches to the issue appeared in the USA. The first approach was to view drug taking as a form of natural behaviour (Einstein 1980) and the promotion of safer drug taking and alternative methods for altering one's consciousness safely. The second has been interpreted as a backlash against the encouragement of rational decision making and responsible drug use (Kurzman 1976) which was beginning to be popularized in the late 1970s. This posited that all use is bad and total abstinence is the only option; thus the 'just say no' media and government-backed campaign reigned. Drug Abuse Resistance Education (DARE) is the most widely dispersed programme based on these ideas (Koch 1994). However, effect sizes are reported to be relatively small and therefore not promising, despite its wide appeal and implementation (Dukes, Ullman and Stein 1996; Ennett *et al.* 1994).

Targeting social influences

The situation in Europe tended to be less policy led and more reliant on research and theoretical developments in the drug use and prevention field. There are various opposing views as to the usefulness and impact of programmes based on different models of behaviour (Hansen 1992; Tobler 1986). There are no clear leaders in the field. Refinements of both the decision-making models and social skills enhancement continue to be both popular and widely supported. Social influence models of prevention are increasingly advocated (Botvin and Botvin 1992; Dorn and Murji 1992). These target the social influences of young people in relation to drugs, particularly among peers, the family and the wider community. These models tend to involve making participants aware of potential influences, teaching specific skills to resist them and targeting perceived social norms regarding substance use. There are not necessarily any knowledge- or decision-making-related objectives to such programmes, but they do often involve peers as tutors or educators. Evidence on the effectiveness of these programmes is promising, even more so when combined with other techniques (Botvin and Botvin 1992; Hansen 1992; Tobler 1992). The journey is not over, as prevention is far from being an exact science. Nevertheless, it is not practical or even necessary to wait until there is definitive knowledge on how to affect behaviour in an ethically acceptable manner (Westermeyer 1989). Sufficient evaluation data exist to enable a best practice model to be developed and there is widespread agreement on the most appropriate forms of interventions for some settings.

Programme evaluation

While methodological difficulties abound in all applied research, especially evaluation, many authors have attempted to tease out the components of successful programmes. The most regularly cited and quoted reviewers in this field are Tobler (1986, 1992) and Hansen (1992). Many authors have been pessimistic about the outcomes from prevention interventions (Moskowitz 1989; Plant 1990, 1994); there is no doubt they are not entirely effective. Knowledge levels and attitudes are more regularly altered (Morgan *et al.* 1996; Nic Gabhainn and Kelleher 1995) than behaviour. There is much controversy surrounding this in the literature (Tobler 1992). As most evaluations are short term and the objectives of most interventions are long term, researchers sometimes argue that there has not been sufficient time for an impact on behaviour to be shown. Others argue that given the low prevalence of most substance use, huge sample sizes would be required to identify behavioural changes with any reliability. Altering of attitudes and knowledge are sometimes characterized as valid outcomes in themselves, which may indeed have the long-term effect of altering social norms in relation to substance use (Montagne and Scott 1993).

Nevertheless, the reviews of Tobler and Hansen have set about comparing approaches with one another. Hansen and O'Malley (1996) examine these two evaluative reviews and find that they do indeed complement each other. Programmes were categorized into four major groups: information only; affect only; social influence; and multicomponent (sometimes referred to as comprehensive). Hansen's collection of 45 evaluations and Tobler's 143 were recategorized according to these four groups and average effect sizes calculated for all those falling into the specific category. Only those that could be adequately categorized and for which it was possible to calculate effect sizes were included. Most effect sizes (ES) range from −1 to +1 (where −1 means that a 100 per cent reduction in a particular behaviour or disorder was noted and +1 means that a 100 per cent increase in the behaviour was found). In this case, the larger the ES, the greater the impact of the programme on drug use. Table 7.1 contains an abridged version of Hansen and O'Malley's (1996) original. N refers to the number of studies included in that group. The Tobler restricted column refers to studies that met certain methodological criteria (e.g. adequate follow-up, control groups). The larger the ES, the greater the impact of the intervention programme.

Table 7.1 Effect size meta-analysis from two prevention outcome reviews						
Source/type	Hansen		Tobler		Tobler restricted	
	N	ES	N	ES	N	ES
Information	5	0.17	14	0.09	3	0.05
Affect	11	-0.01	25	0.05	14	0.02
Social influence	12	0.09	37	0.18	16	0.27
Multicomponent	3	0.13	25	0.37	20	0.37

Tobler (1992) clearly identifies comprehensive or multicomponent prog-rammes as most effective and argues for their adoption. She also reviews the use of peers in social influence initiatives and directs considerable attention to their potential for future interventions. Botvin and Botvin (1992) come to the same conclusion and are particularly impressed by the potential that peer education holds. Hansen (1992) is also clear that social influence and comprehensive programmes are most effective in preventing the onset of substance use. Wodarski and Smyth (1994) discuss these comprehensive models in more depth. They argue that these models are not only characterized by drawing on multiple components within the school setting but for maximum effectiveness include other aspects of the young person's environment. From this perspective, they can also include interventions targeted at the family and community, as well as organizational aspects of the school.

There are, however, numerous other intervening or mediating factors which must also be considered in programme implementation. Hansen (1992) considers the importance of fidelity to original programmes as central in order to ensure effective outcomes. Teacher training and background as well as adherence to the programme contents are equally important. Initiatives developed for one population or target group may not be as relevant or useful with another (Rogers 1995). This issue is particularly relevant to the west of Ireland as the nature of drug use differs from that in large urban conurbations and cities, as does the school system as well as the underlying social system in which potential drug users live. The adaptability of findings from another situation is unknown. Any programme adopted in the west of Ireland should incorporate the possibility of emigration of the young people involved. Other factors known to be of influence in school-based programmes include the length of the programme; short-term interventions are likely to have short-term outcomes (Dryfoos 1991; Lavin, Shapiro and Weill 1992). In addition, the school climate and hidden curriculum, as well as explicit and clear school policy, must work in tandem with the ideology of the intervention (Bushong, Coverdale and Battaglia 1992; North-Western Health Board 1996).

Conyne (1994) reviews elements of successful programmes and suggests that, in order to have the desired primary prevention impact, they must involve a collaborative ethic and have empowerment as a superordinate goal. They should work within a social ecology framework and use multifactorial methods. He also argues that risk and protective factors should be explicitly targeted for change and enhancement respectively. Kroger (1994), in his review of prevention work for the European Commission, converts with the above review on a number of issues. Specifically, he agrees on the primacy of the social influence approach, on the importance of programme length, on the potential use of peer leaders and importance of risk and protective factors, as well as the benefit incurred from a multifactorial approach. He also emphasizes the importance of commencing primary prevention prior to the initiation of drug use. The importance of non-school settings and using risk and protective factors is discussed further below.

Risk factors approach

Social influence models are examples of what are considered universal programmes (Gorman 1992), and as such have been considered suitable for large-scale population intervention. They are founded on a particular model of aetiology which sees adolescence as a vulnerable period (Kandel and Logan 1984) and are based primarily on social learning theory (Bandura

1977) and problem behaviour theory (Jessor 1988). Gorman (1992), while accepting the positive outcome findings associated with social influence models, argues that all adolescents are not at the same level of risk and that a generic model will not have the same potential for prevention as targeting specific groups. Thus, the concept of levels of vulnerability is introduced. There are a number of key risk factors associated with drug use, and their identification and alteration is a key way forward according to Gorman (1992). The competition between universal programmes and targeted risk factor interventions is referred to as Kreitman's (1986) preventative paradox. Should prevention efforts target those at high risk who are characterized by the highest probability of negative outcomes or the population as a whole among whom the largest absolute numbers of problems are found (Grant and Johnstone 1991)? One reason for targeting those with a number of risk factors has been because they are frequently not found among wider population samples such as school students.

A number of authors concur with the risk factor perspective and the aetiology of drug use has been widely discussed (e.g. Hawkins, Catalano and Miller 1992; Newcomb and Bentler 1989). It is important to remember that there are few methodologically sophisticated studies in this area and the majority of what is known stems from correlational designs. Thus, while certain factors may be associated with initiation into drug use or later problematic use, the relationships are not necessarily causal. A large number of correlates or predictors of substance use have been identified, including low self-esteem (Miller 1994) or self-efficacy (Turner, Sklar and Annis 1996), impulsivity (Pogge *et al.* 1996), sensation seeking (Newcomb 1996) and extroversion and neuroticism (Quirk, McCormick and Zegara 1996). There is also evidence that genetics (Tarter 1995) or neurological data (Van Heeringen 1995) can assist in the identification of high-risk individuals.

The most stable indicator is peer drug use (Newcomb and Bentler 1989; Swadi 1992a), but there has been considerable debate concerning the interpretation and usefulness of such a finding. It is not surprising that people who use drugs have friends who also use drugs and it is considered largely impractical, though not impossible, to try and identify people through their friendship networks. Further efforts have been directed at locating factors which can be more easily identified. Many authors break down the range of risk factors into categories such as individual level, family level and community level and argue that it is the combination of a number of risk factors that results in any individual being perceived at high risk (Hawkins *et al.* 1992; Newcomb and Bentler 1989). In addition, the literature has identified what are called protective factors, which are hypothesized to protect or insulate the individual against initiation or problematic use.

Penning and Barnes (1982) review documented influences on adolescent marijuana use and consider them to be personal, social and familial. Early evidence suggested considerable familial influence including increased use among children of non-intact families. The data on childrearing practices is more ambivalent. Depending on the study, both parental permissiveness and parental control have been related to drug use. In general, adolescent drug use tends to the inversely correlated with a positive and well-functioning familial environment (Brook *et al.* 1977). Parental and sibling drug use has also been identified as a salient predictor, although as adolescence progresses it is not as important as peer use (Penning and Barnes 1982). Simcha-Fagan, Gersten and Langner (1986) report on a longitudinal study in which specific risk factors for various substances are examined. While marijuana use only is related to socio-economic and early childhood behavioural factors (isolation from peers and increased dependence), the use of other drugs is more successfully predicted from a host of parental and marital behaviours. Both unhappy marriages and parental coldness predicted other drug use and these relationships were particularly strong for heroin use.

Hawkins *et al.* (1992) provide a thorough review of risk and protective factors and define risk as those factors that precede, and are predictive of, drug use. They divide risk factors into contextual factors and individual and interpersonal factors. Table 7.2 presents an overview of their findings.

Others approach these issues from the perspective of early identification. For example, Swadi (1992b) argues that abuse should be suspected or at least investigated when adolescents or pre-adolescents are in receipt of services associated with parental substance use, sexual or physical abuse, dropping out of school, teenage pregnancy, economic disadvantage, delinquency or mental health problems. Lamarine (1993) reports that longitudinal studies have shown that there are psychological differences between later abusers and experimenters, the abuse being the result of poor psychological health rather than the reverse. Other typologies have been proposed by, for example, Newcomb and Bentler (1989). They suggest that risk factors can be categorized according to the eight groups contained in Table 7.3.

Table 7.2 Risk factors for the onset and problematic substance use (adapted from Hawkins *et al.* 1992)		
Type of risk	**Actual risk**	**Example reference**
Contextual	Laws and norms favourable towards behaviour	Levy and Shefflin (1985)
Contextual	Availability	Maddahian, Newcomb and Bentler (1988)
Contextual	Extreme economic disadvantage	Farrington *et al.* (1990)
Contextual	Neighbourhood disorganization	Fagan (1988)
Individual	Physiological factors	Shedler and Block (1990)
Interpersonal	Family use and attitudes	Brook *et al.* (1990)
Interpersonal	Poor and inconsistent family management practices	Brook *et al.* (1990)
Interpersonal	Family conflict	Simcha-Fagan, Gersten and Langner (1986)
Interpersonal	Low bonding to family	Penning and Barnes (1982)
Interpersonal	Early and persistent problem behaviours	Lerner and Vicary (1984)
Interpersonal	Academic failure	Robbins (1980)
Interpersonal	Low degree of commitment to school	Johnstone, O'Malley and Bachman (1985)
Interpersonal	Peer rejection in early school years	Hawkins *et al.* (1987)
Interpersonal	Association with drug-using peers	Brook *et al.* (1990)
Interpersonal	Alienation and rebelliousness	Shedler and Block (1990)
Interpersonal	Early onset of drug use	Kandel (1982)
Interpersonal	Favourable attitudes towards drug use	Kandel, Kessler and Margulies (1978)

Table 7.3 Risk factors for drug use (adapted from Newcomb and Bentler 1989)

Type of risk	Actual risk
Social structural	Low socio-economic status
Family and socialization	Parental use, disturbed families, low religious commitment
Educational	Poor school performance, early school leavers
Psychological	Low self-esteem, neuroticism, impulsivity
Attitudinal	Tolerance for deviance
Behavioural	Lack of law abidance, deviant behaviour
Emotional	Need for excitement, and sensation seeking
Psychopathological	Stress, anxiety, depression

Table 7.4 Correlations between risk factors and drug use

Risk factor and drug use	Correlation
Perceived attitudes to drugs among others	0.38
Drug use by peers	0.37
Prior or current other drug use	0.36
Attitudes towards drug use	0.29
Drug use by others	0.27
Bonding and commitment to school	0.27
Beliefs about health consequences	0.20
Self-esteem	0.17
Participation in recreational activities	0.14
Home factors	0.13
Gender	0.07

The inherent difficulties in the interpretation of the wide variety of risk factors led Hansen and O'Malley (1996) to introduce data which allow comparison between them. Average correlations between types of risk factors and drug use are presented. It is pointed out that these are correlations with use rather than with abuse or misuse. Correlations are an indication of the type of relationship that exists between two or more variables. Correlations range in size from −1 to +1, where −1 is a perfect negative relationship (negative meaning that as the scores on one variable increases, the scores on a second decrease, such as level of education attained and likelihood of being unemployed) and +1 is a perfect positive relationship (positive meaning that as the scores on one variable increase, the scores on a second also increase, such as children's height and age). In this case, the higher the correlation, the stronger the relationship between the risk factor and drug use. The correlations are presented in Table 7.4 in order of strength.

Irish authors have also addressed the issue of risk factors or predictors of substance use. These are extremely useful in providing culturally appropriate risk factors, but are limited because of the small number of such studies which only provide data on a restricted number of factors. Accordingly, the strength or existence of relationships is only known for those variables that were included in the respective studies. Loftus (1997) provides a comprehensive list of risk and protective factors across the individual, school, family and community. Although very useful and in keeping with the factors discussed here, these are not referenced and it is unknown from where they were derived. Grube and Morgan (1990b) report on the structure of problem behaviours among adolescents in Dublin and conclude that general deviancy did not account for variations in problem behaviours. This is in contrast to findings from the USA and they warn that the general deviance hypothesis (Newcomb and Bentler 1988) may be culturally dependent and not applicable to Irish youth. Grube and Morgan (1990a) also reported on contingent consistency effects in the prediction of substance use for the same sample. They found that regardless of age, current substance use behaviours were predicted by perceived substance use by friends, especially when accompanied by favourable attitudes to substance use. In relation to changes in alcohol use, Morgan and Grube (1997) report that these have increased along with changes in normative perspectives of use. Alterations in beliefs about the consequences of drinking and in the perceived social support for drinking were associated with reported changes in drinking behaviour. These studies all point to the importance of the perceived normality or acceptability of substance use as predictors of use behaviours.

Kiernan (1995) reports on correlates of drug use in Western Health Board adolescents. She found significant correlations for perceived approval of father, mother, best friend and other friends. She also presents large differences in prevalence rates for those who report that they have friends who use drugs (77 per cent who say all their friends use drugs have tried them, while 11 per cent who say none of their friends report trying them). Kiernan (1995) also reports significant associations between perceived consequences of drug use and attitudes to drugs with drug use behaviour. The less severely they thought the consequences and the more favourable their attitudes, the more likely they were to have ever experimented. There were also significant relationships between social bonding and drug use. Those who felt closer to their parents and friends, who felt they got on well in school or in training centres, who were less deviant and who prayed regularly were all less likely to have tried drugs. Finally, Kiernan (1995) also reports significantly higher prevalence rates among early school leavers (33%) as opposed to school students (23%) or travellers (10%). (Travellers are an ethnic minority group indigenous to Ireland, as opposed to the New Age traveller groups of recent years.) Note that while the rates for traveller youth are significantly lower than for either of the other groups, 10 per cent still represents significant involvement in drug experimentation among this cultural group. Taken together, these Irish studies provide good evidence of the importance of perceived social norms on the substance use behaviours of Irish youth.

Protective factors in drug use are those characteristics of the individual or their social world which work to mediate or moderate exposure to risk. Although sometimes conceived as the opposite to risk factors, this concept is more useful when employed to help explain why individuals who appear to be exposed to similar risks respond differently. Rutter (1980) explains this in terms of vulnerability or resilience. Resilient children are perceived to possess more social skills and higher self-efficacy. The extent of the research conducted on protective factors and mechanisms is considerably less than on risk factors. Nevertheless, Garmezy (1985) identified a number of factors which protected children in extremely disturbed families. The possession of a positive temperament, external support systems and external positive value systems were all identified in the more resilient children. Studies of indigenous peoples have indicated that 'cultural wholeness' can also serve as a protective factor or curative agent (Brady 1995). It appears likely that the low levels of any individual risk factor could assist in protecting against high levels of the other (Hawkins et al. 1992). For example, high levels of academic achievement and commitment to school could operate against negative home factors or low social self-esteem.

There is therefore considerable overlap in what are considered to be the main risk factors, but care must be taken not to overstate the case. Some that appear most intuitive (self-esteem) are not as important as others that may be less so (perceived attitudes of others). The individual risk factor approach has not been entirely successful in predicting use, and so individuals with one or two risk factors should not be stereotyped; rather, the existence of a wider range of risks should be present before the issue of use should be investigated. These risk factors are based primarily on characteristics of the individual but for a focused or targeted approach to be taken these characteristics also need to be translated into population groups. For example, early school leavers could be taken to represent those with low academic achievement and low commitment to school. Those with family and behavioural problems will be found in child guidance clinics or by their inclusion in social work caseloads. Those at risk because of peer use could be identified through schools or communities where substance use is known to be relatively widespread.

Case for employing a combination of strategies

Given the variety of populations and professional perspectives on drug use, the variety of risk and protective factors identified and the emerging evidence for a multimodal approach, the case for adopting an integrated combination of strategies is strengthened. While most interventions have been undertaken with school-going populations (Lavin *et al.* 1992), and evidence is mounting that interventions can be successful in school settings (Conyne 1994), advances are also being made with other population groups and settings. Numerous authors have provided overviews of such substance use prevention efforts over the last few years. Logan (1991) categorizes them according to the contexts in which they are used. Wodarski and Smyth (1994) also take this approach, but divide the work they discuss into the three levels of prevention. The basic approaches above are detailed, and specific interventions based upon them are discussed, by Montagne and Scott (1993). The main settings addressed in the literature are schools and peers, families and communities.

The major findings in relation to school-based prevention have already been summarized above. Peer interventions form one part of school- or youth-based interventions that are currently receiving attention in the literature. Peer interventions stem from the theory of social networks and individuals are taken from the peer group for specialized training. Peers are then used to teach and model socially acceptable behaviour (such as not taking drugs) (Logan 1991). Often, peer tutors are older than those they teach and many are actually adults with 'high credibility' to youth. In general, peers are perceived as more credible sources of information than other adults. Wodarski and Feit (1993) report one such intervention among youth in schools involving group work with peers as leaders and supporters of prosocial norms. Evidence regarding the effectiveness of various forms of peer-led interventions is accumulating and thus far the results from such approaches appear promising (Benard 1988; Tobler 1992).

Family-based interventions take a number of forms, one of which is focusing on parental education. Such programmes usually include communication skills, child-management strategies and parenting styles (Bray 1988). These stem from the notion that the family is the primary socialization agent for the child and that, through modelling and coaching, patterns of parental behaviour can impact on child behaviour (Wodarski and Smyth 1994). Through strengthening the family functioning, high-risk behaviours can be prevented or modified (Logan 1991). The other model is to focus on families known to be at health risk, either through social work contact, mental health service provision or early childhood interventions (Zucker and Noll 1987). Evidence is mounting that such programmes can impact on family function (Logan 1991) and the popularity of parenting programmes, especially among parents themselves, is increasing. Wodarski and Smyth (1994) describe the 'Family Teams Games Tournaments Prevention Strategy'. Groups of ten pairs of parents meet weekly for two hours over a five-week period and initially concentrate on learning drug concepts and subsequently on communication and problem-solving skills including positive reinforcement procedures.

Elmquist (1995) reviewed 22 parent-oriented programmes and noted that they vary widely, both in approach and content. In terms of content, some focus on communication skills while others concentrate on child management or parenting styles. Some are delivered face to face, while others comprise programmes for parents to follow independently or with their children. Unfortunately, few of the parenting programmes available have been systematically evaluated, but Elmquist makes the following recommendations for selecting appropriate interventions:

- Ensure that the programme is based on proven instructional principles.

- Do not try and address the needs of all parents with a single programme.

- Focus interventions according to the expressed needs of participants.

- Try to teach a few skills well rather than having a broad base and make sure that issues specific to substance use are included.

Community approaches to drug prevention usually contain a variety of approaches including those already discussed above. They are by definition broad based and often focused on high-risk communities (Wodarski and

Smyth 1994). They regularly include residents' organizations, sports and recreational facilities, have a health service orientation as well as media campaigns, and tend to build on resources already existing in a given locality.

Parents as members of the community are also targeted in this way. Attention is directed towards creating alternatives for youth leisure time and sometimes the provision of employment and training. Given the nature of implementation, most community interventions have been difficult to evaluate summatively (Logan 1991). However, there are a number of well-designed studies which provide excellent evidence for a community-wide approach. The Project STAR (Students Taught Awareness and Resistance) is described by Schinke and colleagues (1991). Its core component is school-based instruction on resistance skills, complemented by patients, media and community organizations. Wodarski and Smyth (1994) report as promising initial outcome data in terms of cigarette and marijuana use.

Pentz *et al.* (1989) report on the six-year Midwestern Prevention Project (MPP) which employed a quasi-experimental design. The aim of the project was to decrease onset of drug use among early adolescents, their parents and other residents in Kansas City and Indianapolis. The MPP included a school programme, mass media, peer education, community organization and health policy components. Collectively the components focus on promoting drug use resistance and counteraction skills by adolescents (direct skills training); prevention practices and support of adolescent prevention practices by parents and other adults, including teachers, expected to serve as role models for adolescents (indirect skills training); and dissemination and support of non-drug use social norms and expectations in the community (environmental support). At follow-up, adolescents in the intervention groups reported significantly less substance use than controls. It is worth noting in this context that the evidence for the effectiveness of broad mass media campaigns held on their own is not encouraging and that those conducted within the context of a more structured and focused intervention are more likely to be successful (Wartella and Middlestadt 1991).

Issues for professionals working in the field

It is important to recognize that drug prevention has broadened its horizons by acknowledging that the support systems required by people are as diverse as their individual needs. It has finally matured away from the singular focus on the individual to explore the context of societal, community and family influences on drug use and the drug user. Helping young people to develop a well-functioning social network can offer protective factors which may assist in counterbalancing or offsetting the risks associated with drug misuse. Given that the family is still the main support network for the majority of young people, it is vitally important to include them in the process of drug prevention and drug education.

In practice, society, the adult population and family are not yet ready to acknowledge fully the part they have to play in drug prevention or education initiatives. This situation may have developed because people were previously alienated by a state health-care service which nurtured a public misconception − that health-care providers alone were perceived to be responsible for the problem of drug abuse. There was little family and community involvement in health-care initiatives and, as a result, little co-operation or joint working arrangements to moderate the damaging effects of drugs. The recognition of a wider range of health determinants with a socio-economic perspective and the arrival of community development approaches offer an opportunity for increased participation in a more democratic health process. The time is ripe to advance the drugs prevention and education issue into the community.

So, how do we involve the adult population in this educational process? How do we convince families that they have a role to play without sounding patronising or prescriptive?

The way forward is partnership and the development of a multicomponent educational process that addresses the fears and concerns about drug taking with a programme of factual information. As detailed earlier, there are numerous methods of drug prevention, so it is important to adopt an effective model that is appropriate to local context. Another important requirement is the recognition of the difference between primary and secondary prevention. It is essential to clarify the messages, roles and skills associated with these very different programmes and approaches. The combination of social influence models and life skills programmes can be adopted in school, but then there must be a consistent reinforcing message in the community setting that involves the adult population. Parents need to be educated and informed to reinforce the messages of the school programmes in order to ensure a consistent approach. Educational life skills programmes should be targeted towards at-risk groups through youth initiatives and out-of-school community programmes. These can be usefully reinforced by peer education programmes and mentoring initiatives.

It is generally accepted that in targeting young people, achieving engagement is the most difficult part of the process. Schools may have a captive audience but are often under-resourced and may perceive themselves to be lacking in the skills to facilitate some of the group-oriented work programmes available to them. The priority is to convince schools of the value of life skills education and enable them to facilitate and evaluate these prog-rammes.

Parenting programmes which address a range of issues in an ever-chang-ing society are ideal for incorporating drug awareness information. It is important for educational programmes to explore parental influences and for parents to recognize their importance as role models. Programmes need to explore issues of parental supervision and management of problems within the family, as well as offering practical advice about drugs and information regarding local prevalence. Allaying parents' fears and concerns by providing them with accurate information will also help them to address drug-related incidents with more confidence and consistency. Recruiting parents to attend courses and training events has to be done in the context of busy lives, so these need to be flexible and local. It is also important to clearly identify the needs of the particular group in planning the training. Equally it is important to evaluate the courses and monitor the effectiveness of the input.

Adults who are not parents should not be ignored. Their role in society needs to be recognized and acknowledged as mentors and role models for young people. It is often more difficult to engage this group, particularly men, with health education and promotion. There are many creative methods of approaching and working with the adult population and selling them the concept and value of drugs prevention and education initiatives. For example, targeting workplace programmes via occupational health departments and trades unions in large firms or collaborating with sports clubs and social and leisure organizations frequented by men are strategies that could be adopted.

In the context of multimodal approaches to the drugs issues, health professionals need to pay special attention to a number of aspects of their role. These include collaborating with one another and with outside bodies, provision of accurate and appropriate knowledge, contribution to the creat-ion of a supportive environment for non-use and identification and screening of high-risk individuals. A number of authors have provided guidelines for the further training of health professionals. For example, Durfee, Warren and Sdao-Jarvie (1994) discuss models of ongoing substance abuse education, while Werner and Adger (1994) concentrate on the potential role of paediatricians. Accept (1981) and Bergmann, Smith and Hoffmann (1995) focus on the role of general practitioners. There is also a large literature on patient education which is relevant here (Simmons-Morton et al. 1992).

The difficulties in inter-professional collaboration have to be acknowl-edged. Strang, Smith and Spurrell (1992) provide an overview of how community drug teams have worked in the UK and the problems which they have encountered, including difficulties associated with involving general practitioners in the process. Nevertheless, they also provide a clear model for action. Taken together with the practical digest for UK drugs action teams (Central Drugs Coordination Unit 1996), which contains guidelines for working together at a community level, these two resources form the basis of an effective model for inter-professional collaboration. Others have written about models of collaboration among professionals, specifically in attempts to help youth at risk in the school and community setting, and it would also be fruitful to borrow from its work (Davis 1996).

Conclusion

It has been widely argued that comprehensive programmes which are not only school based are required to really address this issue. Thus a combination of strategies appears to work synergistically to promote more effectiveness than any single initiative. Work being conducted in schools with family- or community-focused intervention appeared greatly to enhance the effectiveness of prevention efforts. The more successful initiatives that have been theoretically and research based involve integration with other health and prevention programmes, and include multiple modalities and work at various stages across the lifespan.

This chapter has discussed relevant evidence in relation to the prevention of drug misuse. The clear message from that research is the importance of the role of family and community within the context of multimodal strategies. That view is finding increasing support in policy and in practice and as a result it is becoming possible to identify necessary features for these types of programmes. However, there is still a need for much more work in this area if drug prevention is to successfully use the potential of family and community support.

References

Accept (1981) 'What G.P.s can do for problem drinkers.' *Drug and Therapeutics Bulletin 19*, 23.

Azjen, I. and Fishbein, M. (1980) *Understanding Attitudes and Predicting Social Behaviour.* Englewood Cliffs, NJ: Prentice Hall.

Bandura, A. (1977) *Social Learning Theory.* Englewood Cliffs, NJ: Prentice Hall.

Bass, L.E. and Kane-Williams, E. (1993) 'Stereotype or reality: Another look at alcohol and drug use among African American children.' *Public Health Reports 108*, suppl., 78–84.

Becker, M.H. and Rosenstock, I.M. (1984) 'Compliance with medical advice.' In A. Steptoe and A. Matthews (eds) *Health Care and Human Behaviour*. London: Academic Press.

Benard, B. (1988) 'Peer programs: The lodestone to prevention.' *Prevention Forum*, January, 6–11.

Bergmann, P.E., Smith, M.B. and Hoffmann, N.G. (1995) 'Adolescent treatment: Implications for assessment, practice guidelines and outcome management.' *Paediatric Clinics of North America 42*, 2, 453–472.

Blackman, S.J. (1996) 'Has drug culture become an inevitable part of youth culture? A critical assessment of drug education.' *Educational Review 48*, 2, 131–142.

Blum, R.H. (1976) *Drug Education: Results and Recommendations*. Lexington, MA: Heath.

Botvin, G.J. and Botvin, E.M. (1992) 'Adolescent tobacco, alcohol, and drug abuse: Prevention strategies, empirical findings and assessment issues.' *Journal of Developmental and Behavioural Paediatrics 13*, 4, 290–301.

Brady, M. (1995) 'Culture in treatment, culture as treatment. A critical appraisal of developments in addictions programs for indigenous North Americans and Australians.' *Social Science and Medicine 41*, 11, 1487–1498.

Bray, B. (1988) *Family Based Approaches to Reducing Adolescent Drug Use: Theories, Techniques and Findings*. Washington DC: NIDA.

Brook, J.S., Brook, D.W., Gordon, A.S., Whiteman, M. and Cohen, P. (1990) 'The psychosocial etiology of adolescent drug use: A family interactional approach.' *Genetic, Social and General Psychology Monographs 116*.

Brook, J.S., Lukoff, I.F. and Whiteman, M. (1977) 'Peer, family and personality domains as related to adolescents' drug behaviour.' *Psychological Reports 41*, 1095–1102.

Bushong, C., Coverdale, J. and Battaglia, J. (1992) 'Adolescent mental health: A review of preventive interventions.' *Texas Medicine 88*, 3, 62–68.

Central Drugs Coordination Unit (1996) *Tackling Drugs Together: A Practical Digest for Drug Action Teams*. Leeds: CDCU and Resource and Service Development Centre.

Coffield, F. and Gofton, L. (1994) *Drugs and Young People*. London: Institute for Public Policy Research.

Coleman, J.C. (1984) *The Nature of Adolescence*. London: Methuen.

Conyne, R.K. (1994) 'Reviewing the primary prevention of substance abuse: Elements in successful approaches.' In J.A. Lewis (ed) *Addictions: Concepts and Strategies for Treatment*. Maryland: Aspen.

Coombs, R., Fawzy, F. and Gerber, B. (1986) 'Patterns of cigarette, alcohol and other drug use among children and adolescents: A longitudinal study.' *International Journal of the Addictions 21*, 897–913.

Davis, W.E. (1996) 'Collaborating with teachers, parents, and others to help youth at risk.' Paper presented at the American Psychological Association Annual Convention, Toronto.

Dorn, M. and Murji, K. (1992) *Drug Prevention: A Review of the English Language Literature.* London: ISDD.

Dryfoos, J. (1991) 'Adolescents at risk: A summation of work in the field-programmes and policies.' *Journal of Adolescent Health 12,* 630–637.

Dryfoos, J. (1993) 'Preventing substance abuse: Rethinking strategies.' *American Journal of Public Health 83,* 6, 793–795.

Dukes, R.L., Ullman, J.B. and Stein, J.A. (1996) 'Three year follow-up of drug abuse resistance education (D.A.R.E.).' *Evaluation Review 20,* 1, 49–66.

Durfee, M.F., Warren, D.G. and Sdao-Jarvie, K. (1994) 'A model for answering the substance abuse educational needs of health professionals: The North Carolina Governors Institute on alcohol and substance abuse.' *Alcohol 11,* 6, 483–487.

Einstein, S. (1980) *Drugs in Relation to the Drug User.* New York: Pergamon.

Elmquist, D.L. (1995) 'A systemic review of parent-oriented programs to prevent children's use of alcohol and other drugs.' *Journal of Drug Education 25,* 3, 251–279.

Ennett, S.T., Tobler, N.S., Ringwalt, C.L. and Flewelling, R.L. (1994) 'How effective is drug abuse resistance education? A meta-analysis of Project DARE outcome evaluations.' *American Journal of Public Health 84,* 9, 1394–1401.

Fagan, J. (1988) *The Social Organisation of Drug Use and Drug Dealing among Urban Gangs.* New York: John Jay College of Criminal Justice.

Farrington, D.P., Loeber, R., Elliot, D.S., Hawkins, J.D., Kandel, D.B., Klein, M.W., McCord, J., Rowe, D.C. and Tremblay, R.E. (1990) 'Advancing knowledge about the onset of delinquency and crime.' In B.B. Lahey and A.T. Kazdin (eds) *Advances in Clinical Child Psychology,* Vol 13. New York: Plenum.

Friel, S., Nic Gabhainn, S. and Kelleher, C. (1999) *The National Health and Lifestyle Surveys.* Dublin: Department of Health.

Garmezy, N. (1985) 'Stress resistant children: The search for protective factors.' In J.E. Stevenson (ed) Recent Research in Developmental Psychopathology (Book Supplement). *Journal of Child Psychology and Psychiatry 4,* 213–233.

Gorman, D.M. (1992) 'Using theory and basic research to target primary prevention programs: Recent developments and future prospects.' *Alcohol and Alcoholism 27,* 6, 583–594.

Grant, M. and Johnstone, B.M. (1991) 'Research priorities for drug and alcohol studies: The next 25 years.' *International Journal of the Addictions 25,* 201–219.

Grube, J.W. and Morgan, M. (1990a) 'Attitude – social support interactions: Contingent consistency effects in the prediction of adolescent smoking, drinking and drug use.' *Social Psychology Quarterly 52,* 4, 329–339.

Grube, J.W. and Morgan, M. (1990b) 'The structure of problem behaviours among Irish adolescents.' *British Journal of Addiction 85,* 667–675.

Hansen, W.B. (1992) 'School-based substance abuse prevention: A review of the state of the art in curriculum, 1980–1990.' *Health Education Research 7,* 3, 403–430.

Hansen, W.B. and O'Malley, P.M. (1996) 'Drug use.' In R. DiClemente, W.B. Hansen and L.E. Ponton (eds) *Handbook of Adolescent Health Risk Behaviour. Issues in Clinical Child Psychology.* New York: Plenum Press.

Hawkins, D.J., Catalano, R.F. and Miller, J.Y. (1992) 'Risk and protective factors for alcohol and other drug problems in adolescence and early adulthood: Implications for substance abuse prevention.' *Psychological Bulletin 112,* 1, 64–105.

Hawkins, J.D., Lishner, D.M., Jenson, J.M. and Catalano, R.F. (1987) 'Delinquents and drugs: What the evidence suggests about prevention and treatment programming.' In B.S. Brown and A.R. Mills (eds) *Youth at High Risk for Substance Abuse.* Washington DC: US Government Printing Office.

Health Research Board (HRB) (1996) *Drug Misuse in Ireland: Annotated Bibliography from 1980.* Dublin: HRB.

Hirst, J. and McCamley-Finney, A. (1995) *The Place and Meaning of Drugs in the Lives of Young People.* Health Research Institute Report No.7, Sheffield: Hallam University.

Jessor, R. (1988) 'Problem behaviour theory, psychosocial development and adolescent problem drinking.' *British Journal of Addiction 82,* 331–342.

Johnstone, L.D., O'Malley, P.M. and Bachman, J.G. (1985) *Use of Licit and Illicit Drugs by America's High School Students, 1975–1984.* Rockville, MD: NIDA.

Kandel, D.B. (1982) 'Epidemiological and psychosocial perspectives on adolescent drug use.' *Journal of American Academic Clinical Psychiatry 21,* 328–347.

Kandel, D. and Logan, J.A. (1984) 'Patterns of drug use from adolescence to young adulthood: Patterns of risk for initiation, continued use and discontinuation.' *American Journal of Public Health 74,* 660–666.

Kandel, D.B., Kessler, R.C. and Margulies, R.S. (1978) 'Antecedents of adolescent initiation into stages of drug use: A developmental analysis.' *Journal of Youth and Adolescence 7,* 13–40.

Kiernan, R. (1995) 'Thesis on substance use among adolescents in the Western Health Board area.' Thesis submitted to the Faculty of Public Health Medicine, Royal College of Physicians of Ireland.

Koch, K. (1994) 'DARE: Drug Abuse Resistance Education.' In J.A. Lewis (ed) *Addictions: Concepts and Strategies for Treatment.* Maryland: Aspen.

Kreitman, R.E. (1986) 'Alcohol dependence and the preventive paradox.' *British Journal of Addiction 81,* 353–363.

Kroger, B. (1994) *Drug Abuse: A Review of the Effectiveness of Health Education and Health Promotion.* Utrecht: Dutch Centre for Health Education and Health Promotion and IUHPE/EURO.

Kurzman, T.A. (1976) A Minnesota Primer on the Prevention of Chemical Use Problems. St. Paul, MN: Dept of Public Welfare, State of Minnesota.

Lamarine, R.J. (1993) 'School drug education programming: In search of a new direction.' *Journal of Drug Education 23,* 4, 352–361.

Lavin, A.T., Shapiro, G.R. and Weill, K.S. (1992) 'Creating an agenda for school-based health promotion: A review of 25 selected reports.' *Journal of School Health 62,* 6, 212–228.

Lerner, J.V. and Vicary, J. R. (1984) 'Difficult temperament and drug use: Analyses from the New York longitudinal study.' *Journal of Drug Issues 14,* 1–8.

Levy, D. and Shefflin, N. (1985) 'The demand for alcoholic beverages: An aggregate time series analysis.' *Journal of Public Policy and Marketing 4,* 47–54.

Loftus, M. (1997) 'Decisions, dilemmas and strategies.' Unpublished document, Crossmolina, Co. Mayo.

Logan, B.N. (1991) 'Adolescent substance abuse prevention: An overview of the literature.' *Family and Community Health 13,* 4, 25–36.

Maddahian, E., Newcomb, M.D. and Bentler, P.M. (1988) 'Adolescent drug use and intention to use drugs: Concurrent and longitudinal analyses of four ethnic groups.' *Addictive Behaviours 13,* 191–1195.

Miller, L.D. (1994) 'Adolescents, self-esteem and substance use.' In J.A. Lewis (ed) *Addictions: Concepts and Strategies for Treatment.* Maryland: Aspen.

Montagne, M. and Scott, D.M. (1993) 'Prevention of substance use problems: Models, factors, and processes. Special Issue: Substance use review.' *International Journal of the Addictions 28,* 12, 1177–1208.

Morgan, M. and Grube, J.W. (1997) 'Correlates of change in adolescent alcohol consumption in Ireland: Implications for understanding influences and enhancing interventions.' *Substance Use and Misuse 32,* 609–619.

Morgan, M., Morrow, R., Sheehan, A.M. and Lillis, M. (1996) 'Prevention of substance misuse: Rationale and effectiveness of the programme "On my own two feet".' *Oideas 41,* 5–25.

Moskowitz, J.M. (1989) 'The primary prevention of alcohol problems: A critical review of the research literature.' *Journal of Studies on Alcohol 50,* 1, 54–88.

National Institute on Drug Abuse (1986) *Adolescent Peer Pressure: Theory, Correlates and Program Implications for Drug Abuse Prevention.* Rockville, ML: NIDA.

Newcomb, M.D. (1992) 'Substance abuse and control in the United States: Ethical and legal issues.' *Social Science Medicine 35,* 4, 471–479.

Newcomb, M.D. (1996) 'Sex, drugs, and rock-and-roll: Fact, fantasy, or confound?' Paper presented at the American Psychological Association Annual Convention, Toronto, August.

Newcomb, M.D. and Bentler, P.M. (1988) *Consequences of Adolescent Drug Use: Impact on the Lives of Young Adults.* Newbury Park: Sage.

Newcomb, M.D. and Bentler, P.M. (1989) 'Substance use and abuse among children and teenagers. Special Issue: Children and their development: Knowledge base, research agenda and social policy application.' *American Psychologist* 44, 2, 242–248.

Nic Gabhainn, S. and Comer, S. (1996) *Substance Misuse in the Western Health Board: Prevalence, Practice and Proposals.* Galway: WHB.

Nic Gabhainn, S. and Kelleher, C. (1995) *The Lifeskills Evaluation.* Galway: Centre for Health Promotion Studies.

North-Western Health Board (1996) *Young People and Drug Misuse in the North West.* Manorhamilton: NWHB.

Parker, H., Measham, F. and Aldridge, J. (1995) *Drug Futures: Changing Patterns of Drug Use amongst English Youth.* London: ISDD.

Peele, S. (1986) 'The "cure" for adolescent drug abuse: Worse than the problem?' *Journal of Counselling and Development 65*, 23–24.

Penning, M. and Barnes, G.E. (1982) 'Adolescent marijuana use: A review.' *International Journal of the Addictions 17*, 749–791.

Pentz, M.A. (1993) 'Comparative effects of community based drug abuse prevention.' In J.S. Baer, A. Marlatt, A. and R.J. McMahon (eds) *Addictive Behaviours across the Lifespan.* Newbury Park: Sage.

Pentz, M.A., Dwyer, J.H., Mattinno, D.P., Hay, B.R., Hansen, W.B., Yary, E.Y.I. And Johnson, C.A. (1989) 'A multicommunity trial for primary prevention of adolescent drug abuse: Effect on drug prevention.' *AMA 261*, 3259–3266.

Plant, M. (1990) 'Constraints upon policy.' In M. Plant, C. Goos, W. Keup and E. Osterberg (eds) *Alcohol and Drugs: Research and Policy.* Edinburgh: Edinburgh University Press.

Plant, M. (1994) 'Drugs and adolescence.' In M. Plant (ed) *Heroin Addiction and Drug Policy: The British System.* Oxford: Oxford Medical Publications.

Pogge, D.L., Horan, D.L., Borgaro, S., Lloyd, A.L., Lord, J.J., Stokes, J.M. and Harvey, P.D. (1996) 'Attentional predictors of persistent substance abuse in adolescent patients.' Paper presented at the American Psychological Association Annual Convention, Toronto, August.

Quirk, S., McCormick, R. and Zegara, J. (1996) 'Personality, coping styles, and pattern of substance abuse.' Paper presented at the American Psychological Association Annual Convention, Toronto, August.

Robbins, L.N. (1980) 'The natural history of drug use.' *Acta Psychiatrica Scandinavia 62*, 7–20.

Rogers, E.M. (1995) 'Diffusion of drug abuse prevention programs: Spontaneous diffusion, agenda setting and reinvention.' *NIDA Research Monographs 155*, 90–105.

Rutter, M. (1980) *Changing Youth in a Changing Society.* Cambridge, MA: Harvard University Press.

Schinke, S.P., Botvin, G.J. And Orlandi, M.A. (1991) 'Substance use in children and adolescents: Evaluation and interventions.' *Developmental Clinical Psychology and Psychiatry Series, Vol 22.* Newbury Pk, CA: Sage.

Shedler, J. and Block, J. (1990) 'Adolescent drug use and psychological health.' *American Psychologist 45*, 612–630.

Sheppard, M.A., Wright, D. and Goodstadt, M.S. (1985) 'Peer pressure, and drug use: exploding the myth.' *Adolescence 20*, 949–958.

Simcha-Fagan, O., Gersten, J.C. and Langner, T. (1986) 'Early precursors and concurrent correlates of illicit drug use in adolescents.' *Journal of Drug Issues 16*, 7–28.

Simmons-Morton, D.G., Mullen, P.D., Mains, A., Tabak, E.R. and Green, L.W. (1992) 'Characteristics of controlled studies of patient education and counselling for preventive health behaviours.' *Patient Education and Counselling 19*, 175–204.

Strang, J., Smith, M. and Spurrell, S. (1992) 'The community drug team.' *British Journal of Addiction 87*, 2, 169–178.

Swadi, H. (1992a) 'A longitudinal perspective on adolescent substance abuse.' *European Child and Adolescent Psychiatry 1*, 3, 156–169.

Swadi, H. (1992b) 'Drug abuse in children and adolescents: An update.' *Archives of Disease in Childhood 67*, 10, 1245–1256.

Tarter, R.E. (1995) 'Genetics and primary prevention of drug and alcohol abuse.' *The International Journal of the Addictions 30*, 11, 1479–1484.

Tobler, S. (1986) 'Meta-analysis of 143 adolescent drug prevention programs: Quantitative outcome results of program participants compared to a control or a comparison group.' *Journal of Drug Issues 16*, 53–568.

Tobler, S. (1992) 'Drug prevention programmes can work.' *Journal of Addictive Diseases 11*, 3, 1–28.

Turner, N.E., Sklar, S.M. and Annis, H.M. (1996) 'Factor structure of drug and alcohol use, and self efficacy.' Paper presented at the American Psychological Association Annual Convention, Toronto, August.

Van Heeringen, C.K. (1995) 'The prevention of drug abuse – State of the art and directions for future actions.' *Clinical Toxicology 33*, 6, 575–579.

Wartella, E. and Middlestadt, S. (1991) 'The evolution of models of mass communication and persuasion. Special Issue: Communication and drug abuse prevention.' *Health Communication 3*, 4, 205–215.

Werner, M.J. and Adger, H. (1994) 'Early identification, screening, and brief intervention for adolescent alcohol use.' *Archives of Paediatric and Adolescent Medicine 149*, 1241–1248.

Westermeyer, J. (1989) 'National and international strategies to control drug abuse.' *Advances in Alcohol and Substance Abuse 8*, 2, 1–35.

Wodarski, J.S. and Feit, M.D. (1993) *Adolescent Substance Abuse: An Empirical Based Group Preventive Health Paradigm.* New York: Haworth.

Wodarski, J.S. and Smyth, N.J. (1994) 'Adolescent substance abuse: A comprehensive approach to prevention intervention.' *Journal of Child and Adolescent Substance 3*, 3, 33–58.

Yu, J. and Williford, R.W. (1994) 'Alcohol, other drugs and criminality: A structural analysis.' *American Journal of Drug and Alcohol Abuse 20*, 3, 373–393.

Zucker, R.A. and Noll, R.B. (1987) 'The interaction of child and environment in the early development of drug involvement: A far ranging review and a planned very early intervention.' *Drugs and Society 2*, 1, 57–97.

CHAPTER 8

Developing Reciprocal Support among Families, Communities and Schools

The Irish Experience

Sandra Ryan

Schools have long been entrusted to provide young people with the education they need to prepare them for their future role in society. It has become increasingly clear, however, that schools alone cannot educate and socialize children and prepare them for life. Based on over thirty years of compelling research evidence, there is increasing and widespread support for the involvement of families in the education of their children. 'The evidence is now beyond dispute. When schools work together with families to support learning, children tend to succeed not just in school, but throughout life' (Henderson and Berla 1994, p.1). It is important to note, however, that it is a misperception to infer that any type of family involvement leads to 'all good things for students, parents, teachers, and schools' (Epstein 1996, p.223). Rather, as Epstein has emphasized, different types of family involvement such as she defines them 'are expected to affect different outcomes for students, parents, and educators' (p.223) and further research is required to determine 'whether and how results of particular types of involvement generalize over time' (p.224).

This chapter takes up the theme of support between families and schools. It examines the concept and relevance of family support in the context of education and, in particular, in the context of educational disadvantage. Initiatives in Ireland to address educational disadvantage are briefly outlined, as are recent government policies relating to such initiatives. One specific initiative, the Home–School–Community Liaison (HSCL) scheme, is examined in detail as an expression of a reciprocal model of the family–school relationship and examples from an evaluation of this scheme are drawn upon to illustrate this model. The benefits and barriers to family–school involvement are discussed in the context of the HSCL scheme and lessons from that experience are described. Finally, the chapter outlines challenges to developing effective family support in the educational context.

Definition of educational disadvantage

In Ireland, as in other countries, various terms such as 'educationally disadvantaged', 'marginalized', and 'at risk' have been used to describe the combination of low socio-economic status and low scholastic achievement in students. While there have been few attempts to define the term educational disadvantage (see Boldt and Devine 1988) the use of many of its correlates, as above, has implied a discontinuity between children's home and community experiences and the demands of schooling (see Ogbu 1982).

Over the past thirty years or so there have been definite changes in emphasis to the way that disadvantage has been considered. Early thinking reflected what was termed the 'deficit' approach. Students were regarded as being disadvantaged if, because of sociocultural reasons, they entered the school system with knowledge, skills and attitudes that make adjustment difficult and impede learning (Passow 1970). A main assumption underlying the deficit approach was that the home of a child in a low-income community often failed to provide the experiences and stimulation necessary for adaptation to the requirements of school and for success within the school system (Kellaghan et al. 1993).

As thinking developed and further work and research was done in the area of educational disadvantage, it was recognized and acknowledged that the knowledge, skills and attitudes that children bring with them to school reflect the demands and experiences of their environments and should not be judged to be inherently inferior to those required in school. Rather, the differences between the cultures of home and school were recognized and the child was supported in adjusting to the school environment (Kellaghan et al. 1993). This view was referred to as the 'difference' perspective.

Current thinking on educational disadvantage is rooted in the concept of partnership and empowerment. The role of the family as the primary educator of the child is recognized and that right has long been enshrined in the Irish Constitution (Ireland 1937, Article 42.1). The concept of partnership implies that families and teachers (and indeed other relevant parties) should co-operate around the common goal of fostering and enhancing the child's learning. The principle of empowerment is centred on the concepts of power and control and the belief that people can control their own lives and change their circumstances (Kellaghan et al. 1993). Five tenets of a well-known empowerment programme, the Family Matters Project (Cochran and Dean 1991; Cochran and Woolever 1983) are cited in Kellaghan *et al*.:

> First, all families have strengths and these, rather than deficits, should be emphasized. Second, useful knowledge about child rearing resides in parents, communities, and social networks, not just in experts. Third, different family forms are legitimate and can promote healthy children and healthy adults. Fourth, fathers should be integrally involved. And fifth, cultural differences are both valid and valuable. (Kellaghan *et al*. 1993, p.94)

Recent initiatives in Ireland to combat educational disadvantage are largely grounded in this approach, known as the 'empowerment' model. Various programmes have been developed that have attempted to address the problem of educational disadvantage (see ESF Programme Evaluation Unit 1997; Kellaghan *et al*. 1995). One contention in relation to such programmes, however, is that the lack of continuity between home and school presents difficulties for children that contribute to poor school achievement (Powell 1989).

In the context of social support research, Tietjen (1989) describes this phenomenon in relation to children's development of certain competencies relevant to their ecological circumstances:

> The nature of children's social relationships also influences the kinds of opportunities and experiences they will have, and hence the competencies they will develop. When congruence between the function of the child's network and the demands of the ecological context does not exist, support is inadequate, and vulnerability results. (Tietjen 1989, p.38)

There often exists a lack of congruence between children's home circumstances and the requirements of schools. Our schools, by and large, reflect the values and expectations of middle-class society. This poses a difficulty in the context of disadvantage in that the demands placed on children may not be realistic in light of their home circumstances. The competencies that are valued are not those which these children bring with them from their own ecological context. One of the problems is that schools and teachers may lack familiarity with children's home backgrounds. This may mean that teachers therefore cannot help pupils to integrate home and school experiences and cannot take account in their teaching of the categories of meaning that children bring with them to school (Kellaghan *et al*. 1995).

Much work has focused on identifying adaptations which are required of both homes and schools that incompatibilities between them might be reduced. This has been accomplished largely through the development of specific home–school linkage strategies (see Booth and Dunn 1996; Kellaghan *et al.* 1993).

Such discontinuities between home and school are often a manifestation of parent–family characteristics and experiences that mediate their willingness and ability to engage with the school. Eccles and Harold (1996) outline eight such characteristics that are likely to be important:

1. Social and psychological resources (e.g. social networks; time demands; parents' general mental and physical health; community resources; parents' general coping strategies).

2. Parents' efficacy beliefs (e.g. parents' confidence that they can help their child with schoolwork).

3. Parents' perceptions of their child (e.g. parents' confidence in their child's academic abilities; educational and occupational expectations and aspirations for the child; parents' view of the options actually available).

4. Parents' assumptions about their role in their children's education and the role of educational achievement for their child (e.g. what role the parents would like to play in their children's education and what they believe are the benefits to their children of doing well in school).

5. Parents' attitude toward the school (e.g. role they believe the school wants them to play, both at home and at school; the extent to which they think the school is sympathetic to their child and their situation; their belief that teachers only call them in to give them bad news about their child or to blame them for problems their children are having at school versus a belief that the teachers and other school personnel want to work with them to help their child).

6. Parents' ethnic, religious and/or cultural identities (e.g. the extent to which ethnicity, religious and/or cultural heritage are critical aspects of the parents' identity and socialization goals).

7. Parents' general socialization practices (e.g. how the parent usually handles discipline and issues of control).

8. Parents' history of involvement in their children's education (e.g. parents' experiences with the school in relation to their children; parents' experiences with schools which, in turn, affect their

attitudes toward, and interest in, involvement with their children's schools and teachers).

Schools are only one of the contexts in which children spend their lives, and schools on their own cannot hope to succeed with children who are marginalized or at risk. Unless schools can harness the support of families, they will not maximize their potential in working with the children in their care.

Relevance of family support to education

Determining the relevance of family support to education and to the role of schools is largely dependent on our construction of what schools are intended to accomplish. Should schools play a role as equalizing institutions in our society or do they tend to be more responsible for magnifying differences between children from wealthy and impoverished backgrounds than for overcoming these differences? The equity gap relates both to the opportunities children are provided with and to the outcomes they achieve.

While there will always be achievement differences on average between groups of students, these gaps have tended to be much greater than they need to be (Slavin 1997). This is particularly evident if one examines the participation rates in third-level education in Ireland of young people from low-income families. Schools can no doubt have a powerful impact on the educational success of all children. Furthermore, school processes affect children and their families in various ways (see Alexander and Entwisle 1996; Gamoran 1996). While no single policy or programme can ensure the school success of every child, a combination of approaches can (Slavin 1997).

The terminology 'family support' has not been widely used in the context of education in Ireland, but has recently begun to appear in relation to specific intervention programmes (e.g. Ryan 1998; Schuerman and Rossi 1999). While the term 'family support' may not have been commonly used, much of the work that has been carried out in educational contexts has related to the development of family–school links, the development of family involvement in children's schooling and in their learning, and the support of parents and families around such involvement.

In the context of the Child Care Act 1991, the purpose of family support is 'to promote the welfare of children in vulnerable families and to minimise those circumstances where a child may have to be received into the care of a health board...because of severe family problems or family breakdown' (Gilligan 1995, p.61). Gilligan further outlines aspects of family support as promoting children's welfare and normal development in the face of adversity, enhancing the morale, supports and coping skills of all and maximizing the resilience of children and families in the face of stress 'particularly by securing their integration into what hopefully prove supportive institutions such as the (extended) family, the school, and the neighbourhood' (Gilligan 1995, p.61).

Schools have the capacity to act as supportive institutions for children and families and have a responsibility to do so in the context of what is outlined as their main role to promote children's social, emotional, academic and personal development (see Ireland 1992, 1995).

The influence of the family on a child's learning begins long before the child goes to school and extends well beyond the scope of the school. The significant influence of the family on the care and education of the child has long been acknowledged by educators. Over two centuries ago, Pestalozzi (1747–1827) stated that 'the teaching of their parents will always be the core' for children. He saw the teacher's role as providing a decent shell around the core (Pestalozzi 1951, p.26). Research studies in the 1960s and 1970s provided evidence that family variables were more powerful than school variables in predicting academic performance (Coleman *et al.* 1966; Jencks *et al.* 1972).

The identification of home and family process variables (see Bloom 1964, 1981; Iverson and Walberg 1982; Kalinowski and Sloane 1981; Marjoribanks 1979) served to better explain the complex behaviours that characterize children's family experiences and provided further supporting evidence for the importance of such variables in the child's social, emotional, intellectual and physical development.

A more recent review of studies found several near-universal family strengths that pertain directly to their children's education (Moles 1993):

- Parents are the first and foremost teachers of their children.
- Families have vast opportunities to influence children by instruction and by example.
- All parents want their children to do well in school and have good futures.
- Parents want to work with the schools to aid their children's education.

While these family strengths may exist as a potential in each family, there are numerous families that experience increasingly difficult conditions. Many parents have not had the experiences that would enable them to provide the nurturing, structure and security needed to protect their children and to support their learning, either at home or in school (Lloyd 1996). It is in recognition of this need to strengthen and support families that various initiatives such as the Utah Center for Families in Education (see Lloyd 1996) and the Family Involvement Partnership for Learning (see Moles 1996) have emerged in the USA.

Based on their research into the effects of family involvement on children's academic achievement, Henderson and Berla (1994) advance six major conclusions:

1. The family makes critical contributions to student achievement; efforts to improve children's outcomes are much more effective if the efforts encompass the children's families.

2. When parents are involved in their children's learning at school, not just at home, children do better in school and stay in school longer.

3. When parents are involved at school, their children go to better schools.

4. Children do best when their parents are enabled to play four key roles in their children's learning: teachers, supporters, advocates and decision makers.

5. A comprehensive, well-planned family–school partnership fosters high student achievement.

6. Families, schools and community organizations all contribute to student achievement; the best results come when all three work together.

These conclusions provide support for the notion that school initiatives on their own cannot compensate fully for extreme differences across families in well-being, lifestyle, attitudes and values, but parent involvement programmes and home–school partnerships show that motivated parents can learn to be more effective in supporting their children's schooling. By teaching parents how to help their child (e.g. by reading to/with them, listening to their reading, asking them about school), by helping them to understand the school's expectations for their children, by opening lines of communication in both directions, and by making parents feel welcome and respected, schools may make a difference for low SES parents (see Lareau 1987).

There is no doubt that the school is one of the significant institutions in the lives of children and, as such, has the potential to make a real difference to them. If one considers that children spend, on average, 13 per cent of their waking life up to 18 years of age in school (Walberg 1984), the potential for maximizing such contact is highlighted. However, it is also clear that schools should not work in isolation. They are embedded within the context of the wider community. Work with the child cannot ignore this wider context, the most important aspect of which is the family. As part of their efforts to work with children at risk, however, school staff need to be aware of other resources within the community that are also working with families. The roles should be complementary.

Initiatives to address educational disadvantage in Ireland

Since early in the twentieth century, there have been limited schemes in Ireland to provide children in need with food, schoolbooks, clothing and footwear (National Economic and Social Council 1993). Over the past two decades a range of additional educational initiatives to address educational disadvantage have been introduced.

Designation of schools in disadvantaged areas

In 1984 a scheme for providing additional funding to schools in disadvantaged areas was set up. Indicators used to identify a disadvantaged area included: numbers of children living in rented local authority housing; numbers of children whose parents were unemployed; numbers of families holding medical cards; and school inspectors' assessment of needs (National Economic and Social Council 1993). Grants were paid to schools for the purchase of books and equipment and for the development of home–school–community liaison.

Home–School–Community Liaison (HSCL) scheme

In 1990 the Home–School–Community Liaison (HSCL) scheme was introduced as an initiative to counteract disadvantage by increasing co-operation between schools, parents and other community agencies in the education of young people (see Ryan 1994, 1995). The scheme is staffed by a teacher who acts in the role of co-ordinator of programme activities within the school and the community on a full-time basis.

The co-ordinator collaborates with parents to identify their needs in relation to the programme: e.g. parenting courses, courses in curricular areas, self-development or assertiveness courses. The main thrust of the scheme is preventive. Co-ordinators are discouraged from responding to crisis situations. Their role is to establish relationships with parents and to develop trust. Since many parents have had negative experiences of school and since very often they are contacted by the school only in relation to their children's difficulties, it was felt that the HSCL scheme should avoid such negative associations. Therefore a definite effort is made to promote positive experiences.

Early Start preschool programme

In 1994, as part of the government's Local and Urban Renewal Development Programme, a pilot preschool programme, Early Start, was established in eight centres in seven disadvantaged areas. Language and numeracy skills are given priority in the curriculum and parental involvement is also considered central to the work of the preschool units. The units are staffed by teachers and child-care workers who work in teams of two and develop and deliver the preschool programme to a maximum of 15 children of 3 years old.

Breaking the Cycle initiative

In 1996 the Breaking the Cycle initiative was introduced to schools in urban and rural areas. The initiative is multifaceted in that it involves allocation of additional resources, a reduction in class size (maximum 15 pupils in the urban scheme), appropriate curriculum adaptation and the development of five-year school plans.

The 8 to 15 early school leavers initiative

In 1998 funding was allocated for preventative and intervention measures to combat early school leaving. Consortia including primary and post-primary schools, youth and community services, area-based partnerships and statutory and voluntary agencies submitted proposals for funding of programmes integrating in-school and out-of-school actions for young people in the 8- to 15-year-old age group who are considered to be at risk of educational failure. Fourteen project areas (eight in city areas, four in town areas and two in rural areas) were selected to pilot the initiative.

Projects have developed a variety of programmes and specific actions to target the needs of the young people. Parental and family involvement is promoted, as is integration of services, improvement in school attendance, behaviour and attainment, and provision of support for school staff (Ryan 1998). Individual projects may include a wide range of elements. Among these are homework support, individual and group counselling, remediation, meal and transport provision, family support, school attendance monitoring, in-career development and supports for school staff, summer schools, off/on campus provision for children experiencing difficulty, art therapy, outdoor pursuits and others (Ryan 1998).

In the Education Act 1998, the Irish government's commitment to addressing educational disadvantage is again outlined. The Act includes provision for the setting up of an educational disadvantage committee 'to advise on policies and strategies to be adopted to identify and correct educational disadvantage'. The setting up of such a committee can be viewed as further enhancing the support of the government to tackle the problems associated with educational disadvantage.

Home–School–Community Liaison (HSCL) scheme as family support

The Home–School–Community Liaison (HSCL) scheme embodies many of the key principles of effective family support as outlined by Gilligan (1995). One such principle is that family support 'must address the family's definition of the need or problem' (p.71). The work of HSCL co-ordinators is based on their assessments of family needs as presented to them by the parents themselves. Co-ordinators also work with parents to help them develop their concept of need and such needs have been seen to evolve over time (Ryan 1994). For example, many parents of post-primary pupils did not initially identify a need for themselves around parenting issues, but subsequently recognized this need as a result of other activities in which they had participated and resulting out of their discussions with each other and with the co-ordinator.

Another principle identified by Gilligan (1995) is that family support must be 'supportive', not 'threatening, alienating, or demeaning' (p.71). The HSCL scheme is built on the principle of partnership defined as 'a working relationship that is characterized by a shared sense of purpose, mutual respect and the willingness to negotiate' (Pugh 1989, p.9) (see Department of Education 1997; Ryan 1996a). This working principle that permeated the HSCL scheme also reflects Gilligan's principle of a professional orientation as 'respectful ally' rather than 'patronising expert' (p.72).

Another key principle is that 'family support must be offered and available on terms that make sense within the lived reality of its target users', which results in an emphasis on a 'low-key, local…"user-friendly" approach' (Gilligan 1995, p.71). The work of HSCL co-ordinators with parents reflected this principle in several ways. At the outset of the scheme, it became apparent that groups of parents existed who tended to feel threatened and fearful of all school activities. There were various underlying reasons for this, the main one being a lack of literacy skills among such parents and a fear that this would be exposed and cause them embarrassment. As a result, a range of non-threatening courses and activities began to emerge from co-ordinators' discussions with such parents. These included self-development courses (e.g. relaxation, assertiveness) and leisure activities (e.g. aerobics, crafts, sewing, knitting, art) and were designed to help foster and strengthen relationships between the co-ordinator and parents and among parents themselves (Ryan 1994). This philosophy and approach also served to 'enhance rather than diminish the confidence of those being helped', another of the key principles posited by Gilligan (1995).

Another aspect of meeting conditions that were acceptable to parents was reflected in the way in which co-ordinators went to great lengths to offer courses and activities at parents' convenience. This varied somewhat from area to area and the specific arrangements (e.g. timing and duration) were worked out between the co-ordinators and parents. One example of parents' lived reality that was common in all areas was the need for child-care support to enable parents of young children to participate in scheme activities. Arising out of this, crèche or child-care facilities were established in conjunction with HSCL activities.

Other aspects of Gilligan's principles are also evident in the HSCL scheme: the fact that activities were located within reasonable proximity to parents' homes; the fact that parents were free to participate or not and to the extent they desired; the fact that courses and activities were based on parents' expressed needs and wants made them more enticing and attractive and also contributed to parents' own sense of benefit from such involvement. Finally, the fact that the HSCL scheme is focused within schools means that it inherently 'wraps around' the 'child-rearing stage of the family' (Gilligan 1995, p.72).

One aspect of family support that does not underpin the HSCL scheme is the notion of dealing with families 'when they are under stress' and of being responsive and accessible for families who need support 'when they need it' (Gilligan 1995, p.71). While HSCL co-ordinators are sometimes called upon to address an immediate problem (e.g. a child who expresses certain fears and concerns, either verbally or through his/her behaviour that are directly related to a family crisis situation), this would not be viewed as the central role of the co-ordinator. Since a main aspect of the HSCL scheme is to promote positive contacts with families, the involvement of co-ordinators in crisis situations for which other professionals (e.g. social workers) are better equipped to respond is not generally felt to be a main focus of their work. Rather, the co-ordinator's role is viewed as one of liaising with the relevant professionals in the area so that a comprehensive approach may be taken to addressing and resolving the problem. Because of the nature of the work of schools, it seems reasonable that co-ordinators should not become involved in addressing needs of parents that can be better addressed by professionals who are specifically trained and experienced in dealing with such issues. The important role for the school would seem to be to co-operate as far as possible in supporting such work.

Benefits of family support and involvement

When school and families work together in partnership, the benefits that accrue are reciprocal and complementary. By working closely with families, schools can accomplish the task of developing and enhancing children's learning more effectively. In turn, parents who feel supported in their involvement in schools gain in confidence, self-esteem and the ability to participate and thus become more effective in their engagements with their children. Of course, ideally, the ultimate winners in this situation are the children. Figure 8.1 presents this relationship in diagrammatic form.

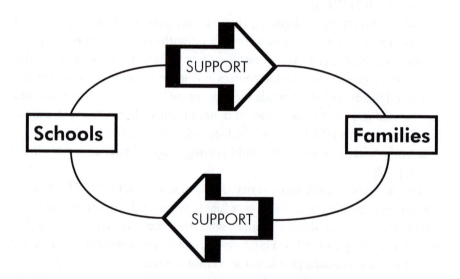

Figure 8.1 Reciprocal nature of the relationship between schools and families

A further aspect of this reciprocal relationship is based on research evidence that school practices influence family involvement. Teachers' practices to involve families are equally or more important than family background variables for determining whether and how parents become involved in their children's education (Epstein 1996). Furthermore, family practices of involvement are as or more important than family background variables for determining whether and how students progress and succeed in school (Epstein 1996). Research evidence shows that if schools invest in practices to involve families, then parents respond by conducting those practices, including many parents who might not otherwise become involved on their own (Dauber and Epstein 1993; Epstein 1986). Another benefit for both families and teachers of parent–teacher involvement is that teachers who frequently involve parents rate them more positively in terms of their helpfulness and follow-through with children at home. Such teachers also tend to stereotype single and less formally educated parents less than is the case for teachers who are not frequently involved with parents (Becker and Epstein 1982).

Subject-specific links have been found between the involvement of families and increases in achievement by students. Results from research suggest that specific practices of partnership may help boost student achievement in particular subjects. Based on the efforts of teachers to involve parents in mainly reading and English-learning activities at home, Epstein (1991) reported increase in involvement by parents on reading activities as well as improvements in the reading scores of students whose parents were involved. Students' mathematics scores were not affected. A similar finding emerged from follow-up of achievement testing of pupils in six selected HSCL schools. Reading scores of first- and third-grade pupils were found to have improved, but no changes were observed in mathematics scores (Ryan 1996b).

Another benefit of the partnership relationship that emerged within the HSCL scheme was the improvement in parent–teacher relations. Since parents were around the school more as a result of the HSCL scheme, they had more contact on an informal basis with teachers. This led to a breaking down of fears of both groups and more friendly exchanges. There was less conflict and greater co-operation and consultation. Parents tended to feel less threatened when they needed to meet their child's teacher. Parents and teachers began to understand each other better. Parents now had a definite purpose for being in the school and took responsibility for activities (e.g. organizing an open day or a social night).

The findings on benefits to parents and families and to schools (the next two headings) are based on evaluation of the HSCL scheme during the first three years of its implementation in schools (Ryan 1994, 1995).

Examples from HSCL of benefits to parents and families

The findings here are based on the responses of parents who were involved in the HSCL scheme. Co-ordinators were also asked to describe their perceptions of effects of involvement on parents. In general, they provided supporting evidence for the findings reported by parents (see Ryan 1994). It should be noted that at the outset of the scheme, numbers of parents who were involved were relatively small, but this increased during the three years. Furthermore, not unlike similar programmes worldwide, the vast majority of involved parents were mothers.

Parents were overwhelmingly positive about their involvement in HSCL activities and noted their enjoyment of such involvement in the school and in courses and activities. This was very important in the context of their lives, which often lack opportunities to fulfil their own interests and enjoyment in a meaningful and beneficial way. An increase in their understanding of schools and of how schools were supporting and enhancing their children's learning was another benefit noted by parents. They also stated that they had an increased understanding of the difficulties faced by teachers, something that helped them to appreciate and understand the work teachers were doing and its context.

Enhanced self-confidence and self-esteem and an increased interest and self-efficacy in relation to children's education were also recorded as benefits that accrued to parents. They noted that they had acquired certain skills to help them engage in their children's learning, both at home and in school. Co-ordinators supported this finding and reported their perception that 'parents had more confidence in themselves as people, in their own skills and abilities, and in their role as educators of their children' (Ryan 1994, p.134). Furthermore, these parents 'were eager to learn for themselves, willing to try out new things, and would persist with whatever activity they had started in the school' (p.134).

Parents also noted a reduction in their fears of schools. Because they were increasingly in the school and meeting staff, both formally and informally, parents benefited from a welcoming aspect of the school that they may not have experienced previously. As a result, their negative connotations around school as an institution gradually dissipated. Parents welcomed increased opportunities for involvement in their children's education. Involvement in the learning process occurred both within home and school. Parents were encouraged to work with their children at home. Examples of such practices included paired reading programmes and helping with homework. Parents were facilitated in this activity by the provision of courses in the school to help them (e.g. courses in Irish or maths). Activities in the school included work both in the classroom with teachers (e.g. working with a group of children while a teacher worked with another group) and outside the classroom (e.g. parents took groups of children for computer activities, arts and crafts, dancing).

Parents also commented that their parenting and home management skills had improved as a result of their involvement in HSCL activities. Co-ordinators confirmed that some parents had become more conscious of the needs of their children and were more aware of good parenting practices to guide children's behaviour. Co-ordinators in some schools also reported improvements in parents' practical home management skills (e.g. children said that their mothers were more adventurous with food recipes following cookery courses) and, in some cases, that children's diet had improved.

The development of networks of support among parents was a very positive aspect of their involvement for many parents. Co-ordinators referred to this as the development of 'mutual support networks' (Ryan 1994, p.135) through which parents made friends, shared problems and began to break the isolation that often surrounded them. This was seen as an important development in that parents began to realize that they shared problems in common with others and that help and support were available from other parents and from the co-ordinator. Co-ordinators also reported improvement in the coping skills of parents. They were perceived to have become more assertive, to have started taking responsibility for their own lives and to deal with ongoing problems in the home more effectively. Another benefit was that the co-ordinator had the time to meet parents informally and to get to know them and develop a relationship of trust. Through these interactions, parents were encouraged to discuss their perceptions of the school and to make suggestions about school policy. An example of this was parent involvement in the development of a discipline code for a school. This proved very successful in that parents had a vested interest in encouraging their children to uphold the discipline code.

The co-ordinator served as a resource to parents in several ways. He or she had the time to meet parents and to talk to them and, as such, became a contact person for them in the school – someone they could approach in relation to needs or problems. The co-ordinator also served as a link with other services within the community and could work with families and identify and address parents' educational, leisure and support needs. In some cases this was done in collaboration with outside agencies or individuals. In other cases the co-ordinator provided the course or activity within the school (e.g. helping with homework, Irish, maths courses).

Examples from HSCL of benefits to schools

Many benefits of the HSCL scheme also accrued to schools as a result of parent involvement. One of the important aspects of the HSCL scheme is the opportunity it affords teachers to meet and get to know the parents of their pupils. In spite of the fact that the school day is highly structured, with little time for staff to interact even among themselves, the very fact that parents are in schools means that teachers meet them, see them in corridors and, in many cases, work with them. Principals also mentioned an improved, more friendly atmosphere in the school and improved relationships with parents.

Teachers gained a better insight into the home circumstances and difficulties faced by families. This helped them in relation to their inter-actions with the children of these families and they were reported to show more sympathy and tolerance to children (Ryan 1994, p.102). Teachers also became more aware of parents' attitudes and aspirations and gained a greater appreciation of parents as individuals with needs and talents of their own.

Attendance at parent–teacher and other meetings improved where it had previously been very difficult to encourage such attendance. As a result of improved parent–teacher relations, problems became easier to deal with, parents were easier to contact and teachers found that parents approached them more openly and were not so much on the defensive. At a more general level, teachers suggested that if parents are involved in and enjoy activities in school, then they are more likely to be involved with children at home and to support the teacher's work. It was clear from teachers' comments, however, that support for the teacher was more obvious and more practical if parents were involved in classroom-based activities. A major benefit to teachers accrued when the number of pupils they had to deal with was reduced because parents took children for computer activities, for junior infant activities or for reading and writing. These practices allowed the teacher to give individual attention to 'weaker' pupils. Teachers found such assistance particularly useful when children were being taught a new concept; the presence of a parent to monitor the progress of most children allowed the teacher to repeat the concept with pupils who needed additional help. When parents helped in the classroom with activities such as arts and crafts or knitting, the children got to do a lot more than they would have done without the parents' assistance. Such assistance eased the workload of the teacher so that teachers frequently referred to the parent in terms of 'an extra pair of hands'. Teachers also derived a sense of support from knowing that a group of parents was available and willing to help on request.

Paired reading was one activity that reached parents which teachers would not normally see (i.e. parents who would otherwise not have ap-proached the school). Parent participation in paired reading was considered to be a support to teachers' work in school. Some teachers noted a preference for activities that involved greater support from parents at home (e.g. completion of homework) rather than having parents involved in other activities in school.

Teachers reported being more aware of what was happening in the community and an increase in the school's profile in the community. In many instances, there appeared to be a more positive attitude towards the school. There was also improved liaison between schools and some community agencies and individuals. Finally, in some schools, there was an improvement in the morale of teachers, parents and pupils. This would be expected to be a significant development in schools where, often, morale can be low as a result of the difficulties that permeate the lives of families in disadvantaged areas.

Lessons from HSCL about family support

Several lessons about the development of parental involvement and the fostering of supportive relationships with parents became apparent as a result of the work of co-ordinators in the HSCL scheme. First, it is crucial to consult with parents in relation to the development of programmes. Otherwise, it is difficult, if not impossible, to match the programme content and methods with the needs and characteristics of parents. What are perceived to be parental needs may not match their own perceptions and, if this is the case, they will not become involved.

Related to consultation of parents, their involvement must have an inherent meaning for them or they will not engage in the programme. Unless parents are convinced that they will derive some benefit (even at the level of enjoyment) from an activity, they will not become involved. Co-ordinators found that using parents' own children as a focus for an activity (i.e. if parents felt their child would benefit from their participation) was probably the most effective approach to elicit and maintain the parents' support.

The building and maintenance of relationships of trust with parents was one of the most difficult aspects of the co-ordinators' work, but also proved to be the cornerstone upon which all other success was based. Co-ordinators found that establishing such relationships was a slow process which required ongoing, frequent, positive interactions and collaboration. Collaborative links with parents also provide a means for parent involvement in decision making and, in addition, may influence parents' interactions with their children. Co-ordinators learned to maximize the potential of such links in terms of spin-offs for other aspects of their work.

At the outset of the scheme, co-ordinators found that they had to work hard not to become entrenched in some of the more intractable problems faced by families. This has been identified elsewhere as a possible pitfall in work of this nature. It is important to remain cognizant of the fact that there will always be some problems which can be solved best by other professionals. This prevents the school personnel from losing focus on the needs of children in relation to their development and learning, which should be the school's main concern (Powell 1989).

Barriers to effective family involvement and support

In order to develop the potential for family involvement in schools and schools' potential role in family support, the barriers to such family involvement that exist in schools at present must be acknowledged, addressed and eliminated. This includes recognizing that school environments may discourage family involvement. A variety of factors contribute to this. The previously predominant institutional culture of schools was one that placed little value on the views and participation of parents. Schools and teachers traditionally concentrated on the needs of children with little, if any, reference to their family life and circumstances. Furthermore, teachers and principals lack adequate time and training in relation to family involvement. Another aspect of this is a lack of policy support within schools that precludes any recognition of teachers' efforts to work with families (Swick and McKnight 1989).

A second major barrier to family involvement in schools relates to the demands of family and household responsibilities (Ryan 1994). This issue is tied in with changes in family demographics and increases in the number of lone-parent households. This factor, combined with lack of time for teachers in which to meet with families, can inhibit the development of supportive relationships between families and schools (Swap 1990).

A further barrier to family involvement in children's schooling is the negative attitude towards such involvement on the part of both teachers and parents. Most teachers do not know most parents' goals for their children; nor do they understand the information parents would like to have in order to be more effective in engaging in their children's learning (Epstein 1996). For example, various studies have shown that most parents want to know how to help their own children at home (Moles 1993). Further, most parents do not know what most teachers are trying to do each year in school. A belief held by some teachers is that parents are neither interested in participating in their child's education nor qualified to do so. For their part, parents sometimes feel intimidated by school administrators, staff and teachers, feeling that they lack the knowledge and skills to help educate their children (Ryan 1994). Teachers may lack confidence to work closely with families and, because of their lack of experience in this area, may feel that they would not be able to motivate parents to become more involved (Epstein 1991).

Fourth, what is defined as family involvement varies widely and is variously acceptable by both parents and teachers (Krasnow 1990). Traditionally, parents attended school meetings and helped out at various other functions such as concerts and sports days. The White Paper on Education (Ireland 1995) stated the government's commitment to promote 'the active participation of parents at every level of the education process' (p.140), and the statutory requirement for school boards of management to promote the setting up of a parents' association has since been put in place. However, while a small number of schools have moved on to involving parents in certain aspects of decision making (e.g. discipline policies, school closures), as yet the practice of such involvement remains far removed from the level of participation espoused in the White Paper. The requirement that all school boards of management 'develop a formal home–school links policy' (Ireland 1995, p.141) will hopefully contribute to the fostering of relationships between schools and families.

Finally, a lack of preparation and support for teachers in working with family members raises another barrier to effective family involvement and support. In order to work effectively with families, teachers clearly need certain skills, knowledge and positive attitudes about family involvement (Burton 1992; Davies 1991; Edwards and Jones Young 1992). Teachers' requirements regarding the context and conditions for such involvement should also be a major consideration in any move towards developing collaborative relationships with families (Ryan 1994).

Challenges for education in relation to effective family support

Education in isolation cannot even begin to tackle the intractable problems of disadvantaged communities. To be effective, work in this area must be multifaceted. There is a need, therefore, for greater co-ordination of services at all levels within the system, from local to national. In recent years, there has been increased evidence of collaboration between government departments in examining policies at national level (e.g. National Anti-Poverty Strategy process). However, this collaboration needs to be taken further so that true collaboration also permeates work at local level.

Recent developments in this area have posited the integrated-services approach as one way to resolve the lack of collaboration between agencies working with disadvantaged families. The integrated approach 'is seen as a way of tackling problems inherent in the relationship between home, school, and community in circumstances where educational disadvantages persist' (Cullen 1997, p.5). Integrative strategies include networking, co-ordination, co-operation and collaboration around administrative and service functions within agencies and also intra-agency and worker–family collaboration (see

Cullen 1997). There is much to be learned from the experiences of other EU countries and the USA in the development of integrated services.

Schools as institutions have traditionally operated in isolation, as indeed have teachers within schools. There is a need to introduce changes in school organization so that family support can be better promoted and become an effective aspect of the work of the school. For example, the standardized curriculum that is recommended for schools can lead to the inclusion of some students while excluding others. Linked to this, students are stereotyped according to their success in school – success that is defined in very limited terms and based on limited criteria. Some work has examined ways in which schools can be more flexible in meeting the needs of disadvantaged students and their families (e.g. Gitlin, Margonis and Brunjes 1993). Such strategies require further exploration.

Another aspect of changes at school level is reflected in the recent requirement for the development of a home–school links policy in every school (Ireland 1995). Family involvement and support is more likely to occur when school policies encourage it and school administrators support teachers and acknowledge their efforts in relation to this work. There is a need for the provision of comprehensive professional development opportunities for teachers in fostering parent and family involvement. Such opportunities must be ongoing to expand educators' abilities to reach out to parents and communities. Furthermore, family involvement and the development of effective strategies to foster and build on such involvement should be an integral part of all teacher preparation.

Another challenge in the area of the development of family involvement and support lies in the fact that the most needy families are also the most difficult to engage. There is a need for the examination of different approaches and strategies to address the needs of such families. This is also linked to the need for integration of services and a collaborative approach to working with families to enable them to reach a readiness for school involvement. A related point is the need for an additional understanding of the nature and effects of fathers' participation in school and family partnerships (Epstein 1996).

Finally, if we are to learn from the work that is being done, there is a need for better designed studies in the area of collaboration between families and schools (Epstein 1996; Moles 1996). Longitudinal studies would be of particular help in determining long-term effects, as well as a better understanding of short-term ones. There is also a need for evaluation of school programmes and practices in fostering partnerships with families (Moles 1996). Such evaluations should address questions about the mechanisms and nature of the changes wrought through various aspects of programmes. Furthermore, issues in implementation should help to determine the most effective strategies for carrying out particular intervention ideas (Bierman 1996).

References

Alexander, K.L. and Entwisle, D.R. (1996) 'Schools and children at risk.' In A. Booth and J.F. Dunn (eds) *Family–School Links: How Do They Affect Educational Outcomes?* Mahwah, NJ: Lawrence Erlbaum.

Becker, H.J. and Epstein, J.L. (1982) 'Parent involvement: A study of teacher practices.' *Elementary School Journal 83*, 85–102.

Bierman, K.L. (1996) 'Family–school links: an overview.' In A. Booth and J.F. Dunn (eds) *Family–School Links: How Do They Affect Educational Outcomes?* Mahwah, NJ: Lawrence Erlbaum.

Bloom, B.S. (1964) *Stability and Change in Human Characteristics.* New York: Wiley.

Bloom, B.S. (1981) *All Our Children Learning: A Primer for Parents, Teachers and Other Educators.* New York: McGraw-Hill.

Boldt, S. and Devine, B. (1998) 'Educational disadvantage in Ireland: Literature review and summary report.' In S. Boldt, B. Devine, D. McDevitt and M. Morgan *Educational Disadvantage and Early School Leaving.* Dublin: Combat Poverty Agency.

Booth, A. and Dunn, J.F. (eds) (1996) *Family–School Links: How Do They Affect Educational Outcomes?* Mahwah, NJ: Lawrence Erlbaum.

Burton, C.B. (1992) 'Defining family-centered early education: Beliefs of public school, child care, and Head Start teachers.' *Early Education and Development 3*, 1, 45–59.

Cochran, M. and Dean, C. (1991) 'Home–school relations and the empowerment process.' *Elementary School Journal 91*, 261–270.

Cochran, M. and Woolever, F. (1983) 'Beyond the deficit model: The empowerment of parents with information and informal supports.' In I.E. Sigel and L.M. Laosa (eds) *Changing Families.* New York: Plenum Press.

Coleman, J.S., Campbell, E.Q., Hobson, C.J., McPartland, J., Mood, A.M., Weinfeld, F.D. and York, R.L. (1966) *Equality of Educational Opportunity.* Washington DC: US Government Printing Office.

Cullen, B. (1997) *Integrated Services and Children at Risk.* Dublin: Combat Poverty Agency.

Dauber, S.L. and Epstein, J.L. (1993) 'Parents' attitudes and practices of involvement in inner-city elementary and middle schools.' In N. Chavkin (ed) *Families and Schools in a Pluralistic Society.* Albany, NY: State University of New York Press.

Davies, D. (1991) 'Schools reaching out: Family, school, and community partnerships for student success.' *Phi Delta Kappan 72*, 5, 376–382.

Department of Education (1997) 'The Home–School–Community Liaison (HSCL) Scheme.' Department of Education Web Site, March.

Eccles, J.S. and Harold, R.D. (1996) 'Family involvement in children's and adolescents' schooling.' In A. Booth and J.F. Dunn (eds) *Family–School Links: How Do They Affect Educational Outcomes?* Mahwah, NJ: Lawrence Erlbaum.

Edwards, P.A. and Jones Young, L.S. (1992) 'Beyond parents: Family, community, and school involvement.' *Phi Delta Kappan 74*, 1, 72–80.

Epstein, J.L. (1986) 'Parents' reactions to teacher practices of parent involvement.' *Elementary School Journal 86*, 277–294.

Epstein, J. (1991) 'Effects on student achievement of teachers' practices of parent involvement.' *Advances in Reading/Language Research 5*, 261–276.

Epstein, J. (1996) 'Perspectives and previews on research and policy.' In A. Booth and J.F. Dunn (eds) *Family–School Links: How Do They Affect Educational Outcomes?* Mahwah, NJ: Lawrence Erlbaum.

European Social Fund (ESF) Programme Evaluation Unit (1997) *Preventive Actions in Education.* Dublin: ESF Programme Evaluation Unit.

Gamoran, A. (1996) 'Effects of schooling on children and families.' In A. Booth and J.F. Dunn (eds) *Family–School Links: How Do They Affect Educational Outcomes?* Mahwah, NJ: Lawrence Erlbaum.

Gilligan, R. (1995) 'Family support and child welfare: Realising the promise of the Child Care Act 1991.' In H. Ferguson and P. Kenny (eds) *On Behalf of the Child: Professional Perspectives on the Child Care Act 1991.* Dublin: A. and A. Farmar.

Gitlin, A., Margonis, F. and Brunjes, H. (1993) 'In the shadow of the excellence reports: School restructuring for at-risk students.' In R. Donmoyer and R. Kos (eds) *At-Risk Students: Portraits, Policies, Programs, and Practices.* Albany, NY: State University of New York Press.

Henderson, A. and Berla, N. (eds) (1994) *A New Generation of Evidence: The Family is Critical to Student Achievement.* Columbia, MD: National Committee for Citizens in Education.

Ireland (1937) *Bunreacht na héireann, Constitution of Ireland.* Dublin: Stationery Office.

Ireland (1992) *Education for a Changing World. Green Paper on Education.* Dublin: Stationery Office.

Ireland (1995) *Charting our Education Future. White Paper on Education.* Dublin: Stationery Office.

Ireland (1998) *The Education Act 1998: Students, Teachers, Parents, Patrons/Owners, Special Needs, Disadvantaged.* Department of Education and Science. Dublin: Stationery Office.

Iverson, B.K. and Walberg, H.J. (1982) 'Home environment and school learning: a quantitative synthesis.' *Journal of Experimental Education 50*, 3, 144–151.

Jencks, C., Smith, M., Acland, H., Bane, M.J., Cohen, D., Gintis, H., Heyns, B. and Michelson, S. (1972) *Inequality: A Reassessment of the Effect of Family and Schooling in America.* New York: Basic Books.

Kalinowski, A. and Sloane, K. (1981) 'The home environment and school achievement.' *Studies in Educational Evaluation 7*, 85–96.

Kellaghan, T., Sloane, K., Alvarez, B. and Bloom, B. (1993) *The Home Environment and School Learning: Promoting Parental Involvement in the Education of Children.* San Francisco: Jossey-Bass.

Kellaghan, T., Weir, S., Ó hUallacháin, S. and Morgan, M. (1995) *Educational Disadvantage in Ireland.* Dublin: Department of Education Combat Poverty Agency Educational Research Centre.

Krasnow, J.H. (1990) *Improving Family–School Relationships: Teacher Research from the Schools Reaching Out Project.* Boston, MA: Institute for Responsive Education.

Lareau, A. (1987) 'Social class differences in family–school relationships: The importance of cultural capital.' *Sociology of Education 60*, 73–85.

Lloyd, G.M. (1996) 'Research and practical application for school, family, and community partnerships.' In A. Booth and J.F. Dunn (eds) *Family–School Links: How Do They Affect Educational Outcomes?* Mahwah, NJ: Lawrence Erlbaum.

Marjoribanks, K. (1979) *Families and Their Learning Environments: An Empirical Analysis.* London: Routledge and Kegan Paul.

Moles, O.C. (1993) 'Collaboration between schools and disadvantaged parents: Obstacles and openings.' In N. Chavkin (ed) *Families and Schools in a Pluralistic Society.* Albany, NY: State University of New York Press.

Moles, O.C. (1996) 'New national directions in research and policy.' In A. Booth and J.F. Dunn (eds) *Family–School Links: How Do They Affect Educational Outcomes?* Mahwah, NJ: Lawrence Erlbaum.

National Economic and Social Council (1993) *Education and Training Policies for Economic and Social Development.* Dublin: NESC.

Ogbu, J.U. (1982) 'Cultural discontinuities and schooling.' *Anthropology and Education Quarterly 13*, 4, 290–307.

Passow, A.H. (1970) *Depreciation and Disadvantage: Nature and Manifestations.* Hamburg: UNESCO Institute for Education.

Pestalozzi, J. (1951) *The Education of Man.* Trans. H. Gordon and R. Gordon. New York: Philosophical Library.

Powell, D.R. (1989) *Families and Early Childhood Programs.* Washington DC: National Association for the Education of Young Children.

Pugh, G. (1989) 'Parents and professionals in pre-school services: Is partnership possible?' In S. Wolfendale (ed) *Parental Involvement: Developing Networks between School, Home and Community*. London: Cassell.

Ryan, C. (1998) 'The 8 to 15 early school leavers' initiative.' *Astir*, December, 10.

Ryan, S. (1994) *The Home–School–Community Liaison (HSCL) Scheme: Final Evaluation Report*. Dublin: Educational Research Centre.

Ryan, S. (1995) *The Home–School–Community Liaison (HSCL) Scheme: Summary Evaluation Report*. Dublin: Educational Research Centre.

Ryan, S. (1996a) *Evaluation of a Home–School–Community Liaison Scheme in Irish Elementary Schools*. Ann Arbor, MI: UMI.

Ryan, S. (1996b) 'Follow-up report on the assessment of first, third, and fifth class pupils for the evaluation of the Home–School–Community Liaison Scheme.' Paper presented to the National Steering Committee on Home–School–Community Liaison. November.

Schuerman, J. and Rossi, P. (1999) 'National evaluation of family preservation services.' Chicago, IL: Chapin Hall Center for Children, University of Chicago.

Slavin, R.E. (1997) 'Can education reduce social inequality?' *Educational Leadership 55*, 4, 6–10.

Swap, S.M. (1990) *Parent Involvement and Success for All Children: What We Know Now*. Boston: Institute for Responsive Education.

Swick, K.J. and McKnight, S. (1989) 'Characteristics of kindergarten teachers who promote parent involvement.' *Early Childhood Research Quarterly 4*, 19–29.

Tietjen, A.M. (1989) 'The ecology of children's social support networks.' In D. Belle (ed) *Children's Social Networks and Social Supports*. New York: Wiley.

Walberg, H.J. (1984) 'Families as partners in educational productivity.' *Phi Delta Kappan 65*, 397–400.

CHAPTER 9

Creating Municipal Structures for Family Support in a Danish City

Peter Steen Jensen

Introduction

Although affected by the waves of the conservatism that swept through Europe and the USA in the 1980s, the Danish state continues to be one of the most interventionist in the world. Comprehensive, well-funded interventions in many areas of social life and, in particular, in the care and support of children represent the norm. Indeed, it could be argued that the Danish experience represents one end of an ideological continuum constructed along the dimension of the responsibilities of individuals and the state.

Rather than argue the relative merits of such an approach to the organization of society, this chapter offers a case study of how the Danish state, operating through its local government structures, supports children and families. The specific focus of the case study is the Child and Youth Authority of the municipality of Odense and it is written from the perspective of a senior manager in that authority. The chapter describes its genesis, organization, the legislative basis of its work, its objectives and the strategies it uses towards their achievement. What emerges are a number of core organizational and intervention concepts which we in Odense believe have general applicability, even in other less universal, more residual state social policy contexts. However, before going on to the specifics of the experience in Odense, it is worth identifying some key characteristics of state services in Denmark.

Big state – local government

Like many nations in the 1980s, Denmark had a neo-conservative government with an alliance of the Conservative and Liberal parties holding power from 1982 to 1992. As might be expected, one of the policy targets of this government was to reduce the level of state intervention in society. One of the legacies of their period in power is an increased level of involvement of third/not-for-profit sector organizations in the delivery of services (Munday 1996, p.34). Perhaps more important has been the overall shift within European Social Democratic parties to the centre. Thus, even Denmark's current era of a Social Democratic party-led coalition has seen changes in the nature of the welfare state. For example, unemployment benefit eligibility has been tightened, its duration shortened and what constitutes a reasonable job offer extended, with sanctions introduced in the case of refusal of offers (European Commission 1998, p.102). However, in spite of these changes, the overall position has altered little. Writing about the Conservative–Liberal era, Christiansen (1994) argues that the welfare state 'was too deeply entrenched in Danish consensus to be dismantled' (p.95). An examination of the growth in social protection expenditure between 1990 and 1995 confirms this. In this period, expenditure grew by 4.3 per cent as against an EU average of 3.4 per cent (European Commission 1998, p.66).

In 1997, state consumption expenditure in Denmark constituted just over one quarter of GDP. In 1996, 31 per cent of the country's employment was in the state sector. In respect of both of these indicators, Denmark was ranked second highest among OECD nations, surpassed only by Sweden. On the other side of the balance sheet, tax receipts are the highest among OECD states, representing 51.3 per cent of GDP in 1995, compared with an EU average of 41.8 per cent and OECD average of 37.4 per cent. What results from this high tax–high spend regime is a comprehensive set of state services. For example, in education, it results in pupil–teacher ratios as low as 11.3 at primary level and 9.8 at secondary, compared with OECD averages of 18.2 and 14.4 respectively (OECD 1998).

One of the most important features of the Danish economic and social system is the extent of female participation in the labour force. In 1996, over 80 per cent of the 25–54 female population was engaged in some sort of work outside the home (European Commission 1998, p.36). In their analysis of family policy in Europe, Hantrias and Letablier (1996) identify Denmark as one of a number of states which has intervened to help parents combine work outside the home with childrearing. Rather than affording special protection for women as mothers, the emphasis in Denmark has been on encouraging sharing between men and women of paid and domestic work. In this context, the provision of comprehensive services in the form of nurseries, kindergarten and after-school supports reflects a Danish tradition of public responsibility for the care of children, established in the early twentieth century (Hantrias and Letablier 1996, pp.126–127).

As the new century begins, the extent of state involvement is increasing. Table 9.1 and 9.2 illustrate the extent of growth of day care in Denmark between 1990 and 1995.

Table 9.1 Day care in Denmark: extent		
In day care	**1990**	**1995**
Day nurseries	24,420	21,130
Municipal day care	65,879	74,884
Kindergartens	88,851	108,398
Youth recreation centres	36,883	31,267
Age-integrated institutions	56,382	96,096
School care schemes	35,419	112,835
Total	307,834	444,610

Source: Danmark Statistik (1999)

Table 9.2 Day care in Denmark: growth		
Number per 100 in respective age groups	**1986**	**1995**
0–2 years	47.2	48.2
3–6 years	71.0	82.7
7–14 years	14.7	28.7
0–14 years total	35.0	48.5

Source: Danmark Statistik (1999)

In 1995, spending on 'family and children' represented 12 per cent of social protection expenditure (4.1 per cent of GDP), higher only in Luxembourg and Finland (European Commission 1998, p.65).

Another important feature of the Danish system is the level of decentralization in the provision of social services, which dates back to local government reform in 1970. There are 275 local authorities, known as municipalities, which are responsible for a full range of services extending from social welfare benefit administration to primary and lower secondary education and public utilities. At the intermediate or regional government level there are 14 counties which take responsibility for functions too extensive for the municipalities to handle; for example, the hospital service. The municipalities not only have a spending remit, but also have a significant role in revenue generation through local taxes. Furthermore, local consultative structures for service users reinforce the ethos of subsidiarity, which runs through all aspects of the state's operation.

Odense

Odense is Denmark's third largest city with a population of 180,000. Situated on the island of Funen, it is a major regional centre. The city itself is over one thousand years old, has a thriving university and is steeped in culture; for example, it is the native city of Hans Christian Anderson. Like any other large urban area, Odense also has its social problems and one of the tasks of the local authority is to try to address these difficulties.

Odense City Council

As stated, local government in Danish cities is under the direction of the municipalities. Odense municipality has five functions delivered via five corresponding departments:

- the Mayor's Department which has overall responsibility for the operations of the local authority in Odense

- the Environment and Technical Affairs Department which caters for all matters relating to environmental issues, including public transport and planning

- the Care and Welfare Department which administers services for the handicapped, elderly and all day-care services

- the Services and Cultural Affairs Department which covers all cultural centres such as museums and libraries, in addition to the administration of the tax system and social welfare operations

- the Children's and Young People's Department which has responsibility for child care, education and all pedagogical services.

Figure 9.1 illustrates the organizational structure of the Department for Children and Young People. Previously, the activities currently under the responsibility of the Child and Youth Department were dispersed among the various sections of the municipality. Their reorganization under one heading in 1994 represents a critical change in the municipality's strategy for meeting the needs of children and young people.

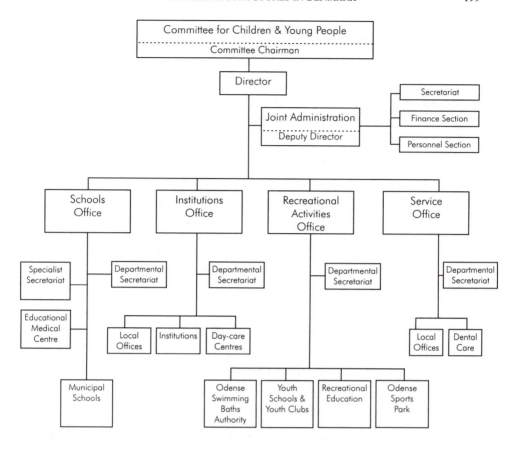

Figure 9.1 The Child and Youth Authority – Organization plan for the Child and Youth Organization

Legislation and objectives

The role of the City Council is to implement what parliament decides through a variety of forms of legislation. In doing so, the local authority adheres to the rules and spirit of the legislation with a view to mobilizing better services and facilities for Danish families. This implies an expectation on the part of the municipality, both in terms of quality of the services on offer to children and families and expectations regarding the performance of staff. For example, the Public Schools Act instructs that the role of the state schools is, in conjunction with parents, to promote pupil's ability to learn skills, working methods and forms of expression which can contribute to the pupil's all-round personal development. This mandates the council to work together with the family with specific emphasis on prevention and family support. Therefore, the role of the council is to act as a bridge between the desire and aspirations of the state, as illustrated through its legislation, and what occurs on a day-to-day basis at the local level in schools and other day-care child and family services.

Deriving from the set of legislation that underpins the work of the authority, there is also a set of centrally defined objectives which act as a guide to the corporation generally and more specifically to the Child and Youth Authority:

- All activities must be co-ordinated, integrated and formulated at all levels towards a total solution.

- All activities must be focused on the individual child and its surroundings.

- Special activities must, as far as possible, be integrated into the normal system and prevention measures within the normal system must be constantly reinforced.

- There is a continuum of devolution of administrative duties to local agents and the development of partnerships at local level.

- The department as a whole must operate with openness and transparency, providing a high level of information to both politicians and service users.

- A high degree of quality and efficiency must be ensured.

It could be argued that the first three objectives at least could easily be principles for the delivery of family support services.

Normal and Special Systems

In order to achieve these objectives, services are delivered through a strategic model combining the Normal System and Special System. Within the Normal System a comprehensive range of educational, social and recreational activities is provided to groups of children and young people. These activities include generic education in schools, as well as evening schools, youth clubs and other social associations. Overall, the Normal System is the primary forum of education within the municipality of Odense.

Some children and young people may need additional support in attaining academic, social and life fulfilment and the Special System represents a mechanism that supports the Normal System in order for this to happen. This assistance is provided in different ways and at varying levels. For example, the Special System may provide individual children and families with one-off help in times of sudden adversity such as death or sudden loss of income. Where children and families are experiencing longer term adversity, it may provide crisis care and in some cases this might include the admission of a child into the care of the Danish state. Whatever the intervention, it is of the utmost importance that actions are taken in consultation with all involved, including the family.

In addition, both systems operate within the philosophy that every citizen has equal and easy access to the services he or she needs. In doing so, it can be seen that the Special System operates as part of the Normal System, not separate to it.

The Child and Youth Authority operates through four designated departments:

- the Institutions Department
- the Schools Department
- the Leisure Department
- the Services Department (which is essentially the Special System).

The first of these, the Institutions Department, ensures adequacy of service to all 0–6-year-olds through preschool and early education programmes. Additionally, the department has a watchdog role relating to the provision of services to specific children and their families, including those with physical and intellectual disability, refugees and immigrants. Overall, within the Institutions Department there is emphasis on prevention, early intervention and an ethos of working together for children and their families.

Just as the Institutions Department promotes services for 0–6-year-olds, so also the Schools Department monitors the performance of schools in accordance with policy decisions by the City Council and relevant legislation. In addition, the department has a specific co-ordinating role in respect of schools. This co-ordination includes administrative and financial functions, as well as the co-ordination of teaching and the replication of models of best practice among all education sites. Thus, the objective of the Schools Department is to seek to provide a cohesive and co-ordinated service for the entire child and youth sector in conjunction with teachers, school committees and other community agents. The Schools Department recognizes that teachers are the key asset to the Danish education system. Therefore, there is high emphasis on teacher training in working with others for families needing support.

School is but one part of a child's life and social legislation in Denmark clearly values the right and need of the individual to leisure pursuits. In Odense the importance of positive leisure activities for young people is emphasized by the fact that there exists a department with specific responsibility for managing and developing leisure and sports facilities. The role of the Department of Leisure and Activities is to enable young people to have adequate access to a range of leisure activities suitable to their needs, including facilities such as swimming pools and sports parks. Additionally this department oversees a public information service; thus it ensures that citizens in Odense know what is available and how, where and when to access such facilities.

Services Department

The Services Department ensures that children and young people receive an adequate service, both in terms of the general services on offer from the other departments and in terms of the child's personal individual need. The department shares a responsibility with other departments to contribute to the family's well-being, in order for as many children as possible to live in conditions that promote growth and development. Specifically, the department monitors initiatives aimed at supporting families experiencing stress and difficulty. In accordance with the law, the service department has a duty to ensure that action is taken in cases where a child is at risk due to conditions in the home or through involvement in crime, for example. Where the system fails children, it is the responsibility of this department to ensure first that a service is provided to the child and family and that this support is effective. It is important to remember that any such intervention by the Services Department occurs early and is implemented in conjunction with the child's wishes, negotiated with the family and occurs in the child's immediate surroundings such as school and community.

Just as the Services Department offers a flexible model of family support, so also is the budgeting system adaptable. Unlike the other departments, the budget for the Service Department is not solely based on the numbers of service users via a 'per capita' grant model. Rather, the Services Department has the facility to move existing resources and access additional monies for child and families dependent on identified need within the Special System.

Examples of Special System services supporting the Normal System

So far this chapter has described the framework of the Normal and Special Systems, the objectives and functions of the Child and Youth Authority and the designated departments through which these objectives are achieved. However, one might ask how in practical terms are families supported by this service network? Such support usually takes varying forms, as illustrated by the following examples:

1. The provision of a specially trained remedial teacher who gives one-to-one attention to a child with a learning disability, with this

support being provided to the child on site at his or her local home/school.

2. If a child had a physical disability, the Special System would offer, arrange and implement a course of physiotherapy.

3. The ongoing provision of a range of paramedical services by the Special System through the forum of the Normal System, i.e. through in-home, school and community-based service sites.

4. Social and life skills work with children and parents, provided for them in their own home.

5. Where a family needs more formal therapeutic support, such a family might be offered therapy/systems work from within the Special System. In such cases, the requisite professional help may be offered to family members singularly or collectively. All these inputs work with an underlying commitment to prevention and the belief that successful family support can halt the admission of children into the formal care system.

6. In exceptional circumstances, care placements for children are provided, but always with a view to the earliest possible return home.

Children and young people in Odense municipality

Whereas the vast majority of young people of Odense enjoy a happy, normal childhood and adolescence, for others this is not the case. They usually have problems with their school work, or at best leave school with a very minimum of education. They may have begun to dabble in petty crime and shoplifting and may be expressing themselves by acting out through violent behaviour. Occasionally this can develop into something worse; for example, more explicitly violent behaviour, prostitution and drug misuse.

In addition to these expected social problems, the number of ethnic groups in Odense is high relative to the rest of Denmark. In fact, Odense has the highest ratio of ethnic groups outside Copenhagen and this ratio is still growing. Immigrants come from all over Europe, the Middle East, Vietnam, Pakistan and Somalia, among others. They tend to experience difficulty with Danish life in terms of fundamental issues of cultural values. For example, they do not speak the expected level of Danish and the mores present in the context of kindergarten, school and after-school facilities such as sports clubs may clash with their own cultural experience.

As in other major cities throughout Europe, it has been difficult to achieve a totally successful housing policy. For example, housing developments for large numbers of people from the same social class exist in our city. In addition, the situation is complicated by the fact that many of these are immigrant families. This often makes the provision of on-site services more difficult. For example, an area in the city known as Vollsmose has a population of around 20,000. Approximately 75 per cent of the population is bilingual, but with different linguistic and ethnic backgrounds. Providing a general education to Vollsmose resident children is already complex, without focusing on the specific problems which individual children experience.

Room for manoeuvre

In reconstituting its approach to working with children and families through the creation of an integrated Children and Youth Authority, a critical focus of the municipality was to be prevention. In concrete terms, this meant stressing the duty of the Normal System to engage in preventive measures and therefore a significant change in attitude among the staff of that system.

The starting point in encouraging a shift in thinking occurred in October 1996, with the drafting and circulation of a working paper among all parts of the authority which introduced the concept of 'room for manoeuvre in the Normal System'. Since then, the idea of seeking to create educational space within the mainstream systems has been dominant in discussions about service development and improvement. The concept strongly reflects the themes of normalization and prevention, very much in line with the objectives of the authority as outlined above.

Like all concepts, however, room for manoeuvre runs the risk of becoming a 'buzzword' and being of little practical use for front-line practitioners. Rather than letting this possibility develop, the various services within the Normal System were asked to express in concrete terms in their annual workplans how the Normal System could support the Special System. The main feature to emerge among the responses was an emphasis on skills development. Staff in Odense's nurseries and kindergartens believed that their skills could be extended in order to help and retain as many children as possible within the mainstream services.

For example, teachers expressed the view that their traditional roles have changed, requiring them to address needs of children which are not purely educational in nature. As well as talking about specific problems relating to the lack of stimulation in the homes of some children, they mentioned the general challenge of teaching children who, although having a sophisticated understanding of computer and telecommunication technologies, lack deeper knowledge and are difficult to engage in the pedagogical process. Changes in society and its younger members require change in the institutions charged with supporting their development.

The concept of room for manoeuvre implies building the skills of service providers, but it also means working from a position of children's strengths. The point here is that there is little dispute that many children prove to be resilient in the face of serious personal adversity:

- They are able to develop confidence in themselves.
- They are able to handle and predict situations and to make strategic choices.
- They have, or establish, a network from which they can draw support.

Clearly, these factors are interlinked. Having a good network allows greater confidence in trying something out, as opposed to being scared to take a chance on a particular course of action. The fact that front-line professionals encounter such factors and scenarios every day is the critical point.

The relationship between teacher or child-care worker and the child should emphasize the idea of support in managing risk situations, instead of simply shielding the child from such events. What makes this strategy so appealing is that it can be applied in the operation of the Normal System. Children encounter stressful situations in their everyday experience within the Normal System and it is within this context that they can be supported in developing the skills needed to cope. Room for manoeuvre therefore implies using the experience of the Normal System in preventing later problems for at-risk children. It also implies providing professionals with the skills to work towards this goal.

Conclusion

The need to refocus our organization and find new strategies, even in the context of what is in comparative terms a comprehensive and well-funded service, suggests some important lessons. Perhaps the most significant is that any family support organization must continuously challenge itself with the question: 'Are we delivering our services in such a way as to achieve the best possible results for all our clients?' It is unlikely that the chief executive of any organization, in any part of the world, could answer this question affirmatively and with fully supporting evidence. The reality of family support work is that it is an ever-changing canvas, requiring dynamic and flexible organizations.

As has been emphasized, the dominant representation of organizational flexibility and dynamism in Odense is in the expansion of the capacity of the Normal System. If there is a message from our experience about how family support services should be delivered it is that, whatever their needs, as many children and families as possible should be catered for in mainstream services. Prior to our reorganization, we felt that within the terms of the legislation, we were achieving the aim of supporting all children and families to participate fully in society. However, even in this context of our good intentions and precise diagnoses, we were sometimes failing to identify and meet the needs of all our children fully. While we cannot yet present evidence of greater success, we can at least say that we now clearly operate from a philosophy that requires our organization to meet individual welfare needs using a variety of methods, without recourse to labelling which often results from referral to special services.

Basic to the approach described in this chapter is the emphasis on the rights of children and families to state support. However, within Denmark some citizens are beginning to ask a different question. For them, the issue is not about children's right to state support; rather, it is about their right to family care and relationships. It is interesting that the Child and Youth Authority's experience with ethnic groups and their desire to retain kin-based supports for their children mirrors some of the concerns of a growing number of native Danes. It looks increasingly likely that it is these questions that will be driving a new agenda of change and ensuring that our organization continues to promote family support.

References

Christiansen, N.F. (1994) 'Denmark: "End of an idyll".' In P. Anderson and P. Camiller (eds) *Mapping the West European Left.* London: Verso.

European Commission (1998) *Directorate General for Employment, Industrial Relations and Social Affairs, Social Protection in Europe 1997.* Luxembourg: Office for Official Publications of the European Communities.

Hantrias, L. and Letablier, M.-T. (1996) *Families and Family Policies in Europe.* London: Longman.

Munday, B. (1996) 'Contexts and overviews.' In B. Munday and P. Ely (eds) *Social Care in Europe.* London: Prentice Hall/Harvester Wheatsheaf.

OECD (1998) OECD in Figures: 1998 Edition. Paris: OECD. (See http://www.OECD.org/publications/figures for more updated information.)

CHAPTER 10

Emerging Agendas for Family Support

John Pinkerton

Introduction

From the preceding chapters it is clear that family support can mean many things, which is both its strength and its weakness. There is a real danger of it being one of those warm and fuzzy terms which by being all inclusive ends up meaning nothing. However, that does not need to be the case and this concluding chapter will argue that family support has the potential to be an invaluable synthesizing term, helping to set the core agenda for child welfare at the start of the twenty-first century. Drawing on the experience of researching the development of family support in Northern Ireland and the wealth of perspectives and experiences presented in the pages of this book, it will be suggested that there are unifying themes within the broad range of ideas and practices that can and should be drawn together under the banner of family support.

This chapter will also argue that by adopting a social policy perspective to provide a very basic conceptual framework for questioning child welfare, it is possible to weave together the variety of ideas and practices which constitute family support at its present stage of development. Through using the framework in this way, it is possible to understand family support within the context of the relationship between civil society and the state through focusing on four key themes: needs, services, process and outcomes. These themes have all been addressed in various ways in the previous chapters and together suggest directions for future developments. These will be presented here in the form of separate but interdependent agendas for policymakers, operational managers, practitioners and researchers. It will also be suggested that politicians and citizens need to take responsibility for advancing the family support agenda.

Finding a framework

Family centres have consistently had a key place in the discussion of family support (Cannan 1992; Holman 1988; Pithouse, Lindsell and Chueng 1998) and one reason for this is that they reflect the diversity of the field. In the early 1980s a conference was held in Northern Ireland which tried to distil the local experience of family centre work under the provocative title: 'The answer is family centres – but what was the question?' Almost twenty years later the paradox within the title of that conference still remained to challenge a research project on family support carried out in the region (Higgins, Pinkerton and Devine 1998; Higgins, Pinkerton and Switzer 1997). The aim of the research was to determine the state of family support after twelve months of it having a clear legislative mandate under the Children (NI) Order 1995 and to compare that to what had existed prior to the new legislation. It was self-evident that something called family support existed. There was not only the new Northern Ireland law but also legislation throughout the UK providing a mandate for it. There was a literature, including both empirical research and some theoretical work, which described, evaluated and promoted it (Audit Commission 1994; Gibbons 1992; Parton 1997; Smith 1996). Yet in looking for a researchable definition of family support, the unsatisfactory result was to be faced with definitions such as 'any activity or facility provided either by statutory agencies or by community groups or individuals, aimed at providing advice and support to parents to help them bring up their children' (Audit Commission 1994, p.39). Such definitions are so general as to be not much more helpful than the tautology offered as a definition by one interviewee in the Northern Ireland study: 'Family Support is what supports families' (Higgins *et al.* 1997).

As is so often the case, in order to move forward it was necessary to take a step back. Rather than pursue an illusory, neatly bounded definition of family support as the predetermined answer on which to base the research, what the Northern Ireland study needed was a set of questions to open out the focus of enquiry. In order to inform research usefully, these questions needed to be based on a coherent conceptual framework. The discipline of social policy within the UK provides a useful perspective for developing such a framework. In a basic introduction to the subject, Alcock (1998) has pointed out that while it has a distinct empirical focus on 'the support of well-being through social action' (p.7), social policy is quintessentially 'an interdisciplinary field – drawing on and developing links with other cognate disciplines at every stage and overlapping at times with these in terms of both empirical foci and methods of analysis...the boundaries...are porous and shifting' (p.7). The resonance with family support as described and discussed in previous chapters should be clear.

The history of social policy is rooted in social administration, which can be defined as the study of state services aimed at improving the welfare of individuals within the wider civil society, but the discipline then

> proceeded from this starting point to take the definitions deeper and ask fundamental questions about the services; what needs are they trying to meet; why do needs arise; on what grounds – political, moral, economic – does society base its attempts to meet need; how effective are its policies and, indeed, what are the criteria for effectiveness in this context. (Brown and Payne 1990, p.3)

From this perspective, child welfare can be narrowly viewed as those state services designed to promote and protect the well-being of children and young people. It is thus clearly situated in the context of the relationship between the 'state' and 'civil society'. For the purposes of this discussion the state can usefully be defined as 'a set of agencies claiming supreme authority for the co-ordination and continuity of a population [civil society, JP] within a particular territory, backed by a virtual monopoly of force' (McLennan, Held and Hall 1984, p.3) and civil society as 'all those social institutions and relationships which arise, through voluntary association, outside the sphere of direct state control' (McIntosh 1984, p.20). These definitions are inter-dependent in that each is defined by contrast to the other. Both definitions also encourage attention to social relationships which constitute the institutions of state and civil society and to the place of power and authority. If family support is seen as an instance of how state agencies relate to social institutions within civil society, it ceases to require definition as a static category, to be applied rigidly to some sets of ideas or practices and not to others.

What become important are the kinds of questions of concern to social policy – questions about the purpose of the relationship between the 'needs' generated in civil society and the 'services' provided by the state; about what is driving the relationship as it unfolds as a particular 'process'; and about whether the resulting 'outcomes' for children and families are desirable, or even those intended. These relationships between civil society, the state, needs, services, process and outcomes provide a framework, as set out in Figure 10.1. It constitutes a very basic conceptual model useful for questioning child welfare in a way that bring into focus key issues. As Titmus, a major figure in the development of post-war British social policy, observed: '...the purpose of model building is not to admire the architecture, but to help us to see some order in all the disorder and confusion of facts, systems

and choices' (quoted by Hardiker, Exton and Barker 1991, p.18). Conceptual modelling has been proved useful to practice (Fisher *et al.* 1986), to
research (Holman 1988; Pinkerton 1994; Pinkerton and McCrea 1999) and
to theory (Roberts 1990). Here it provides a means by which to identify
unifying themes within family support and suggest directions for its further
development and consolidation.

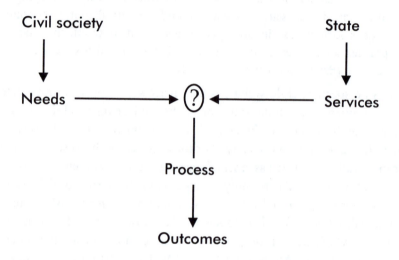

Figure 10.1 A framework for questioning contemporary child welfare

Civil society and needs

From the perspective suggested by the model in Figure 10.1, a key question
for any discussion of family support must be what is the need which is
involved. As clearly illustrated in the previous chapters, family support, to
date, has been primarily concerned with the needs of children and young
people for protective and stimulating conditions in which to grow and
develop in order to take their place in the adult world. To address those needs
also requires attention to the needs of carers. Both are met if three conditions
are present, highlighted by Maluccio, Fein and Oldmstead (1986) in their
discussion of permanency planning for children:

> Continuity: the parent's consistent, constant and predictable availability
> in a child's life.

> Stability: a nutritive environment that supports the parent–child relat-
> ionship and the capacities of both parent and child to engage in the
> bonding process.

> Mutuality: parent–child interactions that are mutually rewarding and that reinforce the importance of one to the other. (Maluccio, Fein and Oldmstead 1986, p.6)

These three aspects of need, reflecting the physical and emotional dependence of children and, to a lesser degree, young people, represent the need for social care which lies at the heart of family support. That term has been defined as 'the sum of helping (and when need be, controlling) resources available to people in adversity' (NISW 1982, paragraph 13.7). While linking the term to 'adversity' accurately reflects the continuing 'problem' focus of much family support, it restricts it unnecessarily. Social care and, by association, family support are a part of coping with the routine challenges of everyday life and not just exceptionally difficult circumstances. Family support as promotion of the 'normal' is one of the recurring themes of the preceding chapters, although they also demonstrate that it is important to go beyond that general truth to identify the particulars of types of need for social care. The form need takes may be age specific or linked to psychosocial well-being, health, education or to impoverished material conditions, be they financial, housing or environmental. Need may also have its own particular rhythm. It may be chronic and corrosive or it may be low key and short lived. There are also important variations in the degree of control possible over different types of need.

The model in Figure 10.1 firmly places need within the context of civil society and within that society needs are not only generated but are also met. Over and over again the preceding chapters have drawn attention to the energy, creativity, stability and sense of belonging provided by neighbourhood and friendship and particularly by kinship and romantic attachment. These informal social care networks within civil society have been shown to provide the resources for children and young people as they deal with the challenges of their physical, social, psychological and educational development. The stable attachment and rich supply of positive reinforcement so necessary to prosocial psychosocial development are generally provided by the birth mother with the support of a partner and the informal social care networks of kinship, friendship and neighbourhood that surround them. Even into the so-called 'storm and stress' years of adolescence, it is primarily within networks of family that young people continue to find the secure base from which they face their expanding world.

At the same time, much of the material in this book emphasizes that it is important not to romanticize either the past or the present nature of the social care networks within civil society. From all the countries represented there have been pessimistic images shared of a fracturing social world: 'We used to raise children to join the larger society. Now, we struggle to protect them from the larger society' (quoted by Cutrona, Chapter 5). It is not only the wider society. The safe haven of family life is recognized as the site of gender inequality, domestic violence, child abuse and exhausting power struggles between children and parents. Adolescent friendships become supply routes for drugs. Concern for the crisis of family life and the collapse of community may be enduring themes given a contemporary spin by more or less sensational media reporting, but as with any 'moral panic' at its root there will be a reality – as much if not more about the context as the subject of concern itself. In this case it is particularly worth noting two important aspects about the reality of need and how it is met within civil society – change and complexity.

Much is made of the pace and direction of change in the so-called postmodern world. Internationally there are major shifts occurring in patterns of family formation and dissolution. These reflect shifting expectations of intimate relationships and family life, as well as the changing patterns of work, housing, transport and leisure. These tend to promote individualization and communities which are more fluid and heterogeneous. Children and young people as much as the adults around them are actively engaged with these changes – not least through the new technologies. The increase in stable couple relationships and births outside the legal institution of marriage, together with higher levels of divorce, remarriage, single and step parenting, have an impact on the nature of need – what forms of support are required and the nature of the social care networks available to meet them. This change is often presented as creating more challenging needs and a weaker capacity for meeting them. In fact it may be that the complexity of the informal networks of family, friendship and neighbourhood are becoming more visible.

Central to this complexity is the contradictory nature of social care. As the definition of social care given above noted, it is the sum of both helping and controlling. As discussed in Chapter 2, behind the solidarity of traditional communities, based on class, shared employment and residence in a clearly defined locality, lay conflict and differences, especially of gender, managed by a matrix of obligation and control that were integral to the social care networks. Relations beyond the family in particular were generally conditional and negotiated and the issues of respectability contested in many subtle ways, including the isolation of 'rough' or unruly families. Within any family, past or present, inside or outside traditional communities, the location of power and direction of coercive influence as well as social care will vary between its members according to age, gender and the particulars of circumstance.

People differ in their overall style of coping and an individual may not cope the same way in every situation. Chapter 5 stressed that there are different types of support (emotional, esteem, nuturant, information, tangible are all listed) which are useful at different times depending on need or type of stress. People also find certain types of support are appropriate from family while others can be obtained from friends or neighbours (Monteith and Pinkerton 1997). All this can make communication about need difficult. The subtle ways that people indirectly signal their need for support, even to those with whom they are most intimate, increase the chances of it being missed.

Thus within the social care networks of civil society there is a contradictory image to be found of need being both generated and met and also being left unmet or even compounded. This reflects a difficult complexity in which the interplay of class, gender, ethnicity, culture, religion, urban/rural divide spins out issues of care and control, costs and benefits, friendly distance and constructive interference. This interplay develops through individuals negotiating explicitly and implicitly over the detail of family, neighbourhood and friendship ties, obligations and boundaries, generating both the 'stressors' and 'protective factors' affecting the resilience of children, young people and their carers and indeed anyone else in need of social care.

The state and services

The model makes clear that family support is not just concerned with what goes on in civil society but is also about the response of state-run or sponsored services to needs generated there. Here again the theme of change is a recurring one from the previous chapters and, while not being matched with quite the same sense of crisis as there is about family and community, it is also linked to a sense of inadequacy, if not failure, of the state. It is important to recall that social care is about control as well as helping. State intervention is based on a 'double mandate: on the one hand for and in the interest of our clients but on the other to ensure norms and conformity of society' (Chapter 3, p.62). The ultimate basis of state power in the welfare arena as elsewhere is, as the earlier definition noted, 'a virtual monopoly of force'. Yet despite this power and authority there is a deep and well-founded concern over the state's capacity to substitute for the caregivers within civil society. Much of this reflects the international experience of high-cost and low-quality residential provision; with the latter reflected in both the care experience and in the capacity of young people to cope on leaving care.

Questioning the state's capacity to care for children is not just a matter of institutional versus community care. Attention has also been drawn to the mismatch between professional services provided or sponsored by the state and the expressed needs of family and community. This has been brought into sharp relief by the predominance now generally given to child protection – particularly in the English-speaking world. This mismatch can be seen as at best a failure to make the right connection between service providers and service users and at worst a form of exploitation of those in need by those making a living as 'poverty merchants' and 'disability parasites' (terms used in a plenary session of the conference linked with this book). Both those views are useful in that they point up two more important themes – the technical difficulties of ensuring effective and appropriate services and the power relations that reflect the politics of welfare which determine choices about the nature of state intervention.

Both the historical accounts and the international comparisons found within the detail of the earlier chapters make it clear that different choices have been and are being made about the nature of the state intervention, the services provided and the resources made available to support families. Hardiker *et al.* (1991), in their work on prevention, suggest there are three basic options in relation to state welfare provision: the residual, the institutional and the developmental. As Table 10.1 shows, these can be linked to particular ways of characterizing needs and the appropriate role for the state in providing services.

In any particular country, at any particular time, history, culture, national economic performance and political expediency will all play a role in what choice is made between the three models of state intervention or whether to hybridize them or move beyond them. As regards the latter, Hardiker and her colleagues recognize a fourth 'radical' perspective that sees state welfare as an inherently unstable attempt to manage the conflicts within a capitalist society in the interest of those holding the economic, political and social power. Whichever choice is made will have major implications for the development of family support. In particular, it will determine whether it is integrated into universal provision (see Chapters 6 and 9) or more narrowly targeted to children in need or at risk. The importance noted in earlier chapters of the legislative mandate for family support emphasizes the point that the choice, or balance, between family support as developmental, compensatory or protective (Chapter 1) is a political one which requires much debate, negotiation and accommodation. It is a debate that needs to be held not just among politicians, professional policymakers and those delivering services, but also with service users and the general public. The importance and the problem of the media's role has to be recognized as a crucial part of this.

Table 10.1 Framework linking types of welfare to need and state provision (modified from Hardiker *et al.* 1991)

Types of Welfare	Needs	State services
Residual	• Individual explanations • Pathology model/individual defect • Individual requires corrective treatment	• Individual/family carries burden of responsibility to provide for all needs • Right to choose/duty to provide • State provides basic social minimum as a last resort/safety net • Informal, voluntary and private sources of care are predominant
Institutional	• Product of faulty interaction between individual and environment • Faulty functioning of either individual or social institutions • Individual needs help to adjust to demands of society • Improvements may be needed in delivery of welfare services	• State has a duty to ensure needs of most disadvantaged members of society are met • State discharges its duty by co-ordinating mixed economy of welfare in which it plays a significant role
Developmental	• Individual difficulties arise from the unequal distribution of power and resources in society • Individuals need to be able to exert more control over their lives, including increased access to resources • Social systems, not people, are required to change	• State guarantees social rights • State accepts predominant responsibility for meeting social need via universal social services and redistributive social policies • State welfare is a means towards a just and equal society

The influence of the politics surrounding the state's contribution to family support should not block out recognition of the technical challenge involved in developing services. In particular, the importance of partnership to family support, which is underscored in various ways by previous chapters, requires both a practice style and organizational structures that are inclusive and provide a broad range of services which are responsive to the varying types of need – not least in relation to education which provides such a fertile site for family support interventions through giving access to the vast majority of children and their families (Chapter 6). This is an administrative and organizational issue requiring skilled management. Earlier chapters have illustrated the challenge of achieving internally integrated organizations and interagency working that can draw together health, education and personal social services. The detail of the complex Danish local government structures bear particular witness to this (Chapter 9).

Family support requires agency structures that are inclusive of service users. This requires not only being receptive to user involvement at all levels, but also working at engaging service users, adults and children, on their terms, through flexible outreach and sophisticated information promotion. The participatory style of work that this requires will inevitably have implications for the internal working of organizations. This has been an area which has not received the attention it deserves in the debate around family support. Staff can only be expected to work in an empowering fashion on behalf of an agency if it is in keeping with their own experience as employees. Organizations must have the capacity to support staff as individuals with personal, professional and training needs. Family support needs to be delivered from a humane and family-friendly workplace.

Process and outcomes

While the dynamic of the relationship between the state and civil society, between service and needs, ultimately determines the process of family support, this is no spontaneous movement. Earlier chapters shared detailed descriptions of disciplined application and rigorous evaluation of methods and skills aimed at achieving change. Interventions were applied at a number of levels: the micro through behavioural work (Chapter 3), counselling (Chapter 4) and parent education (Chapters 3 and 6); the mezo through group work (Chapter 5) and family work (Chapter 8); and the macro through local government organization (Chapter 9). Being clear about which level or levels are being targeted by any particular intervention is an important aspect of ensuring the process moves forward as intended. In addition, there can be a synergy created through the combination of types of intervention and their use at different levels simultaneously. Chapter 4 provided a detailed tabulation of knowledge, skills and values along with associated characteristics of content and process (Figure 4.1). It is clear that in family support, as in other areas of human services, it is competent practice, the reflective combination of knowledge, values and skills (O'Hagan 1996), that drives the process towards its desired outcomes.

Not only is it crucial that methods and techniques are applied skilfully and purposefully, but this must be done in an appropriate way. Some will be used in routine support over lengthy periods of time, while others will be the basis of a short-term, specialist, emergency response. Effective connections need to be made between the help being offered and the capacity and style of those being worked with as individuals, as couples, in families or in common interest groups. Family support is less about 'grafting on' a service than facilitating the flow of existing support (Chapters 1 and 4). This can be achieved through careful and detailed matching, pacing, timing, negotiating and experimenting. The onus is on the service provider to understand the cultural context, to engage with it without necessarily endorsing it (reference to unhelpful gendered expectations occurs in a number of chapters) and to actively solicit ideas, wishes and feelings from service users, both adults and children. Above all, family support as a style of practice depends on a mutual recognition between service provider and service user that they are partners in a 'therapeutic alliance' (Chapter 1) or 'collaboration' (Chapter 3).

The style of working required for moving on the process of family support is not easy to achieve and failure in some situations must be accepted as inevitable, in part because of the demands which the work can make on the service user. Change is never comfortable. It is also made difficult by the 'double mandate' which may well mean that accountability for child protection, underpinned by law, dictates a bottom line in the power relations which disadvantage the user. It is important once again to recall that state power ultimately rests in its 'virtual monopoly of force'. Also, the demands may be too great for the competence of the worker or the remit and resources of an agency or programme. It can require patience over hours, weeks and months from an individual worker and consistency over years from a service. The descriptions in the earlier chapters make it clear that family support involves varied skilled and complex types of work which are at various stages in establishing themselves. Improvisation and experimentation with new approaches, including learning from users (Chapter 6), means taking risks, and with risks go failure.

In order to recognize and learn from failure it is essential that the outcomes of family support are clear. At a general level this again raises the question of the model of welfare which has been chosen and the resulting type of family support – developmental, compensatory or protective. But it also raises difficult questions about outcomes. It has been observed (Parker *et al.* 1991) that it is easy to ask the general outcome question: has a service prevented harm to children, minimized the effect of disability, promoted children's well-being or secured family preservation? The difficulty is to specify, identify and measure actual outcomes and their relationship to particular aspects of the service. A useful distinction made by Cheetam and her colleagues (1992) is between 'client based outcomes', which measure the effects of services on service users, and 'service based outcomes' which are concerned with the process of delivery. It is also helpful to think in terms of a continuum rather than a hierarchy of methods of testing effectiveness; thereby allowing for a 'levels of evidence' approach (Hill 1999) rather than having a 'gold standard' of the randomized controlled trial discussed at the start of this book (Chapter 1). If outcome is understood in this more differentiated way there is considerable encouragement from the work reported in the previous chapters, in addition to the messages from the wider research discussed in Chapters 1, 3, 4 and 7.

Agendas for future development

Through using the basic social policy conceptual model set out earlier in Figure 10.1, it is apparent that there is 'some order in all the disorder and confusion of facts, systems and choices' presented in the previous chapters. Family support can be used as a synthesizing term to create something that is more than the sum of the parts. All aspects of the model were addressed in different ways by the description and discussion contained in the earlier chapters. Yet the material also makes it clear that, despite its long history and the quality and quantity of work which it embraces, there is still much to be done in developing family support if it is to make a place for itself at the core of child welfare. Based on the discussion in the previous sections, some of those future developments will now be suggested. These will be presented here in the form of separate but interdependent agendas for policymakers, operational managers, practitioners and researchers, summarized in Table 10.2.

Table 10.2 Emerging agendas for family support

For policymakers

- Developing a conceptual framework and vocabulary.

- Producing criteria for evaluation.

- Engage community representatives and service users as active partners.

- Promote subsidiarity.

For operational managers

- Ensure organizational structures express family support principles and style.

- Directly engage community representatives and service users in management.

- Promote staff support, supervision and training.

- Develop integrated structures across disciplines, agencies and sectors.

For practitioners

- Link practice to agencies' strategic goals.

- Operationalize conceptual framework and vocabulary.

- Undertake assessments as a means to express.

- Routinely evaluate work against planned outcomes-based evaluation.

- Clarify and develop methods, techniques and skills being used.

For researchers

- Rigorously evaluate 'what works'.

- Deepen understanding through qualitative case studies.

- Explore relationships between forms of family support through locality cluster studies.

- Develop social care economics as a means to cost family support.

First, in relation to policy, there is an onus on those who are promoting family support, in a top-down fashion from the position of making policy which others have to implement, to sustain and build on that position. This requires policy statements that go beyond general restatement of principles to detail a clear conceptual framework, linked to a defined vocabulary. This is necessary to keep the momentum of policy change underway through enabling more precise debate about the policy goals contained within the various aspects of family support. In particular, there needs to be more explicit linkage between family support and the model of welfare being pursued as part of wider social and economic priorities. That would be particularly helpful for ensuring that in the development of the necessary international debate not only apparent similarities but real differences are drawn out. Contrast as well as comparison is helpful to policy development.

Linked to a clearer conceptual framework, policymakers also need to produce policy criteria for evaluating the impact of family support and set the use of these within timetables of operational review and research. Table 10.3 sets out 26 policy criteria developed from the Northern Ireland study for evaluating policy impact on the work of a range of child-care settings.

In addition to improvements in the quality of the policy output, policymakers also need to incorporate into their own working practices the commitment to inclusiveness that is so essential to family support. The various levels of service provider, community representatives and service users, along with politicians and the media, all need to be involved in macro policy development. At the same time as practising inclusive engagement of these other stakeholders in overarching policy development and review, there should be a disengagement by policymakers from the lower levels of policy in keeping with the principle of subsidiarity: that is, detailed policy is left at the lowest appropriate level, whether to operational managers, practitioners or service users.

Table 10.3 Policy evaluation criteria (based on Higgins *et al.* 1998)

Expressed purpose

Criterion 1:   the setting is based on explicit assumptions about the type of welfare it is promoting ('residual', 'institutional', 'developmental').

Criterion 2:   the setting has clearly stated aims and objectives which are couched in the terms used in the relevant legislation.

Criterion 3:   the setting is explicitly targeted at a defined level of intervention.

Criterion 4:   the setting has an expressed commitment to providing one or more of the types of services mandated by the relevant legislation.

Organization

Criterion 5:   the setting includes its service users (adults and/or children) in its management.

Criterion 6:   the setting encourages effective and flexible working across disciplines, agencies and sectors.

Criterion 7:   the setting encourages a close and co-operative relationship with representatives of the neighbourhood(s) in which the children in receipt of its services live.

Criterion 8:   the setting ensures capacity to deliver a range of services.

Criterion 9:   the setting attends to staff needs and creates an effective and integrated staff team.

Need

Criterion 10:   the programme delivers services to users with health or well-being problems.

Criterion 11:   the programme delivers services to users experiencing material deprivation.

Criterion 12:   the programme delivers services to users in need of social support.

Criterion 13:   the programme delivers services to children with a disability.

Services

Criterion 14:   service delivery is through a clearly planned and managed but flexible process.

Criterion 15:   an explicit set of methods, techniques and skills which promote engagement and creativity are used.

Criterion 16:   the expertise of other service providers is drawn on effectively.

Criterion 17:   the contribution of relatives, friends and neighbours is drawn on effectively.

Criterion 18:   service delivery is responsive to the opinions, wishes and feelings of both the children and parents/carers who use them.

Criterion 19:   service delivery enhances existing strengths and skills of the children and parents/carers who use them.

Criterion 20:   service delivery expresses understanding and respect for issues of race and culture in the lives of the children and parents/carers who use them.

Criterion 21:   service delivery incorporates concern for child protection.

Criterion 22:   service delivery minimizes as far as possible the effect of children's disabilities.

Outcomes

Criterion 23:   the setting contributes to children achieving or maintaining a reasonable standard of health or development.

Criterion 24:   the setting contributes to the prevention of significant impairment of children's health or development.

Criterion 25:   the setting contributes to minimizing for children the effects of being disabled.

Criterion 26:   the setting promotes the upbringing of children by their families.

Moving on to operational managers, their primary contribution is to develop organizational structures and working practices that reflect the principles and style of family support – in particular, responsiveness, flexibility and inclusiveness. Alongside the more traditional checks and balances of democratic control through elected politicians plus various administrative means of complaint and representation, ways need to be found to ensure effective direct involvement of service users, adults and children, in operational management. Support in cash and kind to build the capacity of independent user groups should be an important part of this. Similar capacity building for staff within the organization through team working, line management support and training is another important item for the operational management agenda. The organization must model the family support style within its internal workings. Managers also need to further develop and facilitate the workings of integrated structures across discipline, agencies and sectors. Here, drawing in large part on the experience of managing child protection systems, there is now a fairly extensive understanding of not just the difficulties but also of how best to achieve improvement. Again the principal of subsidiarity, including direct control over the allocation of resources, should be applied when addressing any of these agenda items.

Practitioners need to recognize the responsibilities that subsidiarity brings under family support. The potential for decentralized power and authority requires them to mould their agency's strategic goals for family support. These goals need to be consciously pursued and creatively realized in new forms of practice. For themselves, and as a contribution to the wider policy debate, practitioners need to test and develop in an explicit and disciplined fashion the conceptual framework and vocabulary of family support within the everyday worlds of their work. In particular, they need to tease out the knowledge, skills and values components that comprise competence in family support. In their contribution to the process they need to further develop the skills and techniques of assessing need in a way that ensures service users are enabled to express their needs. Competent intervention will combine tried and tested methods, techniques and skills with the novel and innovative. Practitioners will need to constantly evaluate their efforts against the intended outcomes. This will require a transparent, rigorous and self-critical approach to detailing their work. It should also involve openly sharing the results, not least with service users.

It is increasingly recognized that there must be a research dimension to making the conceptual advances required, to building appropriate organizational structures and to furthering understanding of 'what works'. Researchers need to grasp this opportunity and build the necessary relationships through showing what exactly their knowledge and skills have to offer. The challenge is to further develop the scientific sophistication of the research methods being used while more firmly embedding results and analysis in the day-to-day policy and practice process.

There are four areas in particular where there is a need to push forward the research agenda. First, in relation to what works in achieving the desired outcomes of family support there has to be much more rigorous evaluation which accepts that there is a continuum of appropriate approaches, but is willing to include and explore the use of randomized controlled trials. There also needs to be more detailed qualitative case studies to understand the detail of intervention as experienced by both workers and service users. The interdependence of different formal and informal social care networks requires research attention through locality cluster studies, which focus on a specific geographical area to identify and explore the clusters of formal and informal networks and their relationships to each other. Finally, there is the issue of managing what are always finite resources, whether large or small. This requires a much more detailed understanding of the real costs of family support – not just to the state but also to informal carers within civil society. To achieve that there needs to be developed, specifically for application to family support, a much more sensitive and sophisticated social care economics.

Conclusion

It has been argued, and illustrated by material from the previous chapters, that family support encompasses a range of outcomes. These result from a particular type of collaborative process which is driven by the interaction of a wide variety of service users and types of service provider, as disparate needs and services engage. Those needs are generated in civil society and the services are provided or sponsored by the state. Family support, it is being suggested, is an instance of the state's relationship to civil society. In that sense it occupies a political space. To advance the agendas set out above for

the further consolidation, exploration and development of family support requires that this political space is sustained and expanded. This requires
political will: to ensure that will is not only the responsibility of politicians,
but of all who exercise their democratic right at the ballot box and who
participate in the myriad political, professional, trades union and other
special interest organizations through which active citizenship is expressed.

Clarity about the various stakeholders' agendas for consolidating and
developing family support is primarily a means of focusing to ensure that all
the pieces of the jigsaw are taken into account. If those stakeholders do take
forward the agenda for which they are responsible, conscious of how it fits
with the other pieces of this complex field, there is every reason to be
optimistic. Answers can be forged to the central question of how best to
manage the relationship between the state and civil society in a way that
empowers all children and their carers within their extended family, friendship and neighbourhood networks. Family support can be made the centre-
piece of wider social and economic strategies aimed at ensuring the social
capital required for the twenty-first century.

References

Alcock, P. (1998) 'The discipline of social policy.' In P. Alcock, A. Erskine and M.
    May (eds) *The Student's Companion to Social Policy.* Oxford: Blackwell.

Audit Commission (1994) *Seen But Not Heard: Co-ordination Community Child Health
    and Social Services for Children in Need.* London: HMSO.

Brown, M. and Payne, S. (1990) *Introduction to Social Administration in Britain.*
    London: Unwin Hyman.

Cannan, C. (1992) *Changing Families, Changing Welfare, Family Centre and the Welfare
    State.* London: Harvester.

Cheetam, J., Fuller, R., Petch, A. and McIvor, G. (1992) *Evaluating Social Work
    Effectiveness.* Buckinghamshire: Open University Press.

Fisher, M., Marsh, P. and Philips, D. with Sainsbury, E. (1986) *In and Out of Care –
    Experience of Children, Parents and Social Workers.* London: Batsford.

Gibbons, J. (ed) (1992) *The Children Act 1989 and Family Support: Principles into
    Practice.* London: HMSO.

Hardiker, P., Exton, K. and Barker, M. (1991) *Policies and Practices in Preventative
    Child Care.* Aldershot: Avebury.

Higgins, K., Pinkerton, J. and Switzer, V. (1997) *Family Support in Northern Ireland –
    Starting Points.* Belfast: Centre for Child Care Research, Queen's University of
    Belfast.

Hill, M. (1999) 'Effective professional intervention in children's lives.' In M. Hill (ed) *Effective Ways of Working with Children and their Families.* London: Jessica Kingsley Publishers.

Holman, B. (1988) *Putting Families First.* London: Macmillan.

McIntosh, M. (1984) 'The family, regulations and the public sphere.' In G. McLennan, D. Held and S. Hall (eds) *State and Society in Contemporary Britain.* Cambridge: Polity Press.

McLennan, G., Held, S. and Hall, S. (1984) 'Editors' introduction.' In G. McLennan, D. Held and S. Hall (eds) *State and Society in Contemporary Britain.* Cambridge: Polity Press.

Maluccio, A., Fein, E. and Oldmstead, K. (1986) *Permanency Planning for Children.* London: Tavistock.

Monteith, M. and Pinkerton, J. (1997) 'Family friend and neighbours.' In L. Dowds, P. Devine and R. Breen (eds) *Social Attitudes in Northern Ireland: The 6th Report 1996–97.* Belfast: Appletree Press.

National Institute for Social Work (1982) *Social Workers – Their Role and Tasks.* London: Bedford Square Press.

O'Hagan, K. (ed) (1996) *Competence in Social Work Practice – A Practical Guide for Professionals.* London: Jessica Kingsley Publishers.

Parker, R., Ward, H., Jackson, S., Aldgate, J. and Wedge, P. (eds) (1991) *Looking After Children: Assessing Outcomes in Child Care.* London: HMSO.

Parton, N. (ed) (1997) *Child Protection and Family Support: Tensions, Contradictions and Possibilities.* London: Routledge.

Pinkerton, J. (1994) *In Care at Home.* Aldershot: Avebury.

Pinkerton, J. and McCrea, R. (1999) *Meeting the Challenge? Young People Leaving Care in Northern Ireland.* Aldershot: Ashgate.

Pithouse, A., Lindsell, S. And Chueng, M. (1998) *Family Support and Family Centre Services.* Aldershot: Ashgate.

Roberts, R. (1990) *Lessons from the Past: Issues for Social Work Theory.* London: Tavistock.

Smith, T. (1996) *Family Centre and Bringing Up Young Children.* London: HMSO.

The Contributors

Graham Allan is Reader in Sociology at the University of Southampton, England. His research interests include the sociology of the community, family and friendship. He is author of *Kinship and Friendship in Modern Britain*.

John Canavan is a full-time researcher with the Department of Political Science and Sociology at the National University of Ireland, Galway. He is involved in both policy and project evaluation, with a particular focus on health and education service interventions targeting disadvantaged young people. He worked with the European Social Fund Evaluation Unit (Ireland) on its 1997 Report 'Preventive Actions in Education'.

Graham Crow is Senior Lecturer in Sociology at the University of Southampton, England. His research and publications cover the sociology of the community, comparative sociology and the sociology of disability. He is co-author with Graham Allan of *Community Life: An Introduction to Local Social Relations*.

Carolyn E. Cutrona is a Professor of Psychology at Iowa State University, USA, and also has a research appointment at Iowa state's Institute for Social and Behavioural Research. She works at the interface of clinical and social psychology and is currently collaborating on a major research project on 'The Effects of Economic Stress on Rural Parents'. Her most recent book is *Social Support in Couples – Marriage as a Resource in Times of Stress*.

Pat Dolan is Co-ordinator of Adolescent and Family Support Services in the Western Health Board, Ireland. He has worked in the child care field in the areas of practice, policy and management. He has written and researched in the area of social network maps and their use as a tool in working with vulnerable teenagers and their families, and currently lectures on Family Support for the Postgraduate Diploma in Child Protection and Welfare at Trinity College, Dublin.

Robbie Gilligan is a Senior Lecturer in Social Work in the Social Studies Department at Trinity College, Dublin, and Academic Co-Director of that University's Children's Centre. He has publications that cover topics such as social support for children and families; children in public care; and the importance of the school in child welfare. He is author of *Irish Child Care Services: Policy, Practice and Provision*.

Martin Herbert is Professor of Clinical and Community Psychology at the University of Exeter, England, where he directs the doctoral programme in Clinical and Community Psychology. He has published extensively on adult and child/adolescent problems; among his recent publications are *Troubled Families, Problem Children* with Carolyn Webster-Stratton and *Preventing Family Violence* with Kevin Browne.

Saoirse Nic Gabhainn is Assistant Academic Director in the Department of Health Promotion, National University of Ireland, Galway. She is responsible for both basic and applied research in the area of young people and schools health promotion. Her particular interests are the investigation of youth risk behaviour, cross-cultural comparative analyses and methodological innovation.

John Pinkerton is Senior Research Fellow in the Centre for Child Care Research at Queen's University, Belfast, Northern Ireland, where he is a lead researcher on the project 'Developing Family Support in Northern Ireland'. Subjects of his research and publications include children home-on-trial, young people leaving care and social work in Northern Ireland.

Sandra Ryan is a research fellow in the Department of Education at University College, Cork, Ireland. She is involved in the research and evaluation of initiatives to address the effects of social and educational disadvantage and of interventions to tackle early school leaving. She is the author of various evaluation reports including the 1995 evaluation report on the Home–School–Community–Liaison scheme.

Peter Steen Jensen is a General Manager of the Department of Children and Young People in Local Government in Odense, Denmark. A school teacher for eighteen years, he was also Inspector in the Department of Education, Copenhagen.

Fiona Walsh is Regional Drugs Co-Ordinator in the Western Health Board, Ireland. An experienced practitioner and manager, she is responsible for the development of drug prevention, education and treatment services.

Joachim Wieler is Professor of Social Work at Fachhochschule Erfurt-University of Applied Sciences, Germany. His areas of special interest include: social work methods with emphasis on family work; professional growth and self-awareness; and the historical development and internationalization of social work.

Subject Index

Author Index